BEST of the BEST
from
FLORIDA

Selected Recipes from Florida's
FAVORITE COOKBOOKS

BEST
of the BEST
from
FLORIDA

Selected Recipes from Florida's
FAVORITE COOKBOOKS

EDITED BY
Gwen McKee
AND
Barbara Moseley

Illustrated by Tupper Davidson

QUAIL RIDGE PRESS

CONTENTS

Preface 7

List of Contributors 9

Appetizers 11

Soups 29

Salads 43

Seafood 69

Poultry and Game 103

Meats 121

Vegetables 145

Pasta, Rice, Quiche, Dressing, Crepes 165

Fruits 177

Bread and Breakfast 185

Cakes 199

Cookies and Candies 215

Pies and Desserts 231

Index 261

Catalog of Contributing Cookbooks 269

On Anastasia Island, this lighthouse—a remnant of Florida's past—overlooks St. Augustine, the oldest European settlement in the United States.

PREFACE

Florida . . . the land of sunshine and palm trees . . . the haven of pleasure seekers . . . the respite of the winter weary. This beautiful state of tropical climates hosts beach picnics, galley suppers, and poolside parties almost all year long. Good food goes along with good fun, and indeed Floridians love to entertain.

Part of the cuisine of Florida comes from the riches of its soil. Oranges, grapefruits and tangerines account for one third of the state's total agricultural yield. And that's in addition to the more than 25 varieties of melons, strawberries, and winter vegetables that are produced in the central lakes region and in the rich mucklands south of Lake Okeechobee. Recipes are created by Floridians to utilize the abundance of these fresh fruits and vegetables that grow almost everywhere in Florida, even in their own backyards.

Florida's cuisine also comes from the bounty of its seemingly endless shoreline plus its many freshwater lakes and rivers. Since no point in Florida is more than 75 miles from the ocean, Floridians have ready access to a world of seafood. Small wonder that some of the best seafood recipes in the world come from Florida cooks!

We are grateful to the 46 contributing cookbook authors, editors, and publishers whose cooperation and assistance were vital to the development of the book. Each of the contributing cookbooks has its own unique features and flavor. We have attempted to retain this flavor by reproducing the recipes as they appear in each book, changing only the typeset style for uniformity. A complete catalog of these contributing cookbooks begins on page 269. We do beg forgiveness for any books that might have been included that we inadvertently overlooked.

Our thanks to the many food editors from newspapers all over

Florida who recommended cookbooks for inclusion; to Dot Gibson for her suggestions; to the many bookstore and gift shop managers who lent us their knowledge of popular books in their area; and to so many individuals who gave us a suggestion and a smile along the way through beautiful, sunny Florida.

Dixie Lee Nims at the Florida Division of Tourism graciously helped us find Florida photos and information. Tupper Davidson deserves thanks for her Florida-flavored drawings; Carol Mead is always there when you need her to edit and proofread; Waynell Harris never fails to lend her beautiful positive spirit; Jean Harrison simply comes when you say "Help;" and Lonnie and Barney quietly cheer us on from the sidelines. Thank you, dear ones.

We are extremely pleased to share these favorite Florida recipes so rich in fresh, healthful, delicious foods from the leading cookbooks in the Sunshine State.

Gwen McKee and Barbara Moseley

CONTRIBUTING COOKBOOKS

Alone at the Range
Apalachicola Cookbook
Bay Leaves
Beyond the Bay
Canopy Roads
The Colonel's Inn Caterers'—Tallahassee Historical Cookbook
Cook and Deal
Cross Creek Kitchens
The Cuban Flavor
Culinary Arts & Crafts
Cypress Gardens Cookbook
Fare by the Sea
Fiesta
Florida Flavors
Friendly Feasts Act II
Galley Gourmet III
The Gasparilla Cookbook
Gator Country Cooks
Gourmet Cooking
Gourmet Cooking II
Gulfshore Delights
Heart of the Palms
Jacksonville & Company

CONTRIBUTING COOKBOOKS

Juicy Miss Lucy Cookbook
Lost Tree Cook Book
Margaritaville Cookbook
Maurice's Tropical Fruit Cook Book
Ode to the Oysters
The Orange Bowl Cookbook
Palm Beach Entertains
A Pinch of Sunshine
The Prima Diner
Sawgrass and Pines
Seasoned with Sunshine
Seasons in the Sun
Secrets from the Galley
Seminole Savorings
Some Like It South!
Step-By-Step to Natural Food
Sugar Beach
Suncoast Seasons
Sunny Side Up
Sweet Surrender with Advice à la Carte
A Taste of Tampa
Thyme Waves
Through Our Kitchen Windows

Appetizers

Florida beaches like this one at Key West offer surf, sand, sun and fun for all ages.

Cross Creek Tea Blend

If these ingredients don't grow in your garden, buy them at local markets or health food stores.

3 cups dried mint leaves, finely chopped
1 cup dried lemongrass, finely chopped

¼ cup jasmine flower tea
¼ cup dried orange peel, finely chopped

Mix mint, lemongrass, jasmine flower tea, and orange peel in a large glass jar. Keep tightly sealed. Fill half-pint jars with mixture for gifts or fill small cloth bags for fragrant sachets.

Cross Creek Kitchens

Hot Cranberry Tea

1 (32-ounce) bottle of cranberry juice cocktail
1 package red hots
1 small can lemonade concentrate

1 small can orange juice concentrate
2 cups sugar
3 quarts water

Boil 2 quarts water, sugar, and red hots until sugar and red hots are dissolved. Add cranberry juice cocktail, orange and lemonade concentrate; and 1 quart water. Serve hot. Makes 1 gallon.

Canopy Roads

Banana Strawberry Shake

1 banana
5 ice cubes
2 tablespoons yogurt
10 frozen strawberries

1 cup apple juice
1 tablespoon protein powder (optional)

Blend banana, apple juice, plain yogurt and protein powder. When mixed, add ice cubes and strawberries. If you want a thinner shake, add water.

If you decide to kick the milk habit and want a substitute, here is a simple, but very nourishing milk. It is excellent for a cancer control diet, as sesame seeds are a good source of nitrilosides.

Step-By-Step to Natural Food

Banana Punch
Fresh and fruity

8 cups water
4 cups sugar
2 quarts pineapple juice
4 (6-ounce) cans frozen orange
   juice concentrate diluted with
   12 cans water

½ cup lemon juice
5 large bananas, puréed in
   blender
2 quarts ginger ale

Combine water and sugar. Boil 15 minutes and let cool. Add all other ingredients, except ginger ale. Mix thoroughly and freeze.

Take out of freezer 2 hours before serving. Add ginger ale at serving time.

Note: Freeze cubes of orange juice to prevent watering down the punch. Preparation: 15 minutes. Easy. Yield: 50 (4-ounce) cups. Must do ahead.

Culinary Arts & Crafts

 Bananas must have appeal; they're consumed by more people than any other fruit in the world.

Aunt Carrie's Eggnog

1 egg to each person (separate eggs)
1 level tablespoon sugar for each egg

1 tablespoon whiskey for each egg
1 pint whipping cream for 1 dozen eggs

Whip egg whites until stiff. Beat yolks until light and creamy. Mix half of the sugar with the egg yolks. Stir until well blended. Put all of the whiskey, a little at a time, into the yolk mixture, stirring until well blended. Fold the rest of the sugar into the beaten egg whites. Fold the yellow mixture slowly into the whites. After this is well mixed, fold in the whipped cream. (For large amounts, put beaten egg whites into the punch or serving bowl, and add the other ingredients as directed. This makes easier handling.) This eggnog is very thick and needs to be eaten with a spoon. If a thinner drink is desired, use half whipped cream and half milk, adding the whipped cream last.

Note: Part rum and part whiskey may be used in place of the whiskey. If part rum is used, reduce the amount of whiskey and after the cream is folded in, add the rum.

Gator Country Cooks

Lime Luscious

4 cups milk
¼ cup brown sugar
1 (3¾-ounce) package instant vanilla pudding mix

¼ cup lime juice
4 scoops lime sherbet
Mint sprigs, optional

In bowl of electric mixer, blender, or food processor, combine ¼ cup of the milk with the sugar; blend in remaining milk. Add pudding mix and beat smooth. Blend in lime juice and pour into glasses. Float scoop of lime sherbet on top. Mint sprigs make pretty garnish. Makes 4½ cups.

The Orange Bowl Cookbook

Whisper
An after dinner drink

1 quart coffee ice cream
2 ounces crème de cacao

2 ounces brandy

Soften ice cream a little; combine with liqueurs in blender. Mix well. Serve in chilled old-fashioned glasses. Serves 4–6.

Sunny Side Up

Vodka Slush

1 (6-ounce) can frozen orange juice
2 (6-ounce) cans frozen lemonade
2 (6-ounce) cans frozen limeade

3½ cups water
2 cups vodka
1 cup sugar
Sprite

Thaw frozen juices and mix together. Add water, vodka and sugar. Place in freezer for 48 hours, stirring occasionally. Put ⅔ cup slush in an 8-ounce glass and fill with Sprite. Yield: 12 servings.

Some Like It South!

Champagne Punch

1 bottle sauterne
½ bottle peach brandy
1 quart lemon sherbet

1 bottle soda water
1 bottle champagne
1 bottle ginger ale

Mix all ingredients together. Chill and pour over large chunk of ice in punch bowl. Float fresh fruit on top.

Bay Leaves

Smoked Oyster Dip

1 pint sour cream
2 cans smoked oysters
1 tablespoon Worcestershire sauce
1 teaspoon Tabasco sauce (or to
taste)

Mash oysters with fork; stir in Worcestershire sauce and Tabasco sauce. Stir into sour cream. Mix well and let stand overnight. Serve with Fritos corn chips or Ritz crackers.

Variation: Use 1 can oysters and 1 can smoked clams.

Sawgrass and Pines

Mystery Dip

2 (14-ounce) cans artichoke hearts
1 cup mayonnaise
1 small packet Hidden Valley
Ranch Original Salad Dressing

Rinse artichoke hearts. Drain and squeeze all juice out. Chop coarsely. Add salad dressing packet to mayonnaise. Stir. Add artichokes. Mix well and chill. Serve as dip for vegetables, chips, or crackers. Serves 10–12.

A Taste of Tampa

Curry Dip

2 cups mayonnaise
2 cups sour cream
¼ teaspoon turmeric
2 tablespoons curry powder
4 teaspoons sugar
½–2 teaspoons garlic powder
2 teaspoons salt
2 tablespoons lemon juice
½ cup freshly chopped parsley

Mix together and use fresh vegetables as dippers. Should be made several days in advance. Keeps well.

Lost Tree Cook Book

Hot Beef Dip

¼ cup chopped onions
1 tablespoon butter
8 ounces cream cheese
1 cup milk
4 ounces mushrooms, drained

2½ ounces smoked dried beef,
   chopped
¼ cup Parmesan cheese
2 teaspoons chopped parsley

Sauté onion in butter. Add cream cheese and milk; stir over low heat until cheese melts. Stir in rest of ingredients. Serve hot with chips or crackers.

The Colonel's Inn Caterers'—Tallahassee Historical Cookbook

Black Bean Dip

2 (15-ounce) cans Garcia Black
  Beans, partially drained
1 onion, chopped
Salt and pepper to taste

Garlic powder to taste
9–10 drops hot sauce, or to taste
¾–1 cup grated Cheddar cheese
Taco chips

Put black beans in shallow casserole dish. Mix 2 tablespoons chopped onion, salt and pepper, garlic powder, and hot sauce; add to beans. Sprinkle remaining chopped onion over beans. Cover with cheese. Heat at 350° until cheese is melted and heated through. Serve warm with taco chips. Serves 10.

Note: This also may be served cold.

Sunny Side Up

Broccoli Dip

1 stick margarine
1 small onion, minced
1 small roll of Kraft garlic cheese
1 can cream of mushroom soup

1 small can sliced mushrooms, drained
3 packages chopped broccoli, frozen

Cook the 3 packages of broccoli according to package directions. Melt margarine and sauté onion in melted margarine. Add cheese, stirring until it melts. Add soup and mushrooms, mixing well. Drain cooked broccoli and add to cheese mixture. Serve hot in a fondue or chafing dish with Fritos.

To serve as a vegetable, place in casserole dish, sprinkle with herb dressing or crushed Fritos. Bake in 350° oven for 20 minutes.

Canopy Roads

You'd-Never-Guess-It's-Spinach Dip

1 package frozen spinach, uncooked
¼ cup parsley
½ cup onion, chopped

1 teaspoon salt
½ teaspoon pepper
2 cups mayonnaise
Tabasco, to taste

Thaw and squeeze all liquid from spinach. Mix all ingredients in blender. Serve with carrot sticks, celery, and cauliflower.

Bay Leaves

Reuben Dip

1 (3-ounce) package of cream cheese, softened
¼ cup sour cream
½ cup shredded Swiss cheese

4 ounces sliced corn beef, finely diced
¼ cup drained sauerkraut, chopped
2 or 3 tablespoons milk

Heat all ingredients in small saucepan over low heat. Thin with milk if necessary. Serve with rye sticks.

Florida Flavors

Spinach Cheese Squares

4 tablespoons butter
3 eggs
1 cup flour
1 cup milk
1 teaspoon salt
1 teaspoon baking powder

1 pound Monterey Jack cheese or
    any other mild white cheese
    (grated)
2 packages chopped spinach,
    thawed and drained

Preheat oven to 350°. In a 9 × 13 × 2-inch baking pan melt the butter in the oven. Remove from oven. In a large mixing bowl, beat the eggs, then add the flour, milk, salt, and baking powder. Mix these ingredients well. Add the cheese and thawed spinach. Pour all ingredients into baking pan and bake for 35 minutes. Remove from oven, cool for 45 minutes in order to set. Cut into bite-sized squares.

To freeze: Place squares on a cookie sheet and allow to freeze, then transfer into plastic bags. Before serving, remove from bags, place on cookie sheet, heat in oven at 325° for 12 minutes. Yield: 25 appetizers.

Palm Beach Entertains

Spinach in a Bread Bowl

2 loaves round crusty bread
1 cup mayonnaise
1 cup sour cream
1 envelope Knorr Vegetable Soup
    Mix
2 tablespoons fresh minced onion

1 (10-ounce) package frozen
    chopped spinach, thawed and
    drained
1 (5-ounce) can water chestnuts,
    chopped

Combine all ingredients except bread. Cut circle in top of one loaf of bread; hollow it out. Put filling inside bread. Cut remaining loaf into cubes. Serve with small knife to spread filling on cubes.

Sunny Side Up

Stuffed Mushrooms

1 (1-pound) package large fresh
    mushrooms
½ cup butter
3 green onions, minced
½ cup fresh bread crumbs

1 tablespoon minced parsley
1 tablespoon lemon juice
3 tablespoons crumbled bleu
    cheese
½ teaspoon salt

Remove stems from mushrooms. Mince mushroom stems and sauté in butter with green onions (including tops). Blend remaining ingredients and add to mushrooms and onions. Put this mixture in mushroom caps and bake at 450° for 8 minutes or until brown.

Canopy Roads

Cheese and Mushroom Cups

1 cup onion, chopped
2 cups fresh mushrooms, chopped
    (do not chop in food processor)
3 tablespoons margarine
½ cup parsley, chopped
2 egg yolks
¾ cup mozzarella cheese,
    shredded

¼ cup Parmesan, grated
½ teaspoon salt (or a little less)
½ teaspoon pepper
1 teaspoon oregano
8 slices white bread
½ cup butter, melted

Sauté onion and mushrooms in margarine. Remove from heat and add remaining ingredients. Trim crust from bread and cut each slice into 4 squares. Flatten a little with rolling pin. Dip in butter and place in miniature muffin tins. Fill each cup with mushroom mixture. Bake at 350° for 20–25 minutes. Yield: 32 pieces.

Seasoned with Sunshine

Frosted Artichokes With Caviar

1 (8-ounce) package cream cheese, softened
2 tablespoons sour cream
2 teaspoons mayonnaise
1 teaspoon lemon juice

2 teaspoons grated onion
1 teaspoon garlic salt
1 (8½-ounce) can artichokes, drained
1 (2-ounce) jar caviar

Combine first 6 ingredients. Chop artichokes and pack into a mound on a serving plate. Spread cream cheese mixture over artichokes. Sprinkle caviar over top. Serve with mild crackers. Servings: 2 cups. Preparation time: 15 minutes.

Jacksonville & Company

Springtime Filling for Cocktail Sandwiches
Unusual and delicious

2 tomatoes, peeled and seeded
1 cucumber, peeled and seeded
(cut in half lengthwise; scoop
out seeds)
1 green pepper, finely chopped
1 onion, finely chopped
1 cup celery, finely chopped

2 teaspoons salt
1 envelope unflavored gelatin
2 cups mayonnaise
3 medium size loaves very thinly
sliced bread (very fresh), crust
removed and cut in half

Make the day before serving. Combine all vegetables and chop fine. Place in colander over a bowl in which gelatin has been sprinkled. Sprinkle vegetables with salt and let stand 1 hour or more. This allows juice to drip into the gelatin. Heat juice and gelatin; remove from heat and add mayonnaise. Add vegetables and blend. Keep refrigerated in tightly covered jar. When ready to prepare, spread vegetable filling on one slice of bread; cover with another slice. Will keep for a week. Serves 20.

Cook and Deal

Stuffed Raw Cabbage

1 large cabbage head
½ medium onion
1 pound fresh shrimp or
crabmeat, cleaned and peeled,
and cooked
2 (3-ounce) packages cream
cheese, softened

½ cup mayonnaise
Salt and pepper
Red pepper
Worcestershire sauce

Hollow out large cabbage reserving cabbage removed from center. In a food processor blend reserved cabbage, onion, and shrimp. Mix in cream cheese together with mayonnaise, salt and pepper, red pepper and Worcestershire to taste. Put mixture into hollowed cabbage head. Oil large cabbage leaves to put underneath-to make it look like a flower. Serve with crackers.

Beyond the Bay

Shrimp and Clam Mousse

1 cup mayonnaise
1 (8-ounce) package cream cheese
2 cans shrimp (substitute fresh, if desired)
1 can minced clams, drained (reserve juice)
1 package unflavored gelatin

1 cup celery, chopped
½ cup onion (or less), minced
2 teaspoons lemon juice
Tabasco to taste
Salt to taste
Pepper to taste

Cream mayonnaise and cream cheese together. Mash up shrimp and clams; add to above mixture. Heat clam juice with gelatin and let cool. Mix all ingredients together and pour into greased mold. Refrigerate until set.

Seasoned with Sunshine

Shrimp Butter

2 (5-ounce) cans shrimp, drained
1 tablespoon minced onion
1 tablespoon lemon juice
Dash cayenne
½ teaspoon beau monde

4 heaping tablespoons mayonnaise
¾ cup butter, softened
1 (8-ounce) package cream cheese
1 teaspoon dill weed

Combine all ingredients with mixer or in a blender. Serve with crackers or toast rounds. Serves 15 or more.

Heart of the Palms

Shrimp Marinade

1 (6-ounce) jar Creole mustard
1 (5-ounce) jar horseradish
1 cup oil (add more, if necessary)
1 teaspoon Worcestershire sauce
½ cup catsup

¼ cup vinegar
1 medium onion, thinly sliced
8–10 pounds shrimp, boiled, peeled and salted generously

Combine all ingredients, adding shrimp last. Marinate at least 24 hours.

Sugar Beach

Layered Crab or Shrimp Cocktail Spread
Guests gather around this . . . it's a winner

12 ounces cream cheese, softened
1 tablespoon Worcestershire sauce
1 tablespoon fresh lemon juice
1 tablespoon grated onion
Pinch garlic salt

6 ounces chili sauce
8 ounces fresh crabmeat or
  shrimp, cut up
Dried parsley flakes

Blend together the cheese, Worcestershire sauce, lemon juice, onion and garlic salt. Spread mixture evenly in an 8-inch quiche dish or shallow serving dish. Spread chili sauce evenly over the first layer. Spread the crabmeat or cut up shrimp over the chili sauce. Sprinkle generously with dried parsley flakes. Cover with Saran Wrap and refrigerate a minimum of 12 hours. Serve with crackers. Serves 10–12.

Cook and Deal

Baked Brie
Easy, Simple, Elegant!

6 (4½-ounce) rounds of imported
  brie cheese
6 teaspoons butter

6 tablespoons lightly toasted,
  sliced almonds

Place brie rounds in individual ramekins; top each brie with teaspoon of butter and tablespoon of almonds. Bake about 4 minutes
at 400°, or until crusty on outside and runny inside. Serve with hot
French bread, slices of Delicious apples and Anjo pears, and
clusters of green grapes. Serves 6.

Note: A delightful accompaniment to baked brie would be dry
sherry, chianti, red burgundy, chelois, or baco noir burgundy.

Suncoast Seasons

Sherry Cheese Paté

2 (3-ounce) packages cream
  cheese, softened
1 cup shredded sharp Cheddar
  cheese
4 teaspoons Paul Masson cocktail
  sherry

½ teaspoon curry powder
¼ teaspoon salt
1 (8-ounce) jar mango chutney,
  finely chopped
Finely sliced green onions with
  tops
Sesame or wheat wafers

Beat together thoroughly the cream cheese, Cheddar cheese,
sherry, curry powder, and salt. Spread on a serving platter, shaping
a layer about ½-inch thick. Chill until firm. At serving time, spread
with chutney and sprinkle with green onions. Serve paté with
wafers. Makes appetizers for about 8.

Gator Country Cooks

Crystallized Orange Nuts
Great Christmas gift
(Microwave)

¼ cup orange juice   2 cups pecan halves
1 cup sugar

Combine orange juice and sugar in 2-quart, 12×7-inch glass baking dish; mix well. Stir in pecans. Microwave 6 minutes on MEDIUM-HIGH. Stir and continue cooking 4–6 minutes on MEDIUM-HIGH, or until syrup crystallizes. Spread, separate and cool glazed nuts on buttered cookie sheet. Flavor improves with aging. Yields 2 cups.

Fare by the Sea

Pickled Okra

1 cup vinegar	1 clove garlic, cut in two
1 cup water	1 pound okra (small)
1 or 2 small hot red peppers*	Salt

*Use peppers about the size of a small cherry tomato, otherwise use a 1-inch piece of a long skinny hot pepper. These peppers are HOT so adjust to your own personal taste. (Dispose of some seeds.)

Combine all ingredients except okra and bring to a boil.

Wash okra. Don't cut below the stem line as they get slippery. Drop about a quarter of the okra at a time in the hot liquid and blanch for 4 or 5 minutes. Remove and blanch next portion. Pack blanched okra (stand up) in 2 sterile pint jars. Put 1½ teaspoons salt in each jar on top of okra.

Bring liquid back to a boil and pour over okra. Be sure ½ clove of garlic gets in each jar. Seal jars. Let age for several days. Yield: 2 pints.

Cypress Gardens Cookbook

Soups

The Island Hotel in Cedar Key on Florida's west coast.

Gazpacho
A Florida favorite

1 cucumber, peeled and cut in
   chunks
½ green pepper, seeded and cut
   in chunks
1 small onion, cut in chunks
2 tomatoes, peeled

½ ripe avocado, peeled
4 cups tomato juice
3 tablespoons olive oil
2 tablespoons wine vinegar
½ teaspoon oregano
Salt to taste

Using steel blade of food processor, coarsely chop cucumber. Transfer to bowl. Process green pepper and onion until finely chopped. Add to cucumber. Cut tomatoes into ¼-inch cubes. Cut avocado in ½-inch cubes. Add tomatoes and avocado to cucumber along with remaining ingredients. Chill at least 2 hours.

Fare by the Sea

 Gazpacho—A cold vegetable soup, one that usually includes onions, garlic, green peppers, tomatoes and cucumbers.

Cucumber Soup

4 medium cucumbers (raw)
2 lemons (juice only)
1 (11½-ounce) can undiluted
   Campbell's Pea Soup
1 (13½-ounce) can chicken stock
½ medium onion
2 or 3 cloves of garlic

1 teaspoon Worcestershire sauce
3 dashes Tabasco Sauce
1 tablespoon sugar
1 tablespoon salt
Ground pepper to taste
1 pint sour cream

Wash (do not peel) cucumbers and cut up into small pieces. Place cucumbers, onion and garlic in the electric blender. Add all other ingredients except sour cream. Blend until smooth. Blend in sour cream by hand. Best when made day or two ahead. Serve icy cold.

Lost Tree Cook Book

Strawberry Soup

1½ cups water
¾ cup light red wine
½ cup sugar
2 tablespoons lemon juice

1 quart fresh strawberries, hulled
   and puréed
½ cup heavy cream, whipped
¼ cup sour cream

Combine water, wine, sugar and lemon juice. Boil uncovered for 15 minutes, stirring occasionally. Add strawberries, and boil 10 more minutes, stirring frequently. Cool mixture until lukewarm. Combine whipped cream with sour cream and fold into strawberry mixture. Chill. Serves 6. Best if chilled overnight.

Fiesta

What a Crock
Cream of Almond and Zucchini Soup

4 tablespoons butter
1 onion, medium size, minced
2 unpeeled zucchini, medium
  size, scrubbed well
⅔ cup slivered almonds, toasted
4 cups chicken broth

¾ cup heavy cream
1 tablespoon brown sugar (or
  more, according to taste)
1 tablespoon Grand Marnier
¼ teaspoon cinnamon
½ teaspoon nutmeg

Melt butter in a large kettle, add minced onion and cook over medium heat until softened. Add zucchini, sliced thin, and ⅓ cup almonds. Cook for an additional 5 minutes, until zucchini just begins to soften. Add chicken broth and simmer for about 30 minutes, or until mixture is reduced by one-third. Add the additional ⅓ almonds and simmer for 10 minutes. Stir in cream, brown sugar, Grand Marnier, cinnamon and nutmeg to stock and simmer over low heat, while stirring until soup is thoroughly heated. Do not boil. Serves: 6. Preparation: 20 minutes. Cooking: 45 minutes. Difficulty: Easy.

Juicy Miss Lucy Cookbook

Cauliflower Soup

½ cup onion, chopped
1 tablespoon butter
½ teaspoon curry powder
6 cups chicken broth
1½ cups cooked rice

1 cauliflower
1 cup heavy cream
1 teaspoon salt
½ teaspoon pepper

Sauté onion in butter. Add curry powder and 2 cups of chicken broth. Simmer 15 minutes. Add rice to mixture and pour mixture into blender. Blend thoroughly. Wash cauliflower and break into flowerets. Cook in remaining 4 cups chicken broth for 15 minutes. Add mixture from blender to cauliflower mixture. Stir in cream; add salt and pepper. Serves 6.

Fiesta

Cream of Broccoli Soup

4 slices bacon
⅓ cup chopped onion
6 cups shredded raw potatoes
2 teaspoons salt
3 cups boiling water
1 (10-ounce) package frozen
    chopped broccoli
1 cup water

3 tablespoons butter
4 tablespoons flour
1 tablespoon instant chicken
    bouillon
1½ cups milk
1 (13-ounce) can evaporated milk
½ teaspoon pepper
2 teaspoons Aćcent

Fry bacon in deep skillet; remove slices, drain and reserve. Add to the bacon fat, onions, potatoes, salt and boiling water. Cover and simmer about 15 minutes; last 5 minutes add the broccoli that has been puréed with the cup of water in blender. Melt butter in separate saucepan; blend in flour and bouillon. Add milks and cook until thickened. Add to broccoli mixture and heat. Add pepper and Aćcent. Crumble bacon fine; can be added to the soup or sprinkled on top of servings. Serves 6–8.

Note: Use about 6 medium potatoes for the shredded potatoes. Also fresh broccoli can be used, 1½ cups.

Through Our Kitchen Windows

Broccoli, Chicken and Cheese Soup

4 tablespoons butter or margarine
2 medium onions, chopped
6 cups water
6 chicken bouillon cubes
1 (8-ounce) package fine egg
    noodles

2 packages frozen chopped
    broccoli
⅛ teaspoon garlic powder
1 pound process cheese, cut into
    chunks
6 cups milk
Pepper to taste

Melt butter or margarine in soup pot and sauté onion for 3 minutes. Add water and bring to a boil. Add bouillon cubes and boil until dissolved. Add egg noodles and cook 3 minutes. Add frozen broccoli, garlic powder and cheese. When cheese has melted, add milk and pepper to taste. Cook 10 minutes more and serve.

Sawgrass and Pines

Cashew and Carrot Soup
Great meal with fresh baked bread

1 tablespoon butter	6 cups stock
¼ cup oil	2 teaspoons salt
1½ cups chopped onions	½ cup raw brown rice
4 cups grated carrots, packed tightly	1 cup raisins
3 ounces tomato paste	1 cup raw cashews, chopped
1 cup chopped apple	2½ cups milk or half and half
	1 cup sour cream

Melt butter with oil in a 3-quart soup pot or pressure cooker. Sauté the chopped onions for one minute. Stir in the carrots and sauté until onions are soft and transparent. (They may be orange.) Stir in the tomato paste, apple, stock, and salt. Bring the mixture to a boil and stir in the brown rice. Cover and pressure cook for 15 minutes or cook regularly for about 45 minutes until the carrots are tender, but not mushy. Cool. Put mixture by cups into blender. Return mixture to the pot. Add the raisins and cashews. Bring to boil again and simmer until the raisins are plump, about 5 minutes. Add milk and heat through. Top each serving with sour cream. Soup may be refrigerated and reheated.

Preparation: 10 minutes. Easy. Cooking: 45 minutes. Can do ahead. Yield: 2½ quarts.

Culinary Arts & Crafts

Swiss Potato and Cheese Soup

2 (10¾-ounce) cans condensed
  chicken broth
1 (10¾-ounce) can condensed beef
  broth
3 cups water
2 large onions, sliced
4 large potatoes, peeled and diced
2 cups sliced celery
8 mushrooms, sliced
⅓ cup butter or margarine
⅓ cup flour
Salt and pepper to taste
⅓ cup chopped parsley
1 (6-ounce) package Immenthaler
  cheese, shredded

Combine broths, water and vegetables; cover and simmer 30 minutes or until potatoes are tender. In a small skillet, melt butter and blend in flour, stirring constantly over medium heat until mixture becomes golden brown. Add to simmering soup and stir until soup bubbles and thickens. Season to taste with salt and pepper. Sprinkle with cheese and parsley. Serve with dark bread slices.

Secrets from the Galley

Spanish Bean Soup

24 ounces dried garbanzo beans
2 tablespoons salt
1 beef bone
1 ham bone
4 quarts water
8 ounces white bacon
2 onions, chopped
¼ teaspoon paprika
¼ cup vegetable oil
2 to 3 pounds potatoes, peeled
2 pinches saffron
Salt to taste
4 chorizo (Spanish sausages),
  thinly sliced

Allow garbanzos to soak overnight (with salt) in sufficient water to cover beans. After soaking, drain the beans and place the beans and bones in 4 quarts water. Cook 1 hour over low heat. Fry white bacon with paprika and onion in oil; drain and add to beans. Cut the potatoes into medium-size chunks. Add potatoes, saffron, salt and chorizos to soup. Cook for at least 4 hours on low—we just keep ours on until it thickens a little. Tastes better the second day, so make plenty for leftovers. Serves 6.

Seasoned with Sunshine

Pat's Corn Chowder

6 slices bacon
1 pound either/or Italian sausage,
  kielbasa, breakfast sausage
1 medium onion, coarsely
  chopped
3 medium potatoes, peeled and
  cubed

½ cup water
2 cups milk (for richer chowder
  use evaporated milk)
2 (17-ounce) cans cream-style corn
½ teaspoon salt
Dash of pepper

Fry bacon and brown sausage in a Dutch oven until browned; remove bacon and sausage reserving 2 tablespoons drippings in Dutch oven. Crumble bacon, and set aside. Sauté onion in reserved drippings until tender; add potatoes and water. Cover and simmer 15–20 minutes or until potatoes are tender. Stir in milk, corn, salt, and pepper; cook over medium heat, stirring frequently, until thoroughly heated. Add bacon, sausage, and simmer, stirring, 2 minutes longer. Yield: about 8 cups.

Florida Flavors

Conch Chowder

¼–½ pound salt pork or bacon
2 chopped onions
1 diced green pepper
½ cup chopped celery
2 quarts water or more as needed
1 can hominy, drained
2 cans tomatoes
Salt and pepper

2 cloves garlic, minced
1 teaspoon thyme
1 teaspoon oregano
1 can cream of mushroom soup
1 teaspoon curry powder
1½ pounds ground conch
1 large package mixed, frozen
    soup vegetables

In large pot or cooker, fry out salt pork or bacon. Sauté onion, green pepper and celery. Add water, hominy and tomatoes and cook 20 minutes. Add ground conch. Add salt, pepper, garlic, thyme, oregano, mushroom soup, curry powder and soup vegetables and simmer until vegetables are done.

Margaritaville Cookbook

Sea Cloud Chowder

1 (4-pound) red snapper
1 quart cold water
1 teaspoon salt
½ cup salt pork, diced
¾ cup finely diced onion
½ cup diced green pepper

½ cup diced celery
4 cups raw cubed potatoes
1 quart light cream
¼ cup butter
¼ cup flour
Chopped parsley to garnish

Place whole fish in cold water, add salt, and cook until fish flakes, about 15 minutes. Remove fish from pot. Flake and pick out the bones. Return fish head and bones to pot and simmer about 1 hour. Strain stock, and return stock to pot. Fry salt pork until golden brown; add onion and green pepper. Cook 10 minutes, then add to stock along with celery and potatoes. Cook vegetables until potatoes are tender, about 15 minutes. Add cream, heat, then add flaked fish. In a small saucepan melt ¼ cup butter, then stir ¼ cup flour into the butter. Add this mixture to the soup. Sprinkle with chopped parsley or dill before serving. Serves 6–8.

This was a special favorite of the guests of Mrs. Marjorie Merriweather Post. The chowder was named after her 316-foot yacht Sea Cloud.

Palm Beach Entertains

Ajiaco

MEAT:

½ pound jerked beef

½ chicken

1 pound bottom round

1 pound pork meat

1 pound pigs' trotters

7 liters water

VEGETABLES:

2 ears of corn

½ pound yellow yam

2 green plantains

1 pound yucca

1 pound sweet potato

½ pound white root yam

½ pound yam

2 ripe plantains

2 lemons

SAUCE:

2 tablespoons lard

1 large onion

3 cloves garlic

1 green pepper

1 can tomato sauce

2 tablespoons salt

CORN BALLS:

1 pound tender ground corn

1 teaspoon salt

2 tablespoons milk

2 tablespoons lard

2 cloves garlic

Cut beef into four pieces and soak overnight. Discard water the next morning.

Place beef and chicken cut into two in a large casserole and boil for one hour. Add the beef round and the pork cut into pieces. If the pork is fatty, use the lard for the sauce and the corn balls. Add the pigs' trotters and allow to boil a further hour. Remove the fat and foamy substance from the liquid after it has boiled for a while.

While meat is cooking, fry the sauce ingredients and peel the vegetables. When meat is tender, add the vegetables in the order that they appear in the recipe. When adding plantains follow with lemon juice so that soup does not darken. At the same time add the sauce little by little so that it all cooks together. When adding the ripe plantains, prepare the corn balls to be added at the end.

Mix the ground corn with the salt, milk and lard in which garlic has been fried. Take spoonfuls of this mixture and drop the balls

CONTINUED

CONTINUED

over the vegetables in the broth. Cover and cook over low heat for another hour. Do not stir until corn balls are cooked.

To thicken, mash a few pieces of vegetable in a little broth. Serves 12 approximately.

The Cuban Flavor

Ajiaco—A kind of Spanish stew.

Marty's Stew

1 quart oysters	½ teaspoon cayenne pepper
Oyster liquor	1 clove minced garlic
1 teaspoon lemon juice	½ teaspoon salt
½ cup butter	1 quart milk
1 tablespoon flour	1 tablespoon Worcestershire sauce
½ cup chopped green onions	1 cup chopped celery

Simmer the oysters in their liquor and lemon juice until the edges curl. Remove from the heat. Make a roux with the butter and flour, then add the celery, onions, garlic, salt, cayenne pepper and Worcestershire sauce. Let the mixture simmer for 2 or 3 minutes then stir in the milk. Continue to heat for 5 additional minutes then remove and stir in the oysters. Makes 6 servings.

Ode to the Oysters

Baja Bowl

1 (11¼-ounce) can chili beef soup	1 (10-ounce) frozen Italian-style
1 (10½-ounce) can beef broth	vegetables in sauce
1 soup can water	

Preparation time: 5 minutes. Cooking time: 8–15 minutes.

Thyme Waves

Creole Gumbo Apalachicola

BROTH:

1 quart water
2 bay leaves
½ lemon, sliced
2 teaspoons salt
2 pounds fresh small shrimp
¾ pound fresh okra, sliced or 10 ounce package frozen sliced okra

½ small bottle (2½ ounces) Lea & Perrins Worcestershire sauce
1 teaspoon dried parsley
½ teaspoon dried basil
Several dashes of Louisiana hot sauce
2 cups cooked crabmeat
12 ounces standard oysters, drained

Make broth by bringing shrimp to boil in 4-quart heavy saucepan with 1 quart water, bay leaves, lemon, and salt. Remove shrimp immediately, discard lemon and refrigerate shrimp. To broth, add okra, Worcestershire sauce, parsley, basil and hot sauce. Let simmer uncovered while preparing roux.

ROUX:

½ cup oil or bacon drippings
¾ cup plain flour
2 medium onions

1 bell pepper
2 cloves garlic
1 cup water
1 (16-ounce) can tomatoes and liquid

Put onions, bell pepper and garlic in blender with 1 cup of water and chop until fine. Drain, add seasoned water to broth. In black iron skillet, heat oil, add flour and stir constantly on medium high heat until dark brown. Add the vegetables to roux, stirring constantly until moisture disappears. Put tomatoes in blender on low speed or through a sieve; add slowly to roux mixture, stirring constantly. Let cook gently on medium high heat about 10 minutes, stirring frequently. Stir roux mixture into broth; simmer one hour without cover.

Add seafood (peeled shrimp used for broth, 2 cups cooked crabmeat and 12 ounces standard oysters, drained). Bring back to simmer until oysters just curl; turn down to warm. Serve in soup bowls with scoop of cooked rice on top.

Apalachicola Cookbook

Seafood Gumbo

½ pound bacon, diced
½ cup onion, diced
½ cup celery, diced
½ cup green pepper, diced
2 cloves garlic, crushed
1 teaspoon basil
1 teaspoon oregano
2 teaspoons salt
1 teaspoon pepper
2 cups clam juice

2 cups water
1 (2-pound) can tomatoes,
 chopped
2 (10-ounce) packages frozen okra
2 pounds shrimp, cleaned
1 pound fish (flounder or
 haddock), diced
1 pound scallops, cooked
1 cup white wine
1 cup sherry

In large soup pot, sauté bacon until cooked. Add onion, celery, green pepper, garlic and spices. Cook for 10 minutes, until vegetables are tender. Add clam juice, water, tomatoes and okra; cook for 15 minutes. Add remaining ingredients and simmer for 30 minutes.

Secrets from the Galley

Shrimp Bisque
(Bisque des Crevettes)

A very old recipe. Small balls of shrimp and aromatic vegetables are baked and served floating in the rich soup. You will love this one.

3 pounds shrimp. cleaned
1 cup onions, chopped
½ cup celery, chopped
2 tablespoons butter
2 tablespoons flour
1 quart water or shrimp stock
1 quart chicken stock

1 tablespoon tomato paste
½ cup bread crumbs
Salt and pepper
½ cup green onions, chopped
1 tablespoon butter
⅓ cup bread crumbs
1 egg yolk

Grind shrimp in a food processor. Sauté onions and celery in butter. Add flour and cook 2 minutes. Add water, stock, tomato paste and shrimp. Cook for 15 minutes. Add bread crumbs and blend well. Strain and return to low heat. Set half the shrimp mixture aside.

Sauté green onions in butter. Add shrimp mixture and bread crumbs. Remove from heat. Add egg yolk. Roll into small balls. Heat in oven for 5 minutes (350°). Serve soup with 2 or 3 shrimp balls.

Gourmet Cooking II

 Bisque—A kind of creamy soup made with a purée of seafood, meat, and/or vegetables.

Salads

The Singing Tower, a 325-foot carillon tower, keeps watch over the 50-acre Mountain Lake Sanctuary near Lake Wales.

Fantastic 24-Hour Salad
(Seven-Layer)

1 small head of lettuce	1 (10-ounce) package frozen peas,
½ green pepper, sliced	uncooked
½ red pepper, sliced	1½ cups mayonnaise
½ cup celery, chopped	2 tablespoons sugar
½ cup red Spanish onion,	1½ cups grated Cheddar cheese
chopped	8 slices crisp fried bacon,
	crumbled

Line a 9×13-inch pan with bite-sized pieces of lettuce. Sprinkle with red and green pepper slices. Sprinkle celery on pepper slices, then add onion in one layer. Top with green peas, uncooked. Combine mayonnaise and sugar and spread over vegetable layers. Sprinkle cheese over mayonnaise and top with crumbled bacon. Refrigerate overnight. Yield: 10–12 servings.

Florida Flavors

Perkie's Salad

1 (15½-ounce) can French-style	1 medium onion, thinly sliced
green beans, drained	2 teaspoons sugar
1 (17-ounce) can tiny peas,	2 teaspoons seasoned salt
drained	½ teaspoon pepper
1 teaspoon garlic powder	5 bacon slices, cooked, crumbled
10 tablespoons mayonnaise	

Spread half of green beans and half of peas in a shallow 1½-quart dish. Sprinkle with garlic powder. Spread 5 tablespoons mayonnaise evenly over peas. Place half of sliced onion over mixture. Sprinkle with 1 teaspoon sugar, 1 teaspoon salt and ¼ teaspoon of pepper. Repeat layers, omitting garlic.

Cover and leave at room temperature 1 hour. Refrigerate at least 2 hours. Toss gently before serving. Garnish with bacon. Serves 6.

Heart of the Palms

Mushroom-Walnut Salad With Fennel Dressing for a New Leaf on Life

DRESSING:

1 clove garlic
1 teaspoon salt
½ cup olive oil
1 raw egg

3 tablespoons red wine vinegar
2 tablespoons watercress
Pepper to taste
1 teaspoon fennel seed

Mash garlic with salt in a wooden bowl. Add oil and egg, and beat with a whisk. Add vinegar, watercress, and pepper to taste. Add fennel seed to dressing and refrigerate overnight.

SALAD:

1 pound fresh mushrooms
1 head iceberg lettuce, shredded

4 ounces walnuts, chopped

Slice mushrooms thinly. (Recommend the food processor.) Spread mushrooms neatly over a bed of lettuce. Sprinkle with walnuts, and pour dressing over. Serves: 4. Preparation: 15 minutes. Cooking: None. Difficulty: Easy.

Juicy Miss Lucy Cookbook

Marinated Squash

5 medium yellow squash, raw and
   thinly sliced
½ cup green onion, thinly sliced
½ cup green pepper, chopped
½ cup celery, sliced
2 tablespoons wine vinegar

⅓ cup cider vinegar
¼ cup sugar
1 teaspoon salt
½ teaspoon pepper
⅔ cup vegetable oil
⅛ teaspoon garlic powder

Combine squash, green onion, green pepper, and celery in a large mixing bowl; toss lightly. Combine vinegars, sugar, salt, pepper, vegetable oil, and garlic; stir well and spoon over vegetables. Refrigerate overnight. Stir occasionally. Drain and serve with lettuce.

Seasoned with Sunshine

Sauerkraut Salad

1 (16-ounce) can sauerkraut,
  drained
2 cups shredded carrots
1 cup diced green peppers
1 cup diced celery
½ cup diced onion

¼ cup chopped pimiento
⅓ cup vinegar
¾ cup sugar
1 teaspoon salt
Pepper

Mix all ingredients. Let stand to enhance flavor, preferably overnight.

The Prima Diner

Avocado Spinach Salad

Fresh spinach, washed, drained,
  snipped to pieces with kitchen
  shears
½ cup water chestnuts, sliced
2 cups fresh bean sprouts
2 hard boiled eggs, diced

5 slices of bacon, fried crisp and
  crumbled
1 red onion, sliced thin and
  separated into rings
1 avocado, sliced and sprinkled
  with lime juice

Toss all ingredients with *Papaya Seed Dressing*.

Maurice's Tropical Fruit Cook Book

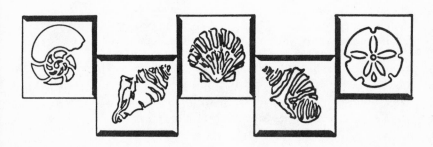

Garden Fresh Slaw

5 cups finely chopped cabbage
2 cups finely chopped lettuce
½ cup chopped fresh parsley
1 cup chopped fresh broccoli
   heads

2 cups grated carrot
1 cup thinly sliced green onion
1 cup diced onion

DRESSING:

16 ounces plain yogurt
2 tablespoons prepared spicy
   mustard
⅓ cup salad oil

2 tablespoons wine vinegar
5 medium garlic cloves, crushed
1 teaspoon mixed fine herbes
½ teaspoon celery seed

In a large bowl, combine all the chopped vegetables and mix thoroughly. In a small bowl, combine dressing ingredients in order listed and mix well.

Pour dressing over vegetables and toss. Chill at least 2 hours. Serves 15.

Cross Creek Kitchens

Fruited Cole Slaw

1 small to medium head cabbage
1 green pepper, diced
2 tablespoons dried, minced onion
   or 1 fresh chopped onion
½ cup raisins
½ cup mayonnaise
¼–⅓ cup cider vinegar

1 teaspoon sugar or 1 packet of
   sweetener
½ teaspoon black pepper
1 (11-ounce) can pineapple
   chunks, drained, or fresh
   oranges, apples or peaches
   when available

Quarter cabbage and cut into coarse chunks. Add green pepper, onions and raisins. Stir enough vinegar into mayonnaise to achieve consistency of heavy cream. Stir in sugar or sweetener and black pepper. Toss cabbage mix with dressing, add fruit and toss again, gently. Keeps well 2–3 days.

Galley Gourmet III

Cauliflower Potato Salad

1 head cauliflower, steamed
½ medium onion, chopped
4 boiled eggs, chopped
1 teaspoon sea salt
1 grated carrot

2 tablespoons parsley
1 stalk celery, chopped
1 tablespoon apple cider vinegar
Mayonnaise to moisten

This "fake" potato salad will really fool people. Many times, no one has guessed that this was actually cauliflower instead of potatoes. Just mash the cauliflower with a potato masher. Add all the ingredients as you would for potato salad. Then add enough mayonnaise to moisten. Sprinkle the top with paprika and serve as potato salad.

Step-By-Step to Natural Food

Sour Cream Potato Salad
There is none better.

5 cups diced, boiled potatoes
1 tablespoon grated onion
½ cup diced cucumber
¾ teaspoon celery seed
1½ teaspoons salt
½ teaspoon freshly ground pepper
1 tablespoon chopped parsley

3 hard-cooked eggs, whites diced,
   yolks mashed
1½ cups sour cream
½ cup Hellmann's mayonnaise
¼ cup vinegar
1 teaspoon prepared mustard

Potato salad is best made from red waxy potatoes, cooked in their jackets and peeled and marinated while still warm. Combine potatoes, onion, cucumber, celery seed, salt, pepper and parsley and mix together lightly. Add diced whites to potato mixture. Combine mashed yolks with sour cream, mayonnaise, vinegar and mustard; add to potatoes and gently blend together. Refrigerate several hours. Taste; some like a little more salt and pepper. Serves 10.

Cook and Deal

Chicken and New Potato Salad

15–18 small new potatoes, unpeeled, cut into bite-sized chunks
2 cups cooked chicken, cut into small pieces

1 cup fresh broccoli or spinach, finely chopped
1 cup grated carrot
½ cup chopped green onion

DRESSING:

1 cup plain yogurt
2 tablespoons mayonnaise
1 teaspoon prepared mustard
2 medium cloves garlic, crushed
1 teaspoon fresh, finely chopped basil or ½ teaspoon dried

1 teaspoon fresh, finely chopped oregano or ½ teaspoon dried
¼ teaspoon freshly ground black pepper

Cook potatoes until just tender. In a large bowl, combine chicken, potatoes, and vegetables and mix well. In a small bowl, combine dressing ingredients and blend well. Pour dressing over salad and toss. Chill at least 2 hours. Serves 8.

Cross Creek Kitchens

Committee's Choice Chicken Salad

SALAD:

½ pound bacon, cooked,
   crumbled

4 cups white chicken meat,
   cooked, diced

1 (14-ounce) can hearts of palm,
   drained, sliced

Lettuce leaves

4 tomatoes, cut into 6 wedges

24 pitted black olives

Combine bacon, chicken, and hearts of palm in a 2-quart bowl. Add bleu cheese dressing and mix well. Cover and refrigerate several hours. Arrange lettuce leaves on individual serving plates and top with chicken mixture. Garnish with tomato wedges and black olives. Serves 6.

BLEU CHEESE DRESSING:

½ cup mayonnaise

½ cup sour cream

3 tablespoons milk

2 tablespoons lemon juice

½ teaspoon seasoned salt

⅔ cup bleu cheese, crumbled

Mix mayonnaise, sour cream, milk, lemon juice, and salt in a blender for 30 seconds. Add bleu cheese and mix for a few seconds. Chill overnight. Makes 1⅓ cups.

Heart of the Palms

Palms

Palms are undoubtedly one of Florida's greatest charms. One such tree, which is a symbol of the real Florida, is the sabal Palmetto, better known as the cabbage palm. The tender inside of this tree's thick trunk is the heart of palm. Another name for this bland, ivory-layered delicacy is swamp cabbage.

The cabbage palm is on the Florida threatened species list and may not be removed from other people's private land or public land without permission. So aside from cutting down trees on your own property, fresh sabal palm stumps can be ordered from AAA Nursery in Okeechobee, Florida, for approximately $2.50 each. This then begins an adventure in itself, as a stump must then be peeled with an ax or chain saw until the heart is exposed. Only the least

CONTINUED

CONTINUED

fibrous center portion is desirable. The heart is white in color and it yellows quickly, so the very crumbly pieces should be put in water as soon as they are cut from the stump. One heart produces about 4 cups, serving small portions to four people.

By far the easiest way to acquire hearts of palm is to purchase them canned from your grocery store or specialty food store. Hearts of palm are produced commercially in and imported from Brazil. This canned product has been specially processed and should be treated like canned asparagus. Serve cold in a salad, mixed with your favorite dressing. The palm hearts may also be heated, drained, and served with a sauce. One 14-ounce can serves 4 or more.

Heart of the Palms

Hot Chicken Salad

1 (2½–3 pound) fryer	½ cup chopped toasted peanuts
Tops from 3 celery stalks	½ teaspoon salt
1 small onion	2 tablespoons grated onion
½ bell pepper	4 tablespoons lemon juice
2 bay leaves	½ cup grated cheese
2 cups thinly sliced celery	1 cup crushed potato chips
1 small can chopped black olives	1 cup mayonnaise

Place chicken in kettle with enough water to cover. Add celery, onion, pepper, bay leaves; bring to boil. Reduce heat and cook until tender. Let chicken cool in broth overnight. Remove skin from chicken. Bone and cut into nice sized chunks. You should have about 2 cups of cut-up chicken. (Strain broth chicken was cooked in and use for soup or gravy.) Heat oven to 400°. Combine chicken with celery, olives, peanuts, salt, onion, lemon juice and mayonnaise.

Pile lightly into casserole or individual baking dishes. Sprinkle with cheese and potato chips. Bake until hot. If baked in individual dishes length of baking time will be approximately 15 minutes. Casserole will take longer. Salad is just as good prepared ahead of time and baked later. Serves 6.

Cypress Gardens Cookbook

Tallahassee Chicken Salad

1 (4–5-pound) hen, boiled with 3–
    4 onions and 3–4 stalks celery
Salt and pepper
1 bunch celery

1 pint mayonnaise
1 jar Crosse & Blackwell pickles
    (Chow-Chow)
Tabasco to taste

Remove chicken from bones and cut up. For each 2 cups chicken, add 1 cup celery. Add pickles (about ½ jar or to taste) and remaining ingredients. Spread a thin layer of mayonnaise over salad to keep moist.

    The Colonel's Inn Caterers'—Tallahassee Historical Cookbook

Chicken and Pasta Salad

CHICKEN:

1 small hen or fryer (about 3 pounds)
1 small onion, chopped
5 stalks celery, chopped
1 small green bell pepper, chopped

Salt and pepper
½ teaspoon lemon juice
½ cup mayonnaise

Cook hen with onion, ½ cup celery, bell pepper, salt and pepper. Cool, bone and skin chicken; dice for salad. Stir in 1 cup celery, mayonnaise and lemon juice.

DRESSING:

¼ cup plus 2 tablespoons cider vinegar
⅔ cup plus 3 tablespoons olive oil
1 teaspoon salt

1 teaspoon sugar
1 teaspoon paprika
⅛ teaspoon Tabasco sauce
¼ teaspoon garlic powder

Shake ingredients together in covered jar or mix in processor.

PASTA:

1 (7-ounce) package vermicelli or other pasta

Lawry's Seasoned Salt
Tabasco sauce

Cook, as directed, in boiling salted water; drain; mix with dressing. Add Lawry's salt and Tabasco to taste. Marinate overnight.

Mix chicken with marinated pasta and refrigerate overnight again. Yield: 8–10 servings.

Note: Chicken and Pasta Salad travels well, making it a good dish for a picnic or boating trip.

Some Like It South!

Pasta Salad

½ pound vermicelli or fusilli
1 green pepper, diced
3–4 stalks celery, thinly sliced
6 scallions, thinly sliced, including
    green tops
2 hard boiled eggs, chopped
1 (4-ounce) jar pimientos, cut up

2 packets ranch style creamy
    Italian dressing prepared
    according to directions on
    packet
1 (¼-inch) slice each of cooked
    turkey and boiled ham,
    julienned
½ cup slivered almonds

Prepare dressing at least 30 minutes before pasta. Cook pasta "al dente." While warm, toss in all ingredients except turkey, ham and almonds. Chill at least 24 hours, preferably 2 days. Just before serving, mix in ham, turkey and almonds. Also excellent with shrimp or crabmeat or both. Serves 6.

Note: If creamy Italian ranch style dressing is unavailable, use regular ranch style Italian and add 1 cup mayonnaise.

Galley Gourmet III

Artichoke-Rice Salad

1 package chicken-flavored (or
    paella-flavored) rice mix
4 green onions, thinly sliced
½ green bell pepper, chopped
12 pimento-stuffed olives, sliced

2 (6-ounce) jars marinated
    artichoke hearts
¾ teaspoon curry powder
½ cup mayonnaise

Cook rice according to package directions, omitting butter. Place rice in a large bowl. Cool. Add onions, green peppers and olives. Drain artichoke marinade, reserving marinade. Cut hearts in half. Combine artichoke hearts, curry powder and mayonnaise. Add artichoke hearts to rice mixture. Toss with dressing and chill. This may be used as a side dish. If shrimp, chicken or ham is added, it may serve as a main course. Servings: 6–8. Preparation time: 30 minutes. Cooking time: 15–20 minutes.

Jacksonville & Company

Ham and Rice Salad

1 boil-a-bag rice (Success)
1 package boiled ham, diced
1 small can pineapple rings
2 green peppers, diced

½ cup sour cream
½ cup mayonnaise
Lettuce

Mix prepared rice, diced ham and green peppers in bowl. Combine mayonnaise and sour cream and mix in. Serve on drained pineapple rings on lettuce. Serves 4.

Alone at the Range

Grapefruit Shrimp Salad

1½ cups fresh grapefruit sections
2 cups cooked shrimp, cleaned
1 cup diced celery
1 tablespoon fresh lemon juice
1 tablespoon heavy cream

½ cup mayonnaise
¼ teaspoon salt
¼ teaspoon white pepper
Salad greens

Combine grapefruit, shrimp and celery. Mix together lemon juice, cream, mayonnaise, salt and pepper. Add to first mixture and toss. Serve on bed of salad greens. Serves 4.

Secrets from the Galley

Cold Seafood and Pasta Salad

MAYONNAISE:

1 egg
½–1 cup vegetable oil
Juice of 1 lemon
2 anchovy fillets (optional)

¼ teaspoon dried orégano or
   dried tarragon
2 tablespoons capers

In a blender or food processor, blend egg briefly. Then add oil slowly until mixture begins to thicken. Add lemon juice, anchovy fillets and orégano. Blend until smooth. Stir in capers.

SALAD:

2 cups pasta, combination of small
   shapes
Mayonnaise
1 head leaf lettuce
½ pound prawns *or* shrimp,
   cooked, shelled and deveined

Lettuce for garnish
2–3 tablespoons capers for
   garnish
1 lemon, sliced for garnish
Fresh snipped parsley for garnish

Cook pasta in a large pot of boiling water until tender. Drain well and place in a bowl, tossing with mayonnaise. Line a serving bowl with lettuce. Stir prawns into pasta. Arrange pasta mixture on lettuce. Garnish with lettuce, capers, lemon slices and parsley. Store, covered, in the refrigerator and remove 30 minutes before serving. Servings: 6. Preparation time: 30 minutes. Chilling time: 30 minutes.

Jacksonville & Company

Prawns—Crustaceans closely related to and resembling shrimp.

Bastille Day Salad
May be an entrée or salad! What a meal with a steak!

1 head iceberg lettuce, cored and
   cubed
1 pound lump crabmeat
35 small shrimp, boiled and
   peeled
2 tomatoes, chopped

⅔ cup red wine vinegar
⅔ cup salad oil
½ cup creole mustard
3 hard cooked eggs (optional)
8 anchovies (optional)

In a large bowl combine lettuce, crabmeat, shrimp and tomatoes. In a smaller bowl combine wine vinegar, oil and creole mustard; beat with a wire whisk. Pour oil and vinegar mixture over lettuce mixture. Chop eggs and anchovies and sprinkle over top of salad. Chill and serve.

Sugar Beach

Tuna and Salmon Salad Mold

2 envelopes unflavored gelatin
1 tablespoon steak sauce
1¾ cups canned tomato juice
½ cup water
¾ cup mayonnaise
1 cup dairy sour cream
1 teaspoon grated lemon rind
½ cup chopped stuffed olives

1 green onion, chopped
1½ cups diced celery
1 (7-ounce) can salmon
1 (7-ounce) can tuna
Salt and pepper to taste
Parsley sprigs
Lemon wedges, sprinkled with
   paprika

Mix 1 envelope of gelatin with steak sauce and ¾ cup of the tomato juice. Heat, stirring to dissolve gelatin. Add remaining juice and pour into 1½-quart fluted ring-mold; chill until firm. In top of double boiler, soften remaining gelatin in ½ cup water; dissolve over hot water. Stir in mayonnaise and sour cream; add lemon rind, olives, onion, celery, salmon and tuna. Season to taste with salt and pepper. Pour mixture on top of chilled, firm tomato gelatin; chill until firm. Unmold onto plate. Garnish with parsley sprigs and lemon wedges. Serves 6.

Secrets from the Galley

Oyster Salad

1 quart oysters
Oyster liquor
1 tablespoon lemon juice
1 cup chopped celery
½ cup chopped green onions
2 tablespoons vinegar
½ cup vegetable oil

Salt
Pepper
½ cup mayonnaise
2 whole lemons
Lettuce, watercress or fresh
  spinach

Simmer the oysters in their liquor and lemon juice until edges begin to curl. Remove, drain, and then marinate in a mixture of the vegetable oil, vinegar, salt and pepper. Chill for 2–3 hours.

Just before serving, add green onions, celery and mayonnaise. Stir gently and serve on a bed of lettuce, watercress or fresh spinach. Top with sliced lemons.

Ode to the Oysters

Crab Louis Salad

1½ pounds fresh crabmeat, flaked
1 cup mayonnaise
¼ cup *Tarragon French Dressing*
  (recipe below)
¼ cup chili sauce

2 tablespoons chopped chives
1 teaspoon horseradish
1 teaspoon Worcestershire sauce
Salt and pepper to taste

Flake crabmeat and arrange on bed of lettuce. Combine remaining ingredients and serve as dressing over crabmeat. Serves 6.

TARRAGON FRENCH DRESSING:
6 tablespoons olive oil
2 tablespoons tarragon vinegar
1 teaspoon salt

1 teaspoon chopped fresh
  tarragon leaves

Blend all together well.

Beyond the Bay

Florida Crab Mold

2 envelopes unflavored gelatin
½ cup cold water
⅔ cup chili sauce
¾ cup water
½ cup mayonnaise
½ cup sour cream
½ cup tomato juice
2 teaspoons instant minced onion
2 tablespoons lemon juice

¼ teaspoon salt
¼ teaspoon dillweed
1 cup celery, diced
½ cup ripe olives, sliced
2 cups lump crabmeat
Salad greens
Olives to garnish
Hard-cooked eggs

Soften gelatin in the cold water. Heat the chili sauce with ¾ cup water; stir in the softened gelatin until thoroughly dissolved. Remove from heat and add mayonnaise, sour cream, tomato juice, onion, lemon juice, salt, and dill. Chill until the mixture is partially set. Stir in celery, ripe olives, and crabmeat. Turn mixture into a 6-cup ring mold and chill until firm. To serve, unmold on salad greens; garnish with whole olives and hard-cooked eggs. The mold can be made 2 days before using. Serves 8.

Bay Leaves

Black Bart's Seafood Ambrosia

1–1½ cups white meat fish,
cooked and flaked
1 medium red onion, chopped
4 stalks celery, chopped
½ green pepper, chopped
1 large dill pickle, chopped
2 tablespoons salad oil

2 tablespoons lemon juice
1 tablespoon parsley flakes
1 teaspoon salt
1 cup mayonnaise
Lettuce leaves
Tomato wedges

Mix thoroughly all but lettuce and tomatoes. Refrigerate in airtight container until ready to use. Serve on lettuce leaves with tomato garnish. Utensil: large mixing bowl. Preparation time: 15 minutes. Servings: 6–8.

Note: To cook fish, filet, leaving skin on, cut into bite-sized pieces, boil in water seasoned with crab boil.

Nice to Know: This is also good served as a dip with crackers or stuffed into jalapeno or banana pepper halves for a fire-breathing surprise!

Thyme Waves

Tomato Aspic Ring

2 tablespoons gelatin
½ cup cold water
2 (8-ounce) cans tomato sauce
2 tablespoons lemon juice
1 cup sour cream
½ cup Rhine wine
½ teaspoon salt
1 tablespoon minced onion
2 tablespoons parsley
1 cup chopped celery

Soften gelatin in ½ cup cold water. Heat tomato sauce to boiling, add gelatin, stir until dissolved. Add lemon juice, sour cream, wine, and salt. Mix in onion, parsley, and celery. Chill until slightly thickened, then top with the following avocado mixture:

AVOCADO MIXTURE:

4 cups mashed avocado
4 tablespoons lemon juice
3 tablespoons gelatin softened in
   ½ cup cold water
1 teaspoon salt
½ teaspoon sugar
⅛ teaspoon red pepper
3 tablespoons onion juice
¾ cup mayonnaise

Mix all together except mayonnaise. Set in refrigerator until partly congealed. Beat with beater and add mayonnaise. Serve with the following shrimp sauce:

SOUR CREAM SHRIMP SAUCE:

Garlic
½ pound cooked, chopped shrimp
1 pint sour cream
½ cup catsup
2 tablespoons Worcestershire
1½ tablespoons grated onion
1 teaspoon salt

Rub bowl with garlic and mix in remaining ingredients.

The Colonel's Inn Caterers'—Tallahassee Historical Cookbook

Tart and Sweet Salad

2 cups boiling water
2 packages lemon Jello
2 tablespoons chili sauce
¼ cup green pepper
1 cup celery

3 tablespoons India relish
¼ cup sliced stuffed olives
¾ cup nuts . . . pecans or English
    walnuts
Pimiento

Dissolve Jello in boiling water and chill. Chop pepper, celery, nuts and pimiento finely; slice olives. Add all ingredients to Jello when it begins to thicken. Taste for seasoning. If desired, a little salt or a bit of lemon juice can be added. Pour into oiled mold or molds. Colorful, sweet and tart. Serves 8.

Cypress Gardens Cookbook

Horseradish Salad

Dissolve:
1 package lemon jello and
1 package lime jello in
2 cups boiling water, cool and
    add

1 (No. 2) can crushed pineapple,
    drained

Blend:
1 (8-ounce) carton cottage cheese
    with

1 cup mayonnaise

Add:
Jello and 1 can condensed
    sweetened milk
2 heaping tablespoons horseradish

3 tablespoons lemon juice
¼ teaspoon salt

Stir and pour into a large mold or individual molds. Serves about 16.

Lost Tree Cook Book

Florida Sunshine Salad

1 (3-ounce) package lemon gelatin
1 (12-ounce) can apricot nectar
1 (6-ounce) can frozen orange
   juice, thawed

1 (3-ounce) package cream cheese
½ cup pecans

Heat apricot nectar to boiling point. Dissolve lemon gelatin in this. **Do not dilute.** Add can of orange juice undiluted. Make small balls of the cream cheese to which pecans have been added and place 3 small balls in each mold. Fill mold with juice mixture and refrigerate until jelled. This is good with fowl, pork or ham. It may also be used at holiday time in place of cranberry sauce. It can be made in one large mold or 6 individual molds. We prefer to use the individual molds.

(Governor Reubin O'D. Askew) *Seminole Savorings*

Besides the usual state symbols, Florida also has a State Mammal (the panther), a State Marine Mammal (the manatee), State Saltwater Mammal (the porpoise), State Saltwater Fish (the sailfish), State Freshwater Fish (largemouth bass), and State Shell (the horse conch).

Celestial Golden Salad

2 (3-ounce) boxes orange Jello
2 cups very hot water
Reserved syrup from mandarin
   oranges

1 (6-ounce) can frozen orange
   juice concentrate, thawed,
   undiluted
1 cup ginger ale
1 (11-ounce) can mandarin
   oranges, drained

Put Jello in bowl, add hot water and stir until Jello is dissolved. Add reserved syrup, orange juice and ginger ale. Chill until slightly thicker than unbeaten egg whites. When Jello is of desired consistency, mix in oranges. Turn into lightly oiled salad mold. Chill until firm. Serves 8–10.

Through Our Kitchen Windows

Fantastic Fruit Salad With Banana Sauce

1½ cups watermelon balls
10 slices of cantaloupe
10 slices of honeydew

10 grapefruit sections
20 orange sections
1½ cups fresh strawberries

Mound watermelon balls in center of platter. Arrange remaining fruit around the center like rays of sun. Serve with banana sauce.

BANANA SAUCE:
2½ ripe bananas
2 tablespoons lemon juice
¼ cup brown sugar

¼ cup honey
1 cup heavy cream, whipped

Combine bananas, lemon juice, sugar and honey in blender and blend till smooth. Fold in whipped cream. Serves: 6–8. Preparation: 20 minutes. Cooking: None. Difficulty: Easy.

Juicy Miss Lucy Cookbook

Cherry Mold

1 can dark pitted cherries (Bing cherries preferred)
1 package lemon gelatin
1 cup Rhine wine (or other dry white wine)

1 cup whipped cream (Cool Whip or other topping may be substituted)
½ teaspoon vanilla (or 1 teaspoon Crème de Cassis)

Drain cherries, reserving juice. Add enough water, if needed, to make 1 cup of liquid. Heat and dissolve gelatin in liquid. Add wine and cherries. Pour into mold or serving bowl. Refrigerate. When firm, unmold and garnish with whipped cream flavored with vanilla. Yield: 6–8 servings

Friendly Feasts Act II

Frozen Strawberry Salad

2 (3-ounce) packages cream cheese
2 tablespoons sugar
2 tablespoons mayonnaise
2 (10-ounce) boxes frozen strawberries

1 (8½-ounce) can crushed pineapple, drained
1 small Cool Whip
3 cups miniature marshmallows (about ⅓ package)
½ cup nuts, chopped

Cream together cream cheese, sugar and mayonnaise. Add strawberries and pineapple. Fold in Cool Whip, marshmallows and nuts. Pour into a mold and freeze. Serve frozen on lettuce leaves.

Note: Can use 1 package of whole frozen strawberries, and increase sugar to 1 cup. Can substitute ½ pint whipped cream for Cool Whip.

Canopy Roads

Papaya Seed Salad Dressing
*Intriguing—you'll learn to always keep
a jar of it in the fridge!*

1 cup red wine vinegar	1 teaspoon seasoned salt
½ cup superfine sugar	2 tablespoons grated onion
1 teaspoon dry mustard	2 cups salad oil
1 tablespoon Pickapeppa sauce	3 tablespoons papaya seeds

Combine first 6 ingredients in electric blender. Add salad oil with blender on high, in infinitely fine stream. It is the little bit at a time that thickens dressing. Add and blend papaya seeds for a short time, or only until dressing looks as if it contained coarsely ground pepper.

Maurice's Tropical Fruit Cook Book

Papaya

Papaya, familiarly known as the "pawpaw," contains the magical *papain*, a digestive aid. Dried, the enzyme is the key ingredient in the commercial meat tenderizers you purchase at the supermarket. Since papaya trees bear year round in Florida's tropical south, why not use the real thing? I spent some years operating a charter boat in the Caribbean and I have seen one of the best cooks in the Islands under a leaf of banana leaves held up by 4 crooked posts, rubbing meat with slices of the green papaya. She also told me that meat wrapped in a bruised papaya leaf is succulently tender.

Never throw away the papaya seeds, but rather refrigerate them in a tightly closed jar. Ground, they are added to marinades and salad dressings for savour pleasure. Or bruise and soak in vinegar before adding.

Papaya juice is an antidote for digestive problems, but the fresh fruit should be approached by allergy prone fanciers with caution.

Native to Central America, the fruit's landing in Florida is not recorded, but probably came via early Incan trade. It is possible to plant a papaya seed, grow the plant, set it out, watch it mature and fruit, harvest the fruit, extract a seed and plant a new crop all in the

CONTINUED

CONTINUED

same Florida year. Why not add a "pawpaw" tree to your backyard garden?

It is sometimes difficult for the uninitiated shopper to even recognize the papaya. It is anything but consistent, growing to sizes ranging from a walnut to 25 pounds and coming in all shapes— spherical, egg, pear, cylindrical.

Maurice's Tropical Fruit Cook Book

Aunt Alice's Grapefruit and Avocado Salad Dressing

2 teaspoons grated onion	2 tablespoons red wine vinegar
1 teaspoon dry mustard	1 cup salad oil
1 teaspoon salt	½–1 teaspoon celery seed
¼ cup sugar	Paprika

Mix dry ingredients in small, deep bowl. Then add onion to make smooth paste. Add salad oil, dripping in a little at a time and beating constantly with an electric beater. The dressing should be very thick. When it gets too thick, thin it down by beating in a little of the wine vinegar. Repeat until all the oil and all the vinegar have been used. Then stir in celery seed to taste and enough paprika to make it an attractive rosy color. (Be sure the oil is very cold, and that you never let it "puddle" while mixing. Also, store the dressing in the bowl in which it was made. Often it will separate if it is transferred to another container.) Use on an avocado and grapefruit salad. This is also good on a fruit salad made of grapefruit sections, orange sections, pineapple chunks, white grapes and mandarin orange slices.

Gator Country Cooks

 Ever wonder why a grapefruit is called a grapefruit? The name is taken from the way the fruit grows, in grape-like clusters. Florida produces over half of the grapefruit consumed through-out the world.

Blender Mayonnaise

1 egg	Juice of 1 small lemon
¾ teaspoon salt	½ cup olive oil
Dash of cayenne	½ cup salad oil

Break whole egg into blender; add salt, cayenne and lemon juice. Process a few seconds until blended. Turn blender on medium cycle and very slowly, but in a steady stream, pour in oils. Taste. Additional lemon juice may be added if needed, and processed for a few seconds.

Variation: A chopped clove of garlic, or 1 teaspoon Dijon mustard may be added with the seasonings for a different taste. Yield: 1 cup.

Friendly Feasts Act II

Seafood

A sport fisherman's catch—the fighting marlin—represents just one of the many kinds of game fish found in the waters off Florida's coasts.

Seafood Medley
A Sarasota favorite

¾ cup flour
¾ cup butter, melted
3 cups half and half
1½ teaspoons salt
½ teaspoon red pepper
2 cups sharp Cheddar cheese, grated
3 teaspoons onion juice
½ cup sherry
⅔ cup water or milk
1 pound crabmeat

1 pound shrimp, cooked, peeled and deveined
1 pound scallops, steamed 2–3 minutes
2 (8½-ounce) cans water chestnuts, drained
2 (14-ounce) cans artichoke hearts, halved
1 cup almonds, slivered
Parmesan cheese, grated

Preheat oven 325°. Add flour to butter. Stir over low heat 3 minutes. Add half and half, salt and red pepper. Stir constantly; continue cooking until thickened. Add Cheddar cheese; stir until cheese melts. Add onion juice, sherry and water or milk. Mix well. Line two 6×12-inch buttered baking dishes with crabmeat, shrimp, scallops, water chestnuts and artichoke hearts. Add cream sauce. Sprinkle with almonds and Parmesan cheese. Bake 30 minutes. Serves 16–18.

Fare by the Sea

Seafood Casserole

1½ pounds boneless fish
2 cans cream of celery soup
  (condensed)
½ cup dry vermouth or sherry
¾ cup mayonnaise
½ cup light cream or half and half

Worcestershire sauce
1 pound shrimp, cleaned
½ pound scallops
Parmesan cheese, grated or
  buttered bread crumbs

Cook fish briefly and cut into pieces. Combine soup, vermouth, mayonnaise and cream and stir into a smooth sauce. Season lightly with Worcestershire. Add all seafood and place in a casserole. Top with Parmesan cheese or crumbs. Bake at 350° for ½–¾ hours, until light brown and bubbly. Yield: 8 servings.

Friendly Feasts Act II

 Scallops can be easily "plumped up" by placing them in salted ice water a few hours before cooking.

Seafood Treasure

1 can shrimp
1 can crab meat
1 can lobster
1 onion, diced
1 (8-ounce) can sliced mushrooms,
  drained
1 tablespoon dried chives

1 teaspoon each: basil, tarragon,
  chervil
½ teaspoon garlic powder
Salt and pepper to taste
4 ounces Cheese Whiz
6 ounces mayonnaise (about ¾ of
  an 8-ounce jar)

Sauté onion and mushrooms. Lower heat, add drained and rinsed seafood. Add seasonings, then mix in Cheese Whiz and mayonnaise. Heat through over low flame, stirring often. Serve over rice and garnish with paprika and chives.

Galley Gourmet III

Mixed Seafood Lasagna
(Lasagna Fruits de Mer)

This variation of Italian lasagna layers broad noodles with shrimp, scallops, crab meat, ricotta cheese and a Velouté sauce. A welcome variation.

1 cup green onions, chopped	1 cup mushrooms, sliced
4 tablespoons butter	4 tablespoons butter
½ cup white wine	4 tablespoons flour
½ pound shrimp (small)	Salt and pepper
½ pound scallops cut in small pieces	1 pound ricotta cheese
½ pound crab meat (dark)	1 pound lasagna noodles, boiled as directed

Sauté green onions in butter. Add wine. Add shrimp and scallops. Cook 5 minutes. Add crab meat and mushrooms, salt and pepper. Strain, reserving both liquid and seafood.

Melt butter in a saucepan. Add flour and cook 2 minutes. Add reserved poaching liquid. Cook until thickened. Salt and pepper. Set aside.

Mix egg with ricotta cheese. In a buttered baking dish place a layer of lasagna noodles. Cover with a layer of ricotta cheese. Spread some of the seafood mixture over ricotta. Cover with a layer of the white sauce. Repeat layers of pasta, ricotta, seafood and white sauce until all is used. Finish with a layer of lasagna and top with a little white sauce. Bake in a 350° oven for 30 minutes.

Gourmet Cooking II

 Veloute—A white sauce made with flour, butter, and a chicken, veal or seafood stock. French for velvety.

Dolphin Pot Pie

1 package frozen puff pastry
2 stalks fresh broccoli, diced
1½ cups mushrooms, sliced
1 medium onion, sliced thin

2 cups (about 1 pound) fresh
  dolphin, cubed
1 egg white, lightly beaten
Zippy Cheese Sauce

On floured board, roll out one layer of pastry, to double its original size. Place in a 2½-quart casserole dish, covering bottom and sides (pastry may lap a little over the sides). Brown pastry in pre-heated 350° oven for about 20 minutes or until browned and puffed. Remove from oven and layer, in order, diced broccoli, sliced mushrooms, sliced onions and cubed fresh dolphin. Roll out second layer of puff pastry on floured board. Pour *Zippy Cheese Sauce* over casserole ingredients. Cover with second layer of pastry, overlapping edges with bottom crust. Trim excess; roll this remaining pastry into thicker dough and cut out fish shape. Place fish cut-out on top of casserole and brush with egg white. Bake at 350° for 30 minutes or until browned on top.

ZIPPY CHEESE SAUCE:

4 tablespoons butter, divided
½ cup minced onion
1 clove garlic, crushed
3 tablespoons flour
2 cups whole milk
1 packed cup grated cheese

1 tablespoon dry white wine or
  sherry
½ teaspoon dry mustard
½ teaspoon prepared horseradish
Dash hot pepper sauce

In medium saucepan, melt 1 tablespoon butter. Sauté onion and garlic; use slotted spoon to lift from pan. Melt remaining 3 tablespoons butter; blend in flour. Remove from heat and gradually stir in milk. Return to heat and bring to boil, stirring constantly. Reduce heat and simmer until sauce thickens. Add cheese, wine or sherry, mustard, horseradish and hot pepper sauce, stirring till cheese is melted and all ingredients are blended into smooth sauce. Pour over casserole as directed.

Secrets from the Galley

Dolphin—Not to be confused with the mammal, the dolphin is a beautiful blue and gold lean fish, often found under patches of sargasso seaweed and very popular in Florida.

Red Snapper With Avocado Sauce

6 red snapper fillets
Salt and pepper to taste
1 cup flour
¼ cup olive oil
3 shallots, minced
3 cloves garlic, minced

6–8 ripe tomatoes, peeled, seeded
and chopped
1 ripe avocado
2 tablespoons lime juice
Dash Tabasco sauce
Salt and pepper to taste

Season fish fillets with salt and pepper and dredge in flour to coat. Pour enough olive oil into a heavy skillet to cover the bottom. Sauté the fillets in the oil 2 minutes on each side. Remove fillets to a baking dish which will hold them in 1 layer. Sauté the shallots and garlic, adding more oil if necessary. When lightly browned, add the tomatoes and cook 2 minutes, mixing thoroughly. Pour sauce over the fish and cover the dish with buttered waxed paper. Bake at 325° for 15–20 minutes or until the fish flakes.

While the fish bakes, mash the avocado with lime juice, Tabasco sauce, salt and pepper. Remove fish from the oven and onto a serving platter. Keep warm. Quickly place the baking pan with the remaining sauce over direct heat and boil to reduce the liquid by ⅓. Remove from the heat and beat in the avocado mixture. Pour over the warm fish and serve immediately. Serves 6.

Seasons in the Sun

Snapper in Foil

1 (4½-pound) snapper, filleted
Seasoned salt
Pepper
2 thick onion slices

2 green peppers, quartered
1½ tablespoons butter
Fresh lemon juice

Place each fillet on a separate piece of heavy duty foil. Sprinkle each with seasoned salt, pepper, and lemon juice to taste. Top with onion slices, butter, and green pepper; seal foil leaving some room for expansion. Place each package on a baking sheet and bake at 375° for 45 minutes. Slit foil at the table being careful not to let the juices escape. This may be prepared ahead of time and refrigerated until baking. Serves 4.

Bay Leaves

Snapper With Sour Cream Stuffing

3–4 pounds fresh snapper, cut into
fillets
1½ teaspoons salt

2 tablespoons margarine, melted,
or oil

Cut a pocket in each fillet in order to stuff. Sprinkle fish inside and out with salt. Stuff fish loosely with *Sour Cream Stuffing*. Close opening with skewers or wooden picks. Place fish on a greased baking pan. Brush with margarine or oil. Bake at 350° for 40–60 minutes, or until fish flakes easily. Baste while cooking. Serves 6.

SOUR CREAM STUFFING:
¾ cup celery, chopped
½ cup onion, chopped
¼ cup margarine, melted
4 cups dry bread cubes
½ cup sour cream

¼ cup lemon, peeled and diced
2 tablespoons lemon rind
1 teaspoon paprika
1 teaspoon salt

Sauté celery and onion in margarine. Combine all ingredients and mix thoroughly.

Sugar Beach

Fillet of Sole, Florentine

4 pieces fillet of sole (or flounder)
3 scallions, chopped
1 package frozen chopped
  spinach, thawed and drained

Salt, pepper, garlic salt, paprika
6 tablespoons sour cream
2 tablespoons white wine
4 tablespoons Parmesan cheese

Sauté scallions and spinach in large frying pan in butter, season with salt and pepper and put in buttered baking dish. Arrange fish on top and sprinkle with salt, pepper and garlic salt. Combine sour cream and wine, spread over fish. Top with the cheese and paprika. Bake at 425° for 15–20 minutes. Serves 4.

Hint: Easy way to cook fish fillets. Put fillet in double thickness of foil, add a package of cream cheese with chives and seal well. Bake at 375° for 20 minutes; makes its own sauce.

Alone at the Range

 Fish that is really fresh will have bulging, clear eyes and bright gills, and will feel firm to the touch.

Barbecued Fish

This recipe came from an old fish camp on the Florida Keys.

½ pound butter
1½ cups brown sugar
¾ cup fresh lemon juice

⅓ cup soy sauce
3–5 pounds white meat fish
  (dolphin, snapper, grouper)

Melt butter and add sugar, lemon juice and soy sauce. Bring to a boil, stirring constantly. Then remove from the heat, set aside to cool. Skin and bone fish. Marinate fish in sauce one hour before grilling. Cook fish on a grill over low fire, basting often with remaining marinade. For additional flavor, add wet hickory chips to the fire. Serves 10.

Seasons in the Sun

Baked Fish With Sour Cream

1 (4-pound) flounder, red snapper
  or other large fish
Paprika

Butter
2 cups sour cream
Sliced almonds

Preheat oven to 350°. Scale, clean, split and remove bones from fish. Flatten it out. Rub inside and out with butter and paprika. Place on ovenproof dish. Cover with sour cream; sprinkle with almonds. Cover the dish. Bake about 45 minutes or until done. Garnish with chopped parsley.

Sawgrass and Pines

Heavenly Broiled Fish

2 pounds skinless fillets, fresh or frozen
2 tablespoons lemon juice
½ cup grated Parmesan cheese
¼ cup butter or margarine, softened

3 tablespoons mayonnaise or salad dressing
3 tablespoons chopped green onion
¼ teaspoon salt
Dash liquid hot pepper sauce

Thaw fish if frozen. Place fillets in a single layer on a well greased ovenproof platter (16 × 10-inch). Brush fillets with lemon juice and let stand for 10 minutes. Combine the remaining ingredients. Broil the fish fillets about 4 inches from source of heat for 6–8 minutes or until fillets flake easily when tested with a fork. Remove from heat and spread with the cheese mixture. Broil for 2–3 minutes longer or until brown.

Florida Flavors

Fish

There are over 50 species of fin-fish harvested commercially each year in Florida. "Fat fish" have an oil content of more than 5 percent. The oil is distributed throughout the flesh of the fish, and hence the flesh color tends to be darker than leaner species. The exact amount of oil in the fish depends on the species and also such variables as season of the year and depth of the water where the fish was caught. Some fat fish in our area include: amberjack, bluefish, croaker, king mackerel, spot, and swordfish. These fish have more flavor, and are generally chosen for smoking.

Lean fish have an oil content of 0.5 percent to 5 percent. The oil in these fish is characteristically concentrated in the liver. During cooking, these fish require more frequent basting. Some lean fish in our area include: black sea bass, black drum, flounder, grouper, jewfish, redfish (red drum channel bass) scamp, shark, spotted sea trout, sheepshead, the snapper family, tilefish, triggerfish, warsaw, weakfish, white sea trout, and whiting. Snook, a local gamefish, is also in the lean category. This treasured prize (for both sporting and

CONTINUED

CONTINUED

eating), is not available commercially, but you may be lucky enough to catch one fishing the rivers. Dolphin is another excellent lean fish and is often found under floating patches of sargasso seaweed. This fish is a beautiful blue and gold and would never be confused with the mammal of the same name.

Florida Flavors

Fillets de Yellowtail aux Bananas

1 pound yellowtail fillets, skinned
   and boned
Salt and pepper to taste
1 cup flour

1 ripe banana
½ cup butter, melted
¼ cup vermouth

Wash fillets and pat dry with paper towels. Season with salt and pepper to taste. Dredge fillets in flour to cover. Place in a small buttered baking dish. Peel banana and cut in half or quarters. Place banana on top of each fillet. Melt butter and add vermouth and pour over fillets. Bake at 450° for 10–15 minutes or until fish flakes when tested. Baste frequently. Spoon pan juices over fillets when serving. Serves 2.

Seasons in the Sun

Shrimp and Crab Stuffing for Flounder, Bass, Etc.

1 minced onion
2 stalks celery, diced
¼ cup diced green pepper
4½ tablespoons butter
1 dozen chopped shrimp
½ pound lump crabmeat
1 small bay leaf

Pinch thyme
¼ cup fresh mushrooms
¼ pound almonds, browned,
  chopped fine
1 tablespoon Worcestershire
½ cup cream
3 ounces sherry

Sauté onion, celery and green pepper in butter till soft. Add shrimp and mushrooms, cover to produce liquid, uncover and continue cooking till shrimp are barely pink. Add all other ingredients, stir and cook 5 minutes. Stuff fish and bake, allowing 10 minutes per pound. A greased sheet of brown paper under fish will keep it from sticking.

SAUCE FOR BASTING:

Blend butter, lemon juice, salt, Worcestershire and Tabasco. Add a little oil, pour over fish and baste often.

The Colonel's Inn Caterers'—Tallahassee Historical Cookbook

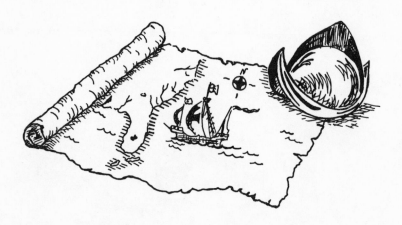

Sweet and Sour Shrimp
(Crevette Sauce Aigre-Douce)

These deep fried shrimp when combined with green pepper, pineapple and tomato provide an eye as well as a taste pleaser. The sweet and sour sauce is especially good.

1½ pounds shrimp, cleaned and deveined	2 onions, cut in wedges
1 tablespoon soy sauce	2 green peppers, cut in chunks
½ teaspoon salt	1½ cups sweet and sour sauce
½ cup cornstrach	1 cup pineapple chunks
Peanut oil	2 tomatoes, cut in wedges

Combine shrimp, soy and salt. Coat shrimp with cornstarch. Deep fry shrimp about 3 minutes. Drain on paper towel.

In wok or large fry pan, heat 1 tablespoon oil. Add onion and pepper. Cook 1 minute. Add sweet and sour sauce and pineapple. Add shrimp and tomato wedges. Cook until heated. Place on serving dish.

SWEET AND SOUR SAUCE:

½ cup sugar	¼ cup orange juice
1 tablespoon cornstarch	¼ cup pineapple juice
2 teaspoons salt	3 ounces tomato paste
½ cup red wine vinegar	

Blend sugar, cornstarch and salt. Stir in vinegar, fruit juices and tomato paste. Cook stirring constantly until thickened.

Gourmet Cooking

 Fresh seafood should be frozen in water in airtight containers or ziploc freezer bags, and thawed in the refrigerator.

Chow Shia
(Stir Shrimp)

Assemble all ingredients before you start. This cooks very quickly.

1½ pounds raw shrimp (or frozen
   raw) peeled and deveined
2 tablespoons cornstarch
½ teaspoon Accent
1½ tablespoons vegetable oil (to
   coat pan)

2 tablespoons water
2 tablespoons soya sauce
Salt to taste (about ½ teaspoon)
½ package frozen green peas
1 can mushroom bits and juice
2 teaspoons sherry

Coat raw shrimp with 1 tablespoon cornstarch; add Accent. Warm frying pan with oil until hot. Add remaining 1 tablespoon cornstarch to 2 tablespoons water and set aside to dissolve. Put shrimp in hot pan and cook about 1 minute over high fire, stirring constantly. Add soya sauce (this gives color to shrimp). Add salt, then remove from fire and put in bowl. Set aside.

Add raw peas, mushrooms and juice to same skillet. Salt. Cook about 1 minute over high heat, stirring constantly. Remove from heat. Return shrimp to peas in skillet. Add sherry.

Stir cornstarch-water mixture well and add to the shrimp for thickening. Return to fire just for a minute to cook thickening. It is now ready to serve over rice or Chinese noodles.

The Chinese word *chow* means "stir." *Mein* means "noodles." "Shrimp" is *shia*.

Cypress Gardens Cookbook

Soy Shrimp

3 pounds shrimp, peeled and
   butterflied
Oil
1 tablespoon vinegar
1 cup soy sauce

Juice of 2 lemons
1 tablespoon onion, grated
Garlic powder to taste
Cayenne pepper to taste

Place shrimp in a cookie sheet or shallow pan. Fill pan about ¼ inch with oil. Combine vinegar, soy sauce, juice from lemons and onion and pour over shrimp. Season lightly with garlic powder and heavily with Cayenne pepper. Broil for 5 minutes or sauté in saucepan.

Sugar Beach

Pleasure Island Shrimp

3 pounds uncooked shrimp	1 small bay leaf
½ cup chopped parsley	6 whole peppercorns
¼ teaspoon ground mace	1 tablespoon salt
1 clove garlic	⅛ teaspoon pepper
3 stalks celery	2 thick slices lemon

Shell and devein shrimp. Cover with water. Add parsley, lemon slices, mace, garlic, celery, bay leaf, peppercorns, salt and pepper. Simmer about 15 minutes. Drain and set shrimp aside.

¼ teaspoon cayenne	6 cups cooked rice
¾ teaspoon salt	8 slices cooked bacon, crumbled
3 tablespoons flour	10 ounces peanuts, chopped finely
½ cup sherry	6 hard-cooked eggs, chopped
1 quart cream	finely

Mix dry ingredients—cayenne, salt and flour. Blend dry ingredients with sherry. Scald cream and add slowly to sherry mixture. Cook slowly, stirring constantly until it is the consistency of a heavy cream sauce. Add the cooked, drained shrimp. Serve over hot cooked rice. In separate bowls, serve bacon, peanuts and eggs. These garnishes may be sprinkled over the shrimp sauce and rice.

Fiesta

Shrimp Boats
(Bateaux Des Crevettes)

Hollowed out crusty rolls become our "boat" container for shrimp, mushrooms and cheese to provide a unique taste treat.

6 brown and serve rolls	1 tablespoon flour
1 tablespoon butter, melted	Salt and pepper
1 egg yolk, beaten	1 cup mushrooms, sliced
¼ cup cream	2 tablespoons pimiento
1 cup American cheese, shredded	2 teaspoons lemon juice
1 pound shrimp, peeled	1 tablespoon dry sherry
⅓ cup green pepper, chopped	2 egg yolks, beaten
2 tablespoons butter	¼ teaspoon paprika
4 tablespoons green onion,	2 tablespoons butter, softened
chopped	Parsley, chopped

Bake rolls as directed on package reducing time by 5 minutes. Cut center out of each roll to form a rectangular shape. Brush inside of rolls with butter. Combine egg yolk, cream and cheese. Half fill roll with cheese custard. Bake at 350° for 15 minutes.

Melt butter in skillet. Sauté green onions, green pepper and shrimp until shrimp are cooked. Add flour, salt and pepper. Stir in cream and wisk until sauce thickens. Add mushrooms, pimiento, lemon juice and sherry.

Blend egg yolks, paprika and butter. Stir into shrimp and sauce. Pour into cheese custard rolls. Garnish with chopped parsley.

Gourmet Cooking

Shrimp and Deviled Eggs
About the best thing you've ever tasted

8 eggs, deviled
24 large shrimp or 32 medium size, cooked and cleaned
4 tablespoons butter
4 tablespoons flour
¼ teaspoon salt

2 cups half and half or light cream
1 cup shredded sharp Cheddar cheese
Several dashes cayenne pepper
Crushed potato chips

Preheat oven to 350°. In a buttered casserole, or 8 individual casserole dishes, place the deviled eggs and arrange the shrimp around them. Melt butter in a heavy-bottomed pan, blend in flour and salt. Over low heat, stir constantly for 3 or 4 minutes until well blended and the taste of raw flour has vanished. Add the half and half, continue stirring, and cook until mixture thickens. Add cheese and cayenne and cook until cheese melts. Pour over eggs and shrimp. Sprinkle the top with crushed potato chips. Bake for 30 minutes. Serves 8.

DEVILED EGGS:

8 hard-cooked eggs
2 tablespoons mayonnaise
2 tablespoons prepared mustard (Dijon type)
¼ teaspoon salt

2 teaspoons vinegar
Several dashes cayenne pepper
¼ teaspoon dry mustard

Cut eggs in half, lengthwise. Remove yolks; put through strainer or mash very well. Add remaining ingredients and blend until smooth. Fill hollow of egg whites. Chill.

Cook and Deal

Memree's Soppin' Shrimp

Memree makes a special trip to the Florida panhandle around Memorial Day and gets the fresh shrimp for this memorable meal.

¼ pound butter	2½ teaspoons black pepper, more
⅔ cup lemon juice	to taste
1 teaspoon grated lemon rind	3 pounds raw shrimp, in shell
1½ cups Italian dressing	

Wash shrimp and remove heads, but leave in shell. Drain. In a medium saucepan, melt butter and add lemon juice, lemon rind, Italian dressing, and black pepper. Bring to a boil. Add shrimp and simmer for about 6 minutes or just until tender.

Serve with crusty French bread. Ladle shrimp into individual bowls with plenty of sauce for soppin' the bread in. You peel your own shrimp, which guarantees the pleasure of slow eating. Serves 4.

Cross Creek Kitchens

Gulf Shrimp Divine
Simply Divine!!

⅔ cup olive oil (no substitute)	3 tablespoons butter (no
½ cup lemon juice	substitute)
½ teaspoon salt	1 clove garlic, crushed
⅛ teaspoon pepper	1 cup blanched slivered almonds
2 pounds fresh shrimp, shelled	Dash of hot pepper sauce
and deveined	½ cup dry vermouth

Make marinade of olive oil, lemon juice and seasonings. Marinate shrimp for at least 2 hours. Melt butter in large skillet; add garlic and shrimp. Reserve marinade. Stir-fry shrimp over medium heat until pink. Discard garlic; remove shrimp to a hot platter. Sauté slivered almonds in butter until brown; add marinade, hot pepper sauce and vermouth. When well blended, pour sauce over shrimp. Serve over saffron rice mixed with chopped chives or finely chopped green onions. Serves 6–8.

Suncoast Seasons

Scampi With Mustard Sauce

MUSTARD SAUCE:

3 shallots, chopped
1 garlic clove, minced
2 tablespoons Worcestershire
  sauce

½ cup fresh lemon juice
1 pound butter
¾ cup prepared mustard
½ cup sherry

In large saucepan, mix all ingredients for mustard sauce. Simmer, stirring constantly, until smooth and slightly thickened, about 10 minutes.

SCAMPI:

36 jumbo shrimp, peeled,
  deveined and butterflied
3 tablespoons olive oil
Salt to taste
Pepper to taste

½ cup fresh bread crumbs
Lettuce for garnish
Red pepper rings for garnish
Lemon wedges for garnish

Arrange butterflied shrimp, split side up, in broiler pan. Brush with oil; season with salt and pepper. Sprinkle with bread crumbs. Broil for about 5 minutes. Place on platter that has been garnished with lettuce, red pepper rings and lemon wedges. Pour ½ cup mustard sauce over shrimp; place remaining sauce in bowl and pass with shrimp. Serves 6. Suggested wine: Saint-Véran.

Gulfshore Delights

Shrimp Florentine

¼ cup finely chopped onion
¼ cup butter
¼ cup flour
1 teaspoon salt
½ teaspoon dry mustard
2 cups milk
½ cup grated Swiss cheese
1 cup grated Parmesan cheese

2 (10-ounce) packages frozen chopped spinach, cooked and drained
1 (8-ounce) can water chestnuts, drained and sliced
1½ pounds shrimp, boiled and peeled
1 tablespoon lemon juice
Paprika

Preheat oven to 400°. Cook onion in butter until tender. Stir in flour, salt and dry mustard. Add milk. Cook, stirring constantly, until thickened. Remove from heat. Add Swiss cheese and stir until melted. Fold in half the Parmesan cheese.

Combine spinach and water chestnuts and spread in a greased, shallow 1½–2-quart baking dish. Drizzle lemon juice over spinach. Add shrimp, then sauce; top with remaining Parmesan cheese. Garnish with paprika. Bake for 15-20 minutes or until hot. Yield: 6 servings.

Some Like It South!

Boiled Shrimp With Butter Sauce

BOILED SHRIMP:

Season boiling water with:	Pickling spices
Salt	Lemon
Garlic	Onion
Bay leaves	Vinegar

BUTTER SAUCE:

1 cup butter, melted	2 tablespoons lemon juice
¼ teaspoon turmeric	Salt
⅛ teaspoon curry	Few drops of Tabasco
¼ teaspoon dry mustard	Dash of Worcestershire

To seasoned, boiling water add washed, unpeeled shrimp (½ pound per person). Do not peel before adding, or at all, as they are served on a plate with cup of butter sauce in do-it-yourself, peel-and-dunk fashion. Cook the shrimp 10 minutes, then drain. For butter sauce: Combine all ingredients. This will serve 4 people. (One-half stick of butter per person when served this way.)

Through Our Kitchen Windows

Shrimp and Crabmeat au Gratin

⅔ stick butter	Sherry to taste
3 heaping tablespoons flour	⅓ stick butter
2 tablespoons sugar	½ pound crabmeat
1 teaspoon salt	½ pound shrimp, cooked
½ teaspoon pepper	1 cup sharp cheese, grated
1 tablespoon paprika	Slivered almonds
2 cups milk	

Melt ⅔ stick of butter in a saucepan and gradually add flour, milk, sherry, sugar, salt, and pepper. Allow it to come to a boil and keep warm. Grease a casserole dish with remaining butter. Place half of shrimp and crab in casserole and half of the cheese followed by a layer of sauce. Repeat layers and sprinkle top with paprika and almonds. Bake at 325° for approximately 45 minutes.

Bay Leaves

Shrimply Delicious

1 pound large shrimp (26–30)   15 slices of bacon, cut in half
1 cup prepared chili sauce

Shell and devein shrimp. Marinate raw shrimp in chili sauce for 1 hour, or overnight.

Wrap each shrimp in ½ piece of bacon and secure with a toothpick. Preheat oven to broil and place shrimp 6–7 inches from heat and cook for approximately 3–4 minutes or until bacon is browned. Turn over and brown other side. Serve hot. Serves: 5–6. Preparation: 15 minutes. Cooking: 8 minutes. Difficulty: Easy.

Juicy Miss Lucy Cookbook

Dolphin Street Broiled Oysters

1 cup butter	¼ teaspoon black pepper
½ cup chopped green onions	½ teaspoon dry mustard
1 cup chopped celery	3 eggs
¼ cup chopped parsley	1 cup dry bread crumbs
1 quart oysters	4 teaspoons dry chablis
¼ teaspoon salt	

Sauté the onions, celery, and parsley in butter until brown. Then add diced oysters, salt, pepper, dry mustard and 3 beaten eggs. Cook over a low heat for about 15 minutes. Stir in the bread crumbs and dry chablis then remove from the heat. Place the mixture in shells or ramekins and stick under the broiler for 2 minutes.

This deserves to be served with a glass of chilled dry chablis. Makes 10 servings.

Ode to the Oysters

Oysters Rockefeller V
Put a star by this one

3 dozen oysters	1 teaspoon lemon juice
1 cup chopped cooked spinach	3 tablespoons dry white wine
¼ teaspoon salt	½ cup milk
¼ teaspoon pepper	¾ cup mayonnaise
½ cup melted butter	1 cup dry bread crumbs
¼ cup minced onions	Dash of paprika
1 teaspoon Accent	

Preheat the oven to 375°. Drain the spinach and blend it with salt, pepper, onions and ¼ cup melted butter. After arranging the oyster shells on the rock salt, spoon 1 teaspoon of the spinach mixture into each shell. Put an oyster on top of the spinach and sprinkle with a little lemon juice and Accent.

Mix the wine with the mayonnaise. When well blended, slowly stir in the milk. Spoon this mixture over the oysters. Now, mix the dry bread crumbs with the remaining ¼ cup melted butter and cover the oysters. Sprinkle tops with a dash of paprika. Bake in the oven for 20 minutes. Makes 6 servings.

Ode to the Oysters

Oysters Lydia

1 bunch parsley, chopped
8 green onions, finely chopped
2 large cloves garlic, minced
¾ stick butter
2 tablespoons olive oil
4 tablespoons Worcestershire
  sauce
1 lemon

¼ teaspoon salt
1 teaspoon Tabasco sauce
2 pints raw oysters, drained
¼ cup Italian seasoned bread
  crumbs
2 small loaves French bread,
  sliced

Preheat oven to 450°. Sauté parsley, onions and garlic in butter and olive oil until tender. Pour into 2-quart baking dish. Add Worcestershire, juice of lemon and remaining lemon rind, salt, Tabasco and drained oysters. Sprinkle with bread crumbs. Bake on upper oven rack for 10–15 minutes, until bread crumbs are lightly browned. Serve at once with French bread. Yield: 6–8 servings.

Some Like It South!

Oyster Club Sandwich

½ tablespoon flour
½ cup milk
¼ pint oysters
2 tablespoons butter
1 egg
¼ cup rolled cracker crumbs

6 slices of buttered toast
1 tomato, sliced
Lettuce
4 slices crisp bacon
Salt and pepper
Mayonnaise

Blend the flour in the milk until smooth and add a well beaten egg. Drain and dry the oysters. Dip them into the batter and roll them in cracker crumbs, then simmer them in the butter until golden brown. Make a two layer sandwich, the first layer consisting of lettuce, tomato, mayonnaise, and bacon, the second layer of oysters, salt and pepper.

Ode to the Oysters

Oysters Golden Rod

½ pint oysters
Oyster liquor
6 hard boiled eggs
2 tablespoons butter

2 tablespoons flour
Salt and pepper
1 cup milk
4 slices buttered toast

Simmer the oysters in their liquor until the edges begin to curl. Remove and drain. Make a roux with the butter and flour, then add salt and pepper to taste. When smooth, stir in the milk and cook at a low heat for 7–8 minutes. Remove yolks from the eggs. Slice up the whites and stir into the sauce. Quarter the oysters and add them to the sauce as well. Continue to simmer over the low heat for 5 minutes. Serve over buttered toast. Sprinkle with sieved egg yolks. Makes 4 servings.

Ode to the Oysters

Deviled Crab

1 pound crab meat	½ teaspoon dry mustard
3 eggs	1 tablespoon Worcestershire sauce
1½ cups crushed Ritz crackers	1 teaspoon onion juice
1 stick melted butter	1 tablespoon lemon juice
¼ cup milk	¼ cup sherry
2 teaspoons celery salt	Paprika

Save ½ cup crackers for top of casserole and combine all other ingredients. Put in buttered casserole dish or individual shells. Sprinkle top with crackers and paprika and bake at 350° for 30 minutes. Serves 6–7.

Gator Country Cooks

Crabmeat Yummies

½ cup butter or margarine, softened	½ teaspoon garlic salt
1 (5-ounce) jar Old English cheese spread, softened	1 (7-ounce) can crabmeat, drained or 1 (6-ounce) box frozen crabmeat, thawed
1½ teaspoons mayonnaise	6 English muffins, split in half

Mix butter and cheese with mayonnaise and garlic salt. Stir in crabmeat. Spread on muffins. Freeze at least 10 minutes. Remove from freezer, cut into quarters and broil 5–10 minutes until hot and bubbly. Serve warm. Serves 4.

May be made several weeks ahead and frozen until ready to cook.

Gulfshore Delights

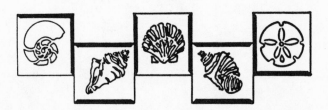

Crabmeat Stuffed Baked Avocado

2 avocados, halved and sprinkled
  with lime juice
1 stick of butter
1 small onion, finely chopped
2 tablespoons flour

3 cups milk, scalded
1 pound lump crabmeat
1 teaspoon prepared mustard
1 tablespoon Pickapeppa Sauce

Sauté onion in butter but do not allow to brown at all. Make roux with flour and cook for 2 minutes.

Add milk, a small amount at a time, guarding against lumping. Cook and stir until smooth and thick. Remove from heat. Combine these ingredients and add sauce. Fill avocado cavities with mixture, sprinkle with Parmesan cheese and bake at 400° for 15 minutes or until avocado is heated through.

Maurice's Tropical Fruit Cook Book

Avocados are sold unripened; allow a few days for them to ripen before you need them for a recipe. You can speed up the ripening process by putting the avocado in a brown paper bag. When pureed with a little lemon juice, they can be frozen in an airtight container for later use.

Ollie's Crab Cakes

1 pound crabmeat (claw meat
  preferred)
2 tablespoons mayonnaise
2 eggs, beaten
1 tablespoon parsley

½ teaspoon dried onion
½ teaspoon prepared mustard
Cracker crumbs
1 tablespoon flour
½ cup butter

Mix well the crab, mayonnaise, eggs, parsley, onion and mustard. Shape into cakes and roll in cracker crumbs to which 1 tablespoon of flour has been added. Fry in butter just long enough to warm, but not cook.

Note: Can use cooked flaked fish also.

Florida Flavors

Stuffed Crab
(Crabe Farci)

A very old family recipe for stuffed crabs combines luscious crab-meat with onions and seasonings to produce a memorable experience.

2 medium onions, finely chopped
8 scallions, chopped
3 tablespoons butter
½ cup breadcrumbs
1 pound crabmeat
⅓ cup parsley, finely chopped

1 clove garlic, chopped
1 egg
⅓ cup pimiento, chopped
Salt and pepper
Breadcrumbs

Sauté onions in butter until well done. Add crabmeat and blend well. Add breadcrumbs and stir well. Add parsley and garlic. Add egg, blending well. Cook until mixture is thick and smooth. Add pimiento and seasonings.

Stuff clean crab shells or scallop shells. Sprinkle with breadcrumbs. Bake in 350° oven for 10 minutes. Garnish with lemon.

Gourmet Cooking

Crab "Meeting Street"

4 tablespoons margarine
4 tablespoons flour
1 cup light cream or half and half
½ teaspoon salt

Ground black pepper
4 tablespoons dry vermouth
1 pound crab meat
½ cup grated Parmesan cheese

Melt margarine over medium heat. Stir in flour, and add cream, making a rich, smooth cream sauce. Season with salt and pepper and stir in vermouth. Add crab meat and place in small greased casserole. Sprinkle Parmesan cheese over top and bake, uncovered, at 350° for 20 minutes. Yield: 4 servings.

Friendly Feasts Act II

Stone Crabs

14 large stone crabs, cooked
1 cup butter

3 key limes, squeezed
1 clove garlic, crushed

Refrigerate the stone crabs until serving time. Ladies usually can eat 3 claws, men, 4 claws. Melt the butter in a saucepan over medium low heat, add the lime juice and garlic. Simmer at least 15 minutes before serving. Do not boil. Serve the stone crabs cold, in the cracked shell, with the melted butter sauce in a dish alongside. Serves 4.

Seasons in the Sun

Tuna Burgers (or Crab)

1 can tuna, drained and flaked
½ cup Italian bread crumbs
2 tablespoons minced onion
⅓ cup mayonnaise

2 tablespoons chili sauce
1 teaspoon lemon juice
Margarine

Combine tuna, crumbs and onion. Blend mayo, chili sauce and lemon and stir into tuna. Shape into 4 patties and sauté in margarine. Serve on a bun with lettuce and tomato. Serves 4.

Hint: Keep a tray of lemonade ice cubes in freezer for iced tea.

Alone at the Range

Crawfish Enchilado

1 chopped onion
½ chopped sweet pepper
3 crushed cloves of garlic
Oregano
½ cup olive oil

1 (16-ounce) can tomato sauce
1 small can tomato paste
Hot pepper flakes
Salt and pepper
6–8 crawfish tails

Brown onion, sweet pepper, garlic and oregano in oil until golden. Add tomato sauce, paste, hot pepper flakes, salt and pepper; bring to a boil. Cut raw crawfish tails into bite-size pieces and add to sauce. Reduce heat, cover and cook for about 1 hour. May be served over rice. Can also be made with raw shrimp.

Margaritaville Cookbook

Crab-Stuffed Artichoke Entrée

4 artichokes
2 tablespoons minced green
  onions
1 clove garlic, minced
2 small bay leaves, crumbled
4 tablespoons butter
¼ cup all-purpose flour

⅛ teaspoon pepper
¾ cup clam juice
¼ cup dry white wine
1 pound crabmeat
¼ cup grated Parmesan cheese
1 (1-ounce) triangle Gruyère
  cheese

Preheat oven to 375°. Cut off top third of artichoke. Trim base and tips of leaves. Cook artichokes in boiling salted water for 25 minutes or until tender. Drain upside down and let cool. Remove choke by gently removing a few center leaves and scooping out the fuzzy center. Place artichokes in an 8 × 8 × 2-inch baking dish.

In a medium skillet, sauté onions, garlic and bay leaves in butter until tender but not brown. Blend in flour and pepper. Add clam juice. Cook quickly, stirring constantly, until mixture thickens and bubbles. Stir in wine, crab and Parmesan cheese.

Spoon into artichokes and place a fourth of the Gruyère cheese on top of each. Pour boiling water around artichokes in baking dish to ½-inch depth. Cover loosely with foil. Bake for 25–30 minutes. Serve with rice pilaf and drawn butter as a main course. Servings: 4. Preparation time: 30 minutes. Cooking time: 30 minutes. Baking time: 30 minutes.

Jacksonville & Company

Crab and Shrimp Hot Dish

1½ pounds crabmeat
½ pound small shrimp
½ green pepper, chopped
⅓ cup chopped parsley
2 cups cooked rice

1½ cups real mayonnaise
2 packages frozen peas, thawed
  but not cooked
Salt and pepper to taste

Toss lightly. Place in a greased casserole. Refrigerate covered. Bake at 350° covered for 1 hour. Serves 6.

Lost Tree Cook Book

Lobster Thermidor

3 lobsters
2 cups heavy cream
¾ cup butter
3 tablespoons flour
1½ teaspoons salt

Freshly ground pepper
½ cup milk
¼ cup prepared mustard
½ cup grated Parmesan cheese

Boil lobsters and remove from shells; cut into bite-sized pieces. Heat cream to a simmer, stirring occasionally; do not boil. Melt 4 tablespoons butter. Stir in the flour, salt, pepper and milk, stirring constantly until thick. Mix in the warmed cream. Combine lobster and sauce and pour into a baking dish that has been rubbed well with mustard. Sprinkle with Parmesan cheese, dot with butter and bake in 400° oven uncovered for 10 minutes. A very rich dish.

Note: Mixture may be placed in cleaned lobster shells (colorful), or served over pastry shells or rice. Chicken may be substituted for variation.

Florida Flavors

Florida Lime Seviche

Use any variety of white meat fish, cleaned and cut into bite size pieces. The less adventurous eaters reject the thought of eating "raw" fish, but in reality seviche is not raw at all but is rather "cooked" by the lime acid.

Diced raw fish
2 cups lime juice
⅓ cup finely chopped onion
3 cloves garlic, finely chopped
2 hot peppers, finely chopped
1 teaspoon chili powder

1 teaspoon salt
1 teaspoon sugar
¼ teaspoon oregano
Freshly ground black pepper
¼ cup olive oil

Combine all ingredients and mix well. Add fish pieces, cover tightly and allow to marinate in refrigerator overnight.

You can serve seviche as an appetizer or as an accompaniment to end-of-the-day cocktails. It's great for lunch or at poolside. In place of fish, you may substitute scallops.

Maurice's Tropical Fruit Cook Book

Fast and Easy Scalloped Scallops

2 pounds small bay scallops (or ocean scallops, halved)
½–¾ cup homemade mayonnaise made with lemon juice (or Hellman's with lemon juice added)
3–4 twists of peppermill

¼ teaspoon shallot powder (or ½ teaspoon very finely chopped shallots)
Salt to taste
Cracker meal or non-flavored bread crumbs
Butter

Mix mayonnaise, pepper, shallot powder, salt, and scallops. Use just enough mayonnaise to moisten scallops well. Butter scallop shells or small au gratin dishes. Add scallop mixture; top with meal or crumbs. Dot with butter. Broil for 5–8 minutes under hot broiler until browned. Yield: 6 as an appetizer, 4 as an entrée.

Florida Flavors

Conch Fritters

1 pound ground conch	1 small green pepper, chopped
1 small onion, chopped	1 teaspoon salt
2 cloves garlic, minced	¼ teaspoon black pepper

To all of the above ingredients, add 1 cup of self-rising flour and mix into a batter. Spoon out by the teaspoonful into deep frying fat over medium-high heat. Cook until browned.

Conch—marine-life mollusk, a purported aphrodisiac delicacy enjoyed either raw in salads or cooked in chowders and fritters.

Conch—native of nearby island ancestry or born in the Florida Keys. So-called because of character and habitual similarity to mollusk. Tough, close to home, proud of their unique heritage and protective of their way of life.

Margaritaville Cookbook

Tartar Sauce

⅔ cup mayonnaise
1 teaspoon grated onion
2 teaspoons chopped chives
1 teaspoon chopped parsley

2 drops Tabasco
1 teaspoon chopped dill pickles
1 teaspoon capers

Blend all together.

The Colonel's Inn Caterers—Tallahassee Historical Cookbook

Beer can be a great help in cooking seafood; it can be used as a marinade to produce flaky fish, or as a flavor enhancer. Cooking fish in beer also eliminates unwanted fish odor.

Poultry
and Game

Reminiscent of pirate days, The Billy Bowlegs Festival in Fort Walton Beach provides rollicksome fun, including burying treasure and capturing and sacking the city.

Chicken Breasts With Orange Sauce
A gourmet's delight

3 large chicken breasts, boned,
  split and skinned
1 teaspoon salt
¼ cup butter
2 tablespoons flour

2 tablespoons sugar
¼ teaspoon dry mustard
¼ teaspoon cinnamon
⅛ teaspoon ginger
1½ cups orange juice

Sprinkle chicken breasts with ½ teaspoon of the salt. Melt butter in a large skillet. Add chicken and brown both sides. Remove from skillet. Add flour, sugar, mustard, cinnamon, ginger and remaining ½ teaspoon salt to drippings in pan. Stir to a smooth paste. Gradually add orange juice and cook, stirring constantly, until mixture thickens and comes to a boil. Add chicken breasts. Cover; simmer over low heat until chicken is tender; about 25–30 minutes. If you wish, 3 cups of hot cooked rice may be served with the chicken. May be done ahead. Reheats well. Serves 4–6.

Cook and Deal

Chicken à la Grecque

Breasts of 5 chickens, halved and
  boned
2 cups milk
¼ teaspoon white pepper
4 tablespoons butter
½ cup olive oil
1½ cups chopped onion
1 cup sauterne

1 cup green seedless grapes
1 cup pitted black olives
1 teaspoon chopped mint
1 teaspoon chervil
Dash of salt
Dash of garlic salt
Dash of white pepper

Preheat oven to 325°. Soak chicken breasts in milk seasoned with
pepper for several hours. Melt butter and olive oil in large heavy
skillet and add onion. Sauté over medium heat until lightly
browned. Remove onion with slotted spoon and set aside. Drain
the chicken and brown quickly over high heat in the butter and oil
remaining in the skillet. Transfer to a heatproof casserole and add
the browned onions, sauterne, grapes and olives, mint, chervil,
salt, pepper, and garlic salt. Bake uncovered for 1 hour. Serves 6–8.
  Note: This can be assembled hours ahead of time and then
baked as directed.

Palm Beach Entertains

Chicken Breast Baked in Wine

4 large chicken breasts
Juice of one lemon
Salt and pepper to taste
1 large onion, chopped
1 teaspoon dry mustard

4 teaspoons parsley, fresh or dried
1 stick butter
Paprika
½ cup white wine

Place chicken breasts in open baking pan, skin side up. Sprinkle
with lemon juice, salt, pepper, onion, dry mustard and parsley.
Dot with butter. Sprinkle with paprika and bake in 350° oven for 1
hour or more. When nearly done add wine and baste with juices in
pan. Don't overcook. Delicious with rice.

Fiesta

Baked "Fried" Chicken
(Microwave)

½ cup butter or margarine
1½ cups cracker crumbs (Ritz)
½ cup Parmesan cheese
¼ cup parsley flakes
½ teaspoon garlic powder

1 teaspoon salt
½ teaspoon pepper
1 (2½–3 pound) chicken, cut into
    pieces

Melt butter in dish that is large enough to dip chicken pieces (12 × 9-inch). Mix crumbs and seasonings together in separate bowl. Dip chicken into butter and roll in crumb mixture and place in baking dish. Be sure to put large pieces to outer edge of baking dish. Cover with waxed paper and microcook for 10 minutes on HIGH. Turn pieces over, cover and cook for another ten minutes on HIGH. Test by piercing with sharp knife and if more cooking time is needed, uncover and cook as needed, 2–4 minutes. Preparation time: 10–15 minutes. Cooking time: 20–24 minutes. Serves 4–6.

Conventional Method: Place in shallow pan and bake at 350° for one hour.

Thyme Waves

Coca-Cola Chicken

1 chicken, cut up
1 cup ketchup
1 cup Coca-Cola

1 tablespoon Worcestershire sauce
Salt and pepper

Place chicken in large frying pan or electric cooker, and salt and pepper. Mix ketchup, Coca-Cola, and Worcestershire sauce together and pour over chicken. Simmer for 1 hour covered, turning once during cooking time. Serve with rice.

Canopy Roads

Chicken Alma Peyroux
(Poulet à La Duchess)

A very old specialty of my mother was this unusual French way of cooking chicken. All skin is removed from the chicken which is then seasoned. As it is fried it is placed into a dutch oven. The potatoes are then fried in the same oil and added to the chicken along with chopped parsley and garlic. The chicken is good but the potatoes are delicious.

3 chickens, cut for frying
Peanut oil for frying
6 pounds potatoes, peeled and cut for French frying

3 cloves garlic, chopped
½ cup parsley, chopped
Salt and pepper

Remove the skin from chicken pieces (except wings). Salt and pepper each piece. Heat peanut oil in a large skillet. Fry chicken first. Fry potatoes in the same oil. As chicken and potatoes are cooked, place them in a large dutch oven over low heat. Sprinkle with garlic and parsley. Cover. Let rest for 10 minutes, covered. Arrange chicken and potatoes on serving plate.

Gourmet Cooking II

Baked Chicken Breasts Supreme

2 tablespoons butter or margarine
2 tablespoons salad oil
6 large chicken breast halves
  (2½–3 pounds)
1 (10¾-ounce) can condensed
  cream of chicken soup
  (undiluted)
½ cup light cream (20%) or dairy
  sour cream plus 2 tablespoons
  milk

½ cup dry sherry or white wine,
  divided
1 teaspoon tarragon leaves
1 teaspoon Worcestershire sauce
¼ teaspoon chervil leaves
¼ teaspoon garlic powder
1 (6-ounce) can sliced mushrooms,
  drained, or ¾ cup fresh
  mushrooms, sliced and sautéed
  in butter

Heat oven to 350°. In oven, heat butter and oil in 13½ × 9 × 2-inch baking dish, until butter is melted. Place chicken in baking dish, turning to coat with butter. Arrange skin side up: bake, uncovered, 1 hour. In saucepan, heat soup, cream and remaining wine or sherry, stirring occasionally. Stir in tarragon leaves, Worcestershire sauce, chervil leaves, garlic powder and mushrooms. Remove chicken from oven; drain fat from dish. Pour soup mixture over chicken. Cover tightly; cook 15–20 minutes longer or until fork-tender.

Variation: Omit tarragon, Worcestershire, chervil and garlic; instead stir 1 (13½-ounce) can pineapple tidbits, drained, and ½ cup sliced seedless green grapes into soup mixture with the mushrooms.

Note: This recipe can be made faster in an electric skillet. Brown chicken at 325°, pour off fat; add ¼ cup wine or sherry and simmer, covered, at 225° for 30 minutes. Add soup mixture and heat till warm, about 10 minutes.

Secrets from the Galley

Chicken Key West
(State Finalist Winner)

¼ pound butter or margarine
1 broiler-fryer chicken, cut in
  parts and skinned
1 teaspoon salt
1 teaspoon freshly-ground pepper

¼ teaspoon paprika
1 large onion, thinly sliced
3–4 cloves garlic, crushed
¼ cup Key lime juice

Melt butter over medium heat in large frying pan with cover. Add chicken and cook until light brown on all sides. Sprinkle with salt, pepper and paprika. Add onion and garlic. Cook, stirring occasionally, 5 minutes. Pour lime juice over chicken. Cover and simmer 25 minutes or until fork can be inserted with ease. Remove cover and cook a few minutes until chicken is a golden color.

Margaritaville Cookbook

Chicken Breast Parmesan
(Microwave)

½ cup seasoned fine bread
  crumbs
¼ cup grated Parmesan cheese
1½ pounds boneless chicken
  breast
1 egg, well beaten
2 tablespoons olive oil

1 cup shredded mozzarella cheese
1 (15-ounce) can tomato sauce
¼ teaspoon oregano leaves
Grated Parmesan cheese

Combine on waxed paper bread crumbs and Parmesan cheese. Dip chicken breast in egg and then bread crumb mixture until well coated. Heat oil over high heat and quickly brown crumb mixture on chicken on both sides. Place chicken in glass baking dish and sprinkle mozzarella cheese over chicken. In small bowl combine tomato sauce and oregano leaves. I add a bit of sugar too. Spoon tomato sauce over chicken. Heat covered in microwave 5–6 minutes or until sauce is bubbly and meat is tender, or bake at 350° for about 30 minutes. Sprinkle with grated Parmesan cheese and heat uncovered until cheese is melted.

Florida Flavors

Chicken Asparagus Casserole

8 chicken breasts
Salt, poultry seasoning, onion, celery
1 medium onion, chopped
1 stick butter
1 (10-ounce) can cream of mushroom soup
1 (10-ounce) can cream of chicken soup
1 (5-ounce) can evaporated milk
½ pound sharp cheese, grated
½ teaspoon Tabasco sauce
2 teaspoons soy sauce
1 teaspoon salt
½ teaspoon pepper
Accent to taste
2 tablespoons chopped pimiento
2 cans asparagus
1 (8-ounce) can sliced mushrooms
½ cup slivered almonds

Cook chicken breasts with salt, poultry seasoning, onion and celery until tender. Bone and cut in bite-size pieces. Sauté chopped onions in butter. Stir in remaining ingredients except asparagus, mushrooms and almonds.

In 3-quart casserole, layer chicken, asparagus, mushrooms, and sauce, ending with sauce. Top with slivered almonds and bake at 350° for 45–60 minutes.

The Colonel's Inn Caterers—Tallahassee Historical Cookbook

Sweet and Sour Chicken

1 (8-ounce) bottle 1,000 Island dressing
1 package dry onion soup mix
1 (12-ounce) jar apricot or peach preserves
1 chicken, cut up

Mix the dressing, onion soup mix and preserves together and pour over chicken, which has been placed in a large baking pan or dish. Bake at 350° for 1½ hours. Do not cover.

Note: This is delicious when served over yellow rice.

Through Our Kitchen Windows

Chicken Breasts Mediterranean
(Blanc de Volaille Mediterranée)

Thin chicken breasts breaded and sautéed are garnished with a light tomato sauce enriched with onions, mushrooms, garlic and black olives. Chicken and sauce are served over a bed of thin pasta.

6 chicken breast halves, deboned
2 tablespoons flour
Salt and pepper
2 tablespoons butter
2 tablespoons peanut oil
2 cloves garlic, minced
1 cup onion, chopped
½ pound mushrooms, sliced
2 cups tomatoes, peeled and
   seeded

½ cup white wine
½ cup chicken stock
½ cup black olives, pitted and
   sliced
⅓ cup parsley, chopped
1 pound vermicelli, cooked
   according to the package
   directions

Pound the chicken breasts lightly between wax paper. Salt and pepper to taste. Dredge in flour lightly.

Heat butter and oil in a skillet. Sauté chicken about 3 minutes on each side. Remove and keep warm. In the same skillet sauté the onions, garlic and mushrooms. Add tomatoes. Pour in the wine and stock. Place chicken breasts in sauce. Lower heat to simmer. Cook about five minutes. Add olives and heat through (1 minute). Cover a large serving dish with pasta. Arrange chicken breasts over pasta. Pour sauce over the chicken. Garnish with parsley.

Gourmet Cooking II

Baked Chicken and Brown Rice

1 whole fresh frying chicken	¼ pound mushrooms, sliced
1 stalk celery, sliced	½ onion, chopped
1 carrot, sliced	1 clove garlic, chopped
1 cup brown rice, rinsed	½ cup yellow squash, chopped
4 cups water	¼ cup green bell pepper
Parsley	½ cup zucchini, chopped
½ teaspoon coriander	Sea salt

Take all skin off chicken and place in large roaster. Place all vegetables, brown rice, water and seasonings around chicken. Be sure to sprinkle seasoning on the chicken. You may use any vegetables, such as broccoli, cauliflower, zucchini squash, or whatever you have on hand. Bake covered at 350° for 1½ hours or until rice is soft.

Step-By-Step to Natural Food

Rice With Chicken

2 chickens	1 can asparagus tips
3 cloves garlic	1 tablespoon salt
1 sour orange	½ teaspoon pepper
⅓ cup oil	1 bay leaf
1 green pepper	3½ cups dry wine
1 large onion	2 cups broth
1 can tomato sauce	2 pounds rice
2 cans red peppers	Saffron to color
1 can petit pois	

Prepare broth with chicken giblets. Cut chicken into quarters and cover with crushed garlic and sour orange juice and leave to stand for a while. Heat oil and brown chicken. Add chopped onion and green pepper, tomato sauce, 1 can of red peppers and their liquid, the liquid from the peas and the asparagus, salt, pepper, bay leaf, saffron, dry wine, broth and water. Wash and soak rice. When chicken is half cooked, add the rice and allow to cook over low heat until rice is loose and soft. Add the petit pois, and garnish with remaining red peppers, asparagus, petit pois and hard boiled eggs. Serves 8 approximately.

The Cuban Flavor

Chicken Tetrazzini

1 (3½-pound) stewing chicken
2 teaspoons salt
⅛ teaspoon pepper
½ pound fine noodles
7 tablespoons butter
½ pound sliced mushrooms
¼ cup all-purpose flour
½ teaspoon salt

1 cup light cream
¼ cup sherry or cooking sherry
1½ cups grated natural cheese or
   ⅓ cup Parmesan cheese
Paprika
1 stalk of celery
1 small onion
½ cup parsley

Simmer chicken with 2 quarts water, celery, onion, parsley, 2 teaspoons salt, and pepper, covered, 3–4 hours. Remove chicken from broth; add noodles, cook 8 minutes. Drain, reserving broth; boil down to 2 cups; strain. Cut meat into pieces; pre-heat oven to 450°. In 3 tablespoons hot butter, sauté mushrooms, set aside. Into 4 tablespoons melted butter, stir flour, ½ teaspoon salt, broth, cream. Cook until thickened. Add chicken, mushrooms, sherry; heat. Place noodles in greased casserole and pour sauce over them. Top with cheese and paprika. Bake 10 minutes in 450° oven. Serves 8. This may be prepared and frozen ahead of time.

The Gasparilla Cookbook

Chinese Chicken Cashew

1 pound chicken breasts, cut in bite-size pieces	½ cup chopped onion
3 tablespoons soy sauce	½ cup bamboo shoots
1 teaspoon sugar	½ cup diced green pepper
1 tablespoon cornstarch	½ cup diced celery
2 tablespoons peanut oil	¼ cup pimento, chopped
½ cup carrots, sliced thin	1 cup salted cashews

SAUCE:

1 tablespoon soy sauce	¼ teaspoon ground ginger
1 teaspoon sugar	3 or 4 tablespoons water
3 tablespoons sherry	

Combine 3 tablespoons soy sauce, 1 teaspoon sugar and 1 table-spoon cornstarch, mixing until lumps disappear. Pour this over chicken and refrigerate overnight. The next day combine sauce ingredients.

Preheat wok to 375° with 2 tablespoons peanut oil. Pour chicken and marinade into hot wok. Begin stirring immediately with the same motion as tossing a salad, stirring constantly for 4 minutes, until peppers change color and carrots are tender. Add bamboo shoots, pimento and cashews. Then add sauce and cook for 1 minute. Serve over rice. Serves 4 or 5.

Apalachicola Cookbook

Chicken With Garlic
(Poulet à l'Ail)

All the unpleasant characteristics usually associated with garlic completely disappear when cooked for a long time and produces a delicious vegetable. The chicken is fantastic.

1 chicken, cut in 10 pieces	6 tablespoons butter
Pepper	Salt
20 cloves garlic	1 cup chicken stock

Pepper chicken pieces. Separate garlic head into individual cloves. Do not peel. Melt butter in skillet. Add chicken and garlic. Sauté covered about 8 minutes. Turn chicken pieces. Sauté covered another 8 minutes. Remove chicken. Salt chicken. Add chicken stock and bring to a boil. Reduce to ¾ cup. Return chicken to sauce and heat. Serve with rice.

Note: To eat the garlic, cut skin away from pulp with a knife and fork or suck the tender cloves from the skin.

Gourmet Cooking

Hot Chicken Sandwich

12 slices Pepperidge Farm bread

Cut crusts from bread. Butter each slice.

FILLING:

2 cups cooked chicken, chopped	¼ cup olives, chopped
⅓ cup onion, chopped	1 small can mushrooms
2 hard-boiled eggs, chopped	½ cup mayonnaise

Combine filling ingredients; spread on bread and make a sandwich.

SAUCE:

1 cup sour cream	1 can cream of mushroom or cream of chicken soup

Combine sour cream and soup. Pour over sandwiches and refrigerate overnight. Bake at 325° for 45 minutes. Sprinkle with paprika.

Seasoned with Sunshine

Mary Ann's Cornish Game Hens

4 Cornish game hens
1 can Le Sueur peas, drained
4 medium potatoes
4 large carrots

1 (10-ounce) bottle soy sauce
1 (10-ounce) bottle A-1 sauce
3–4 medium onions

Place hens in the middle of a large piece of 18-inch aluminum foil. Fill the cavities of the hens with peas. Make a pocket of the aluminum foil by tightly closing the two sides. Place pieces of potatoes, carrots and onions around the edges of the hens. Pour ¼ bottle of soy sauce over each hen, coating the entire top. Next pour ¼ bottle A-1 sauce over each hen, coating the top of each. (You may use a little more of the sauce if you desire. I usually do because it makes the most unbelievably good gravy-type sauce, but thinner.) Put 1 tablespoon of water in each foil pocket, salt and pepper to taste; tightly seal the tops of the foil so that no steam or juice can escape. Bake at 350° for 1½ hours. Just before serving, fold back the foil just enough to brown the tops of the hens. Serve on a plate in the foil pockets with the foil folded down so that the sauce cannot run out. Serve with salad and French bread for a complete meal.

Seasoned with Sunshine

Cornish Game Hen Tropical
A marvelous idea for a memorable twosome picnic.

2 Cornish game hens
Seasoned salt
Freshly ground black pepper
2 tablespoons olive oil
3 cloves garlic, chopped
2 tablespoons lime juice
3 bay leaves

1 (6-ounce) can orange
  concentrate
½ teaspoon thyme
½ teaspoon dry mustard
1 teaspoon horseradish
1 cup chablis

Split hens in half, season and brown lightly in olive oil in heavy skillet. Remove birds to baking pan lined with aluminum foil. Add remaining ingredients to skillet in which hens have been browned in order given. Bring mixture slowly to boil and simmer for 1 minute. Pour sauce over hens and bake for 40 minutes or until tender. Baste from time to time and if birds brown too soon, shield with foil. When done, remove from baking dish and chill.

Maurice's Tropical Fruit Cook Book

Sour Cream Noodle and Venison Bake

1 (8-ounce) package medium
  noodles
1 pound ground venison (or
  ground beef)
2 tablespoons butter
1 teaspoon salt
½ teaspoon pepper

½ teaspoon garlic salt
1 (8-ounce) can tomato sauce
1 cup creamed cottage cheese
1 cup sour cream
6 green onions, chopped
¾ cup shredded sharp Cheddar
  cheese

Cook noodles, rinse, drain. Brown meat in butter. Add salt, pepper, garlic salt, then tomato sauce. Simmer 5 minutes. Combine cottage cheese, sour cream, onions and noodles. In a 2-quart casserole, alternate layers of noodle mixture and meat mixture, beginning with noodles and ending with meat. Top with cheese. Bake at 350° for 25 minutes or until cheese is melted and browned.

Florida Flavors

Venison Swiss Steak

¼ cup flour
¾ teaspoon salt
Few grains cayenne pepper
Dash thyme, nutmeg and cloves
3 pounds venison steak
2 tablespoons beef suet, melted
  (or vegetable oil)
3 large onions, thinly sliced
2 cups tomatoes, peeled and
  quartered (or 2 cups stewed
  tomatoes)
1½ tablespoons Worcestershire

1½ cups red Burgundy wine
½ clove garlic, minced
Bouquet garni (2 sprigs parsley, 1
  bay leaf and 2 sprigs English
  thyme, tied together)
1 cup mushroom caps
1½ tablespoons butter
Salt and pepper, to taste
2 tablespoons red currant jelly
  (optional)
Wild rice

Sift flour with salt, cayenne and spices. Vigorously pound this into steak. Heat melted beef suet or vegetable oil in Dutch oven and sear meat on both sides. Add onions and brown. Add tomatoes, Worcestershire, wine, clove, garlic and bouquet garni. Cover pot tightly. Place in 350° oven and cook for 2½ hours or until meat is tender. Remove bouquet garni. Sauté mushroom caps in butter. Stir into meat with salt and pepper. Mix in jelly. Serve with wild rice. Serves 6–8.

Seminole Savorings

Doves With Rice

12 doves
½ cup butter (1 stick)
Salt and pepper
1 cup rice

2¼ cups chicken bouillon
¼ cup chopped onion
1 small can mushrooms or fresh

Brown doves in butter and set aside. In same pan, sauté onions. Then add rice and brown. When rice is a medium brown, add bouillon and mushrooms. Place these ingredients in a 2-quart casserole with doves on top. Cover and bake 45 minutes–1 hour at 325°. A 10-inch Corningware skillet is perfect.

Apalachicola Cookbook

Orange and Wine Roasted Duck

1 (4–5 pound) wild duck	⅛ teaspoon pepper
Water, to cover	1 tablespoon salad oil
3 onions, quartered	¼ of an orange
2 bay leaves	¾ cup water
1 stalk celery, coarsely chopped	¾ cup orange juice
½ teaspoon salt	¼ cup sherry wine

Place duck in deep saucepan; cover with cold water. Add 1 onion, bay leaves, celery, salt and pepper. Bring to boil. Reduce heat, cover and simmer 20 minutes. Take duck from pan and set oven at 350°. Brush bird with oil. Put orange and 2 onions in cavity. Set duck in roasting pan, breast side up. Add ¾ cup water. Roast for 1 hour, uncovered, basting with orange juice combined with sherry. Serves 4.

Seminole Savorings

Duck Casserole

2 ducks	1 (6-ounce) can mushrooms
1 whole onion	1½ cups duck broth
2 ribs celery	1½ cups light cream
1 (6½-ounce) package long-grain and wild rice	1 tablespoon chopped parsley
½ cup butter	1½ teaspoons salt
½ cup chopped onion	¼ teaspoon pepper
¼ cup all-purpose flour	1 (4½-ounce) package slivered almonds

Boil ducks for 2 hours with whole onion and celery. Cook rice according to package directions; set aside. In deep skillet melt butter; sauté chopped onion, stir in flour. Add mushrooms and broth. Add cream, parsley, salt, pepper and rice. Debone duck and add to other ingredients. Place in 2-quart casserole; sprinkle with almonds. Bake at 350° for 25 minutes. Serves 6–8.

Beyond the Bay

Good-Bye Turkey Casserole

7½ tablespoons sifted flour
⅜ teaspoon onion salt
1½ teaspoons salt
⅜ cup butter, melted (6 tablespoons)
3¾ cups light cream or Half and Half
¼ cup sherry wine

2½ cups cubed, cooked turkey or chicken
2¼ cups instant rice
2¼ cups turkey or chicken broth
¾ cup shredded American cheese
1½ (15-ounce) cans asparagus spears
3 tablespoons toasted slivered almonds

Stir the flour, onion salt, and half of the salt into the butter. Stir in the half and half. Cook over hot water, stirring occasionally, until thickened. Let cool, add the sherry, and set aside. Add the turkey or chicken and the rice, and put into a 2-quart shallow baking dish. Combine the turkey or chicken broth with the remaining salt and pour over the rice mixture. Sprinkle half of the cheese over the rice mixture. Place the asparagus on top and pour the reserved sauce over this. Sprinkle with the remaining cheese and top with the almonds. Bake at 375° until bubbly, approximately 20 minutes. Serves 8–10.

A Pinch of Sunshine

Meats

The massive Villa Vizcaya in Miami was completed by multimillionaire James Deering. Its price tag, even back in 1920, was a staggering $15 million.

Father's Day Steak

1 (3–4 pound) London broil or top
   round steak
½ cup sherry
½ cup soy sauce
¼ cup oil

¼ cup lemon juice
2 tablespoons brown sugar
½ teaspoon ginger
1 garlic clove, minced
⅛ teaspoon hot sauce

STEAK SAUCE:
Reserved marinade
4 teaspoons cornstarch

½ pound mushrooms, sliced
¼ cup sliced scallions

In saucepan, mix together all ingredients except steak. Cook 10 minutes. Cool. Place steak in plastic bag. Add marinade; tie securely. Refrigerate for 24 hours. Remove steak, reserving marinade to make sauce. Place meat over hot coals or on broiling rack in oven with meat 4–5 inches from heat. Broil 25–40 minutes for rare to medium steak. Brush with marinade; turn occasionally. Carve thin slices diagonally across grain. Serve with sauce. To make sauce, stir cornstarch into small amount of water. Add to remaining marinade. Bring to a boil. Add mushrooms and scallions. Cook slowly until thickened. Dilute with water until sauce is desired consistency. Serves 6–8.

Sunny Side Up

Steak au Poivre
If you like steaks and pepper, you'll love this.

4 (1¼-inch) thick filets, 6–8 ounces
   each
Salt to taste
1 tablespoon peppercorns
3 tablespoons vegetable oil

2 tablespoons butter, divided
3 tablespoons finely chopped
   shallots
½ cup white wine or vermouth
½ cup heavy cream or sour cream

Salt steaks. Crush peppercorns in plastic bag with mallet or rolling pin. Press the crushed peppercorns into both sides of steaks. Cover with wax paper. Let stand at least 10 minutes, preferably 2–3 hours. Heat oil over medium high heat in heavy skillet. Cook steaks 3 minutes, then turn. Cook 1½–3 minutes and remove steaks to heated serving platter. Keep warm while preparing sauce.

Pour fat from skillet. Add 1 tablespoon butter and shallots; cook until wilted. Add wine; cook on high until reduced by half. Add cream and cook 1 minute. Swirl in remaining butter; pour over steaks. Serve immediately. Serves 4.

Suggested wine: Cabernet Sauvignon or Côte Rôtie.

Gulfshore Delights

Brisket in Beer
Make the day before

3–4 pounds beef brisket
½ teaspoon garlic powder
½ teaspoon salt
¼ teaspoon pepper

1 cup Heinz Chili Sauce
1 cup beer
4 cups cooked noodles, rice or
   mashed potatoes

Put salt, pepper, and garlic powder on both sides of the brisket. Place the meat in a roasting pan and cover with the chili sauce and beer which has been mixed in a bowl. Cover the pan with foil and bake 2½–3 hours at 350°. Let cool a few minutes and slice. Serve the gravy over rice, noodles, or mashed potatoes. Preparation: 5 minutes. Easy. Serves: 6–8. Cooking: 2½–3 hours. Can do ahead.

Culinary Arts & Crafts

Beef Wellington

1 (4-pound) beef tenderloin	¼ cup green onions, chopped
1 teaspoon salt	1 tablespoon flour
½ teaspoon pepper	½ teaspoon summer savory
1 package crescent dinner rolls	1 tablespoon parsley
1 pound fresh mushrooms, chopped	¼ cup beef consomme
1 stick butter	¾ cup ham, chopped
1 teaspoon salt	3 tablespoons melted butter

Salt and pepper roast; bake at 425° for 30 minutes. Remove from oven; let stand to cool. Trim all fat. Sauté mushrooms and onions in butter until tender; add flour, salt and spices. Stir constantly until thickened; it will resemble paste. Add ham; cool.

Unroll rolls; press side by side out flat, long and wide enough to cover tenderloin. Press ham sauce mixture onto top of pastry; lay tenderloin on pastry and close seams tightly. Place seam side down in baking dish. Bake at 400° for 30–35 minutes, until dough is brown. The last 10 minutes brush dough with melted butter. Let stand 15 minutes before cutting.

Sawgrass and Pines

 Savory—an aromatic herb with a slightly salty taste. Both summer and winter savory are often used as salt substitutes.

Boeuf aux Champignons à la Crème

4 tablespoons butter or
  margarine, divided
2 tablespoons vegetable oil,
  divided
½ pound fresh mushrooms, sliced
4 green onions, finely chopped
Salt and pepper to taste

2 pounds flank steak, partially
  frozen
¼ cup dry white vermouth
1 cup beef stock
1 cup whipping cream
2 teaspoons cornstarch
Fresh parsley

Heat 2 tablespoons butter and 1 tablespoon oil in skillet; add mushrooms and sauté 4–5 minutes to brown. Add green onions and cook for 1 minute longer, seasoning with salt and pepper; set aside. Cut partially frozen meat into pieces and slice. Heat remaining butter and oil in skillet in which mushrooms were cooked and brown a few pieces of meat at a time. Meat should remain rare. Set aside as the meat is cooked. Pour vermouth and beef stock into hot skillet and reduce liquid to about ⅓ cup. Beat in cream and cornstarch (blended with 1 tablespoon cream) with a wire whisk; simmer 1 minute, add the mushrooms and simmer 1 minute more. Season beef lightly with salt and pepper and return to skillet with any juices that may have escaped; stir gently to combine. Correct seasoning. When ready to serve, reheat slowly, but do not overdo it. Serve over rice or noodles garnished with parsley.

Beyond the Bay

Beef and Vegetable Stir-Fry

1 pound round steak, partially
   frozen
2 onions or 1 dry onion and
   several green onions

6–8 large mushrooms
½ small head cabbage
½ pound fresh spinach

SAUCE:
2 cups beef broth
1 tablespoon sugar
½ cup soy sauce

3 tablespoons cornstarch
3 tablespoons water

Preheat electric skillet to 350°. Any cut round steak will do; cut into strips ⅛-inch thick. Slice the onions thin and include tops of green onions if they are used. Mushrooms are optional; if used slice thin. Sliver the cabbage and cut the spinach into 1-inch strips. Add oil to skillet, test for correct temperature. Place beef strips in pan, stir-fry quickly. Add onions, sauté till golden, also add mushrooms and cabbage. Add spinach last. Stir-fry 3–5 minutes. Pour sauce over, heat through. Serve at once with hot rice. To make sauce: In small pan or bowl, heat the beef broth (bouillon cubes may be used) and add the sugar and soy sauce. Stir in cornstarch which has been dissolved in water. Simmer till sauce clears or add uncooked sauce to vegetable dish and then simmer.

Note: This may be made with chicken and chicken broth. Also tuna may be used; instead of stir-frying it first, add it at the end so that it is simply heated.

Through Our Kitchen Windows

For People Who Aren't Afraid to Come Out of Their Shell Beef With Cashews

1 pound top sirloin	⅔ cup roasted cashews, unsalted
4 tablespoons oil	½ cup beef bouillon
½ pound asparagus, cut in 1" pieces	1 tablespoon cornstarch (dissolved in bouillon)
2 cloves garlic, minced	4 teaspoons soy sauce
3 thin slices ginger root, skin removed and chopped fine	1 teaspoon sesame oil
5 green onions, sliced on diagonal or 1" pieces	1 teaspoon oyster sauce

Trim all fat from top sirloin and cut across the grain into thin bite-size slices. Heat 2 tablespoons oil in wok over high heat. Stir-fry beef 3–5 minutes until brown. Remove from wok and set aside.

In a large skillet, cook asparagus in boiling water to cover 3–5 minutes until tender but still crunchy. Drain and rinse in cold water.

Heat remaining 2 tablespoons oil in wok over high heat. Add garlic, ginger, onion and cashews. Stir-fry for 1 minute. Add beef and asparagus to wok along with remaining ingredients. Cook until it boils and thickens. Serves: 4. Preparation: 20 minutes. Cooking: 15 minutes. Difficulty: Easy.

Juicy Miss Lucy Cookbook

Stuffed Sirloin Roast

1 (3-pound) sirloin tip roast	1 or 2 cans mushrooms, sliced
1 clove garlic, minced	2 tablespoons stuffed olives, sliced
1 onion, thinly sliced	½ cup bread stuffing
1 green pepper, slivered	1 tablespoon pimiento, minced
2 tablespoons butter	Pepper
1 can cream of celery soup	

Cut a large pocket in roast with a small opening. Sauté onions, garlic, and green pepper in butter until tender. Stir in soup, mushrooms, olives, bread stuffing, pimiento, and season with pepper. Bring to a boil and remove from heat. Fill pocket and place in a shallow roasting pan. Bake at 450° for 15 minutes; reduce heat to 350° and bake 30 minutes longer. Roast will be medium rare. Serves 6.

Bay Leaves

Hamburger-Spinach Casserole

1 (10-ounce) package frozen
 chopped spinach
1 (8-ounce) package cream cheese,
 softened
½ cup sour cream
3 tablespoons milk
3 tablespoons onion, finely
 chopped

4 ounces wide noodles
1 pound ground beef
1 (15-ounce) can tomato sauce
2 teaspoons sugar
Salt, pepper and garlic powder, to
 taste
Cheddar cheese, shredded

Cook spinach according to directions; drain well. Mix cream cheese, sour cream, milk and onion in a separate bowl and let set to continue softening. Cook noodles in boiling salted water for 10 minutes. Drain well. Brown ground beef and drain well. Add tomato sauce, sugar, salt, pepper, garlic powder and noodles. Heat thoroughly.

In a 2-quart casserole, place a layer of hamburger-noodle mixture (use ½). Top with ½ of the cream cheese mixture. Top with spinach and finish with remainder of hamburger-noodle mixture. Bake in covered casserole at 350° for 40 minutes.

Remove from oven and top with remaining cream cheese mixture. Cover completely with shredded Cheddar cheese. Return to oven uncovered for approximately 10 minutes or until cheese melts completely. Serves 4.

Seminole Savorings

Zucchini Casserole With Ground Beef

2 pounds zucchini squash
1½ pounds ground beef
1 medium onion, chopped
½ pound Cheddar cheese, cubed
1 teaspoon salt

1 teaspoon pepper
1 (10¾-ounce) can cream of
 mushroom soup
1 cup herb stuffing mix or bread
 crumbs, approximately

Boil the squash until tender and drain well. Brown the beef and onion. Cube the cheese and place in a greased casserole dish. Add the zucchini, beef, onion, salt, and pepper. Pour the soup over the top and cover with bread crumbs. Bake at 350° for 45 minutes.

A Pinch of Sunshine

Tomatoes Yemistes
(Greek, Meat-Stuffed Tomatoes)

8 large fresh tomatoes
1 pound ground round steak
2 teaspoons tomato paste
⅔ cup rice, uncooked
1 onion, chopped fine
3 tablespoons olive oil

2 tablespoons green celery,
   chopped
2 tablespoons parsley, chopped
½ teaspoon cinnamon
Salt and pepper
Fine bread crumbs

Brown onion and ground meat in olive oil. Add tomato paste, tomato pulp, chopped and drained, approximately 2 cups hot water, celery, parsley, salt and pepper, rice and cinnamon to meat mixture and cook about 15–20 minutes, stirring frequently.

Prior to this preparation, wash the tomatoes and cut a thin slice off the tops, leaving other end of top attached. Carefully scoop out the pulp. After meat mixture has cooked, stuff each tomato with mixture, allowing sufficient liquid within. Sprinkle the tops with bread crumbs and a little olive oil. Cover with the tomato tops. Arrange tomatoes in a buttered pan, adding remaining mixture around the stuffed tomatoes and bake in a moderate oven until tomatoes are tender and well browned, approximately 1½ hours.

Apalachicola Cookbook

Stuffed Burger Bundles

1–2 cups packaged herb seasoning
   stuffing
Warm water and butter
1 pound hamburger
⅓ cup evaporated milk

1 (10-ounce) can cream of
   mushroom soup
2 teaspoons Worcestershire sauce
1 tablespoon catsup

Soften stuffing with warm water and a little butter. Combine meat and milk. Divide in 5 patties on waxed paper. Pat each to 6-inch circle. Put ¼ cup stuffing on each; draw meat over stuffing and seal. Place in baking pan. Combine soup, Worcestershire sauce and catsup and pour over meat. Bake uncovered at 350° for 35–40 minutes.

Through Our Kitchen Windows

Swedish Meat Balls

⅓ cup minced onion
2 tablespoons butter or margarine
1 egg
½ cup milk
½ cup fresh bread crumbs
1¼ teaspoons salt
2 teaspoons sugar
½ teaspoon allspice
¼ teaspoon nutmeg

1 pound ground chuck
¼ pound ground shoulder pork
2 tablespoons butter or margarine
3 tablespoons flour
1 teaspoon sugar
1¼ teaspoons salt
⅛ teaspoon pepper
1 cup water
¾ cup light cream

In large skillet, sauté onion in 2 tablespoons butter until golden. Meanwhile, in large mixing bowl, beat egg; add milk and crumbs. Let stand 5 minutes; add salt, sugar, allspice, nutmeg, chuck, pork and onion. Blend well with fork. In same skillet, heat 2 tablespoons butter. Using 2 teaspoons, shape the meat mixture into small balls, about ½–¾ inches in diameter. Drop some balls into skillet, brown well on all sides; remove to warm casserole; repeat until all meat is brown. Then, stir flour, sugar, salt and pepper into fat left in skillet; add water and cream slowly; stir until thickened. If desired, pour gravy into casserole with meatballs and heat thoroughly. The gravy may be served separately if desired. May be prepared the day before and refrigerated. Serves 6.

Meatballs are good served as hors d'oeuvres on toothpicks—with or without gravy, of course.

Cypress Garden Cookbook

Elegant Spicy Meat Balls

2 pounds lean ground beef, chuck
  preferred
2 eggs, beaten
1 cup applesauce
2 tablespoons grated onion
½ cup seasoned bread crumbs
1 tablespoon chopped parsley

1½ teaspoons salt
¼ teaspoon pepper
1 cup water
1 (16-ounce) can whole
  cranberries
1 (12-ounce) can chili sauce
2 tablespoons lemon juice

Mix meat thoroughly with the next eight ingredients. Form into meat balls (marble size for cocktails, large for main course). Place in lightly greased 3-quart casserole; do not crowd, layering them carefully. Combine cranberries, chili sauce, and lemon juice; mix well. Pour over meat balls; do not stir. Bake, uncovered, at 325° for 1½ hours. Occasionally shake pan gently and baste. Freezes well. (Defrost and heat at 325° until bubbly. For appetizers, keep hot in chafing dish.) Yields 8 for entrée, 20 for appetizers.

The Prima Diner

Picadillo II

1 pound ground beef
1 pound ground pork
2 medium onions
1 large green pepper, (optional)
Olive oil
6 small tomatoes (or 2 small cans)
2 teaspoons salt
1 teaspoon garlic powder
Pepper to taste

1 tablespoon brown sugar
¼ cup vinegar
¼ cup stuffed green olives,
  chopped
½ cup raisins
1 tablespoon capers
½ cup red wine or ½ cup tomato
  juice or bouillon

Chop onions and green pepper very fine and brown in the olive oil. Add chopped tomatoes, salt, garlic, pepper, and meat, stirring constantly to break in small bits. Add remaining ingredients slowly until meat is tender, about 1 hour. Serve over rice, mashed potatoes, or split buttered and toasted hamburger buns. Serves 10.

The Gasparilla Cookbook

Empanada
(Spanish Meat Dish)

1 cake active dry or compressed yeast	1½ heaping tablespoons vegetable shortening
1 cup lukewarm water	6¼ cups flour
½ cup plus 2 tablespoons butter	2 teaspoons salt

In a small bowl, sprinkle yeast over 1 cup lukewarm water. Let stand 2 minutes; then stir to dissolve. Set bowl aside. Melt butter and vegetable shortening; cool till lukewarm. Combine flour and salt in large deep bowl. Make a well in the center; pour in eggs, yeast and butter mixture. Slowly stir together. (If too dry, add another ½ cup of lukewarm water as needed.) Work dough until mixture becomes a medium-firm dough that can be lifted up in a moist-solid mass. Place dough on lightly floured surface and knead by pressing down, pushing it forward several times with heel of hand. Fold it back onto itself and knead for at least 10 minutes or until dough is smooth and elastic. Sprinkle a little flour over and under dough to prevent its sticking to board. Gather dough into a ball and place in a large, lightly buttered bowl. Drape a towel over bowl and set it in a warm place for approximately 1½ hours or until dough doubles in bulk.

FILLING:

1–1½ pounds ground beef	2 large green peppers, seeded and cut into ½-inch squares
3 tablespoons oil	Parsley, chopped
3 large onions, finely chopped	1 (2-pound) can crushed tomatoes
½ teaspoon garlic, finely chopped	Salt and pepper to taste

In a skillet, brown ground beef; set aside. In oil, cook onions, garlic, green peppers and parsley for 8–10 minutes or until vegetables are soft, but not brown. Add tomatoes and raise heat to cook mixture briskly, till most of the liquid in pan has evaporated. Add cooked ground beef, salt and pepper and cool to room temperature. Preheat oven to 325°.

To assemble: Divide the dough into thirds. On lightly floured surface, roll each third into a rectangle to fit 9 × 13-inch pan. Place first third in bottom of a 9 × 13-inch pan. Spread ½ of the filling over

CONTINUED

CONTINUED

it and layer the top with another ⅓ of the rolled out dough. Spread other ½ of filling over the top again. Cover with remaining ⅓ of dough. Fold in rim and press around to seal securely. Make small hole in center to release steam. Bake at 325° for approximately 1½ hours.

Secrets from the Galley

Burt's Beef Stew

3 slices bacon
2 pounds of lean beef (chuck is juicy)
Flour (enough to cover meat)
Salt and pepper, to taste
1 tablespoon sugar
1 onion, chopped
1 clove garlic, minced
6 ounces tomato sauce

½ can of beef broth or water
1 cup dry Burgundy wine
1 bay leaf (if you like it)
Pinch of thyme
2 carrots, coarsely chopped
2 stalks celery, coarsely chopped
2 large potatoes, quartered
½ cup fresh mushrooms, sliced

Cut bacon into small pieces; cut beef into 1-inch cubes. Cook bacon in large heavy pot. Salt and pepper beef and dip into flour. Brown in bacon fat, turning often. Add a little oil if needed. Sprinkle with sugar. Add onion and garlic and brown a little. Add tomato sauce, water or broth, wine, bay leaf and thyme. Cover and cook slowly for about an hour and a half. Add carrots, celery, then potatoes and mushrooms. Uncover and cook until meat and vegetables are tender. Serves 4–6.

(Burt Reynolds) *Seminole Savorings*

Lucy's Spaghetti Meat Sauce
None better . . . makes a lot . . . freeze some

3 large onions, chopped
2 cloves garlic, minced
¼ stick butter
¼ cup oil
3 pounds ground chuck
1 pound fresh mushrooms, sliced
(use stems, too)
2 (28-ounce) cans Italian tomatoes
(Progresso brand is good)

1 (12-ounce) can tomato paste
1 tablespoon chili powder
1 tablespoon sugar
¼ teaspoon each of marjoram,
oregano, basil, thyme
3 bay leaves
Salt and pepper to taste

Cook onion and garlic in butter and oil until clear. Add meat and brown. Stir in sliced mushrooms. Combine tomatoes, tomato paste and all seasonings; add to meat mixture. Simmer, uncovered, until thick; at least 3 hours. When cool, put in refrigerator. Before reheating to serve, or freezing, skim off fat. Serve over very thin spaghetti. Serves 10–12.

Cook and Deal

Male Chauvinist Chili

6 slices bacon
10 ounces hot Italian sausage, cut
   into 1-inch slices
10 ounces lean ground beef
1 large Spanish onion, cut into
   chunks
1 bell pepper, cut into large
   pieces
2 cloves garlic, minced
1 chili pepper
1 cup red wine
½ cup Worcestershire

6 cups Italian (pear shaped)
   tomatoes
1 teaspoon hot dry mustard
1 teaspoon celery seeds
1½ teaspoons chili powder
½ teaspoon salt
1½ teaspoons black pepper,
   freshly ground
1 (15-ounce) can pinto beans
1 (15-ounce) can kidney beans
1 (15½-ounce) can garbanzo beans

Brown bacon in chili pot (preferably a large cast iron pot) or 4½-quart Dutch oven. Drain; crumble and set aside. Pour bacon fat from pot, leaving only a film. Brown sausage; set aside with bacon. Pour sausage fat from pot, again leaving only a film. Fry ground beef; drain and set aside with other meats. Pour excess fat from pot.

Cook onion, pepper, garlic and chili pepper over low heat 2–3 minutes. Stir in wine and Worcestershire sauce; simmer uncovered about 10 minutes. Mash tomatoes and add with liquid. Add meats to onion mixture. Heat to boiling; reduce heat and simmer covered 30 minutes, stirring occasionally.

Stir beans, with liquids, into chili; heat to boiling. Reduce heat; cover and simmer 1 hour; stirring occasionally.

Hint: This recipe is best made a day ahead and reheated, as flavors will meld to their spicy best.

Seminole Savorings

Victory Skillet Veal

2 tablespoons all-purpose flour
½ teaspoon salt
¼ teaspoon white pepper
½ teaspoon paprika
6–8 small veal loin chops
2 tablespoons vegetable oil
1 medium onion, thinly sliced and separated into rings
1 (10½-ounce) can beef broth
2 teaspoons lemon juice
½ teaspoon lemon rind, grated
1 (7-ounce) can pitted ripe olives, drained and cut in half
1 (2-ounce) jar pimentos, drained and diced
Hot buttered egg noodles
2 tablespoons fresh parsley, snipped

Combine flour, salt, pepper and paprika. Coat veal chops lightly with flour mixture, reserving remainder of mixture for sauce.

Brown chops in vegetable oil. Remove chops, drain and set aside. Add onion to pan drippings and sauté until tender. Sprinkle in remaining flour mixture and stir until smooth. Add broth. Bring to a boil, stirring constantly. Add lemon juice and grated rind.

Return chops to skillet. Cover; reduce heat and cook 45 minutes. Add olive halves and pimentos. Cook an additional 5 minutes. Serve over hot buttered noodles. Top with fresh parsley. Serves 3–4.

Seminole Savorings

Veal or Round Steak Lausanne

2 pounds veal cutlet or beef round steak
Flour for coating
Salt and pepper to taste
3 tablespoons shortening, melted, or bacon drippings
1 cup sliced raw onion rings
1 (4-ounce) can button mushrooms, drained
⅓ cup light cream
3 tablespoons dry white wine

Coat the meat in the flour and sprinkle with salt and pepper. Brown the meat in the shortening. Arrange in a shallow baking dish. Sauté the onions in the same skillet; pour over the meat. Garnish with the mushrooms. Add the cream and wine. Bake covered at 375° approximately 40 minutes or until tender. Yields 4–6 servings.

A Pinch of Sunshine

Veal Meat Balls Italian Style
(Boulettes de Viande à l'Italienne)

Veal and sausage meat balls are combined with wide egg noodles and aromatic vegetables bound together with a rich sauce.

1 onion, chopped	3 stalks celery, sliced
1 tablespoon butter	2 bell peppers, red or green,
1 tablespoon oil	sliced
1½ pounds ground veal	½ pound mushrooms, sliced
⅔ pound sausage, bulk	½ cup white wine
¼ teaspoon marjoram	1 cup beef stock
Salt and pepper	4 tablespoons tomato paste
Flour for dredging	Salt and pepper
3 tablespoons butter	½ pound egg noodles, wide
3 tablespoons oil	3 tablespoons parmesan cheese
3 onions, sliced	½ cup Swiss cheese, grated

Sauté the chopped onion in butter and oil for 2 minutes. Add the sausage and cook about 5 minutes. Remove sausage to a bowl with veal, marjoram, salt and pepper. Mix well and prepare meat balls. Roll in flour. Sauté meat balls in butter and oil about 5–6 minutes. Remove and keep warm. Sauté the onions, celery, peppers and mushrooms in the same skillet about 5 minutes. Add the wine, stock, tomato paste, salt and pepper. Simmer about 15 minutes.

Add the cooked noodles to the meatballs. Add the vegetables and sauce and mix gently. Add the parmeasan. Mix gently. Sprinkle with Swiss cheese. Place in a 350° oven for 10 minutes.

Gourmet Cooking II

Sausage Stuffed Rigatoni

1 large onion, finely chopped
3 tablespoons olive oil
2 (6-ounce) cans tomato paste
1 (28-ounce) can Italian tomatoes
4 cups water
1 tablespoon sugar
1 teaspoon salt
½ teaspoon pepper
½ teaspoon oregano
1 bay leaf

2 pounds ground hot Italian
  sausage
¾ cup Italian-style bread crumbs
⅓ cup milk
2 eggs
1 (16-ounce) package rigatoni
  noodles, cooked 5 minutes and
  drained
Grated Parmesan cheese

Sauté onion in olive oil. Pour onions, tomato paste, tomatoes, water, and seasonings into a 3-quart saucepan. Stir well; cover and simmer for 1 hour. Remove bay leaf.

Brown sausage and add bread crumbs. Mix milk and eggs together and add to meat mixture. Mix well. Cool.

Stuff each rigatoni with meat mixture. Place a layer of rigatoni in a 4-quart casserole. Pour some of the tomato sauce over noodles and sprinkle with cheese. Repeat layers. Bake at 350° for 1 hour. Serves 10.

Heart of the Palms

Fruited Pork

8 small pork tenderloins
1 tablespoon oil
1 small onion, thinly sliced
½ cup apple juice
Salt, pepper, thyme, paprika

7–8 dried apricots
7–8 dried pitted prunes
⅓ cup sweet cream or non-dairy
  creamer

On medium to high heat, brown tenderloins in oil. Add onions, sprinkle with seasonings—being especially generous with the paprika—and continue to cook until browned on both sides, about 8–10 minutes in all. Lower heat, add apple juice and dried fruits. Cover and simmer 7–8 minutes or until meat is well done. Add cream, stir well and cook a minute or two longer.

Galley Gourmet III

Orange Pork Chops

4–6 pork chops	¼ cup brown sugar
½ cup orange juice	¼ teaspoon pepper
1 teaspoon salt	½ teaspoon dry mustard

Put pork chops in a 7 × 11-inch pan. Mix remaining ingredients and pour over chops. Bake covered at 350° for 45 minutes; uncover and bake 15 minutes more basting with juice in bottom of pan.

A Taste of Tampa

When buying oranges, consider their weight, not their color. An orange that feels heavy is a juicy one! Expect a yield of about 2½ ounces of juice from a medium-size orange.

Pork Chops With Beer

4 rib or loin pork chops, about 1-inch thick	2 tablespoons vegetable oil
	1 cup light beer
3 garlic cloves, minced	1 tablespoon prepared mustard
½ teaspoon caraway seeds	1 cup canned beef broth or stock
½ teaspoon salt	or 2 bouillon cubes dissolved in
½ teaspoon pepper	1 cup water
2 tablespoons flour	

Rub each pork chop on both sides with garlic, caraway seeds, salt and pepper. Dredge in flour. Brown chops on both sides in oil in a large skillet. Remove and keep warm. Drain off all fat in skillet, leaving brown bits in pan. Add beer and bring to a boil over high heat, stirring and scraping skillet to loosen brown bits; simmer liquid until reduced to ½ cup. Stir in mustard and beef broth. Simmer until sauce is reduced to 1 cup. Arrange browned pork chops in skillet, cover and simmer for 45 minutes, turning once. Serve with sauce.

Fiesta

Southern Shredded Pork

3½ pounds fresh pork	¼ cup water
2 tablespoons margarine	3 tablespoons Worcestershire
⅔ cup chopped onion	sauce
¼ cup vinegar	1 teaspoon prepared mustard
2 tablespoons brown sugar	2 teaspoons salt
1 cup catsup	

Place pork in a large pot and cover with water. Bring to a boil. Reduce to simmer and cook until tender and easy to shred (approximately 1–1½ hours). Remove from water and pull meat apart, discarding all fat. To prepare sauce, in a saucepan melt the margarine. Add onion and brown slightly. Add other ingredients and simmer until blended. Add shredded pork, then simmer 15–20 minutes. Serve on buns or as a main course over rice. Serves 6–8.

Note: Beef may be used instead of pork. Substitute 3½ pounds stew beef and treat in same manner. Served in buns, this is a great item for a teen party.

Palm Beach Entertains

"Pickin Pork"
Men love it.

Fresh pork ham, whole or	Vinegar
shoulder or butt half (must be a	Seasoned pepper
fresh ham, not smoked or	
cured)	

Trim ham, leaving small amount of fat for flavor during cooking. All skin and brine should be removed. Rub the fresh ham with a liberal amount of vinegar. Cover the ham completely with seasoned pepper, pressing the pepper into the sides so most of it adheres. Wrap the ham in heavy-duty foil tightly. Place in roasting pan and bake at 200° overnight—at least 10 hours. When unwrapped, the pork should "fall apart" or shred when pulled with a fork. Place on a large wooden platter on a buffet table and your guests will "pick" at it forever. Serve with your favorite barbecue sauce. Also great for sandwiches.

Seasons in the Sun

Pork Chops Sarasota

3 or 4 medium-thick pork chops   Orange juice
Flour for dredging (optional)   Powdered ginger
Oil   4 sliced apples (optional)

Cut extra fat from chops. Dredge in flour and brown in hot oil. Pour off all fat. Barely cover chops with juice; shake ginger over each chop. Simmer. After 20 minutes, check amount of orange juice, adding more if needed. Turn chops; sprinkle ginger again on each chop. Add apples during last 20 minutes of cooking. Test with fork for tenderness, cooking about 1 hour.

The Prima Diner

Stuffed Leg of Pork

1 leg of pork (10 pounds)
1 garlic head
2 tablespoons salt
1 teaspoon cumin

1 teaspoon oregano
½ teaspoon pepper
1 pound onions
2 sour oranges

STUFFING:
2 tablespoons butter
2 tablespoons minced onion
½ pound pork meat
½ pound ham
1 cup bread crumbs
½ cup milk
½ cup dry wine

½ cup raisins
½ cup almonds
½ cup apples
1 teaspoon gravy seasoning
⅛ teaspoon nutmeg
⅛ teaspoon thyme
⅛ teaspoon pepper

Remove bone from the leg without opening with a sharp pointed knife. Marinate meat for at least an hour with crushed garlic, salt, cumin, oregano, pepper, onion rings and orange juice.

Sauté the onion in the butter, add ground pork and ham and cook for a few minutes stirring constantly. Add the remaining 'stuffing' ingredients and cook for a further few minutes. Pile into leg and sew up the ends. Place in roasting pan fat side up. If desired, cover with brown sugar or malta. Cook in a 325° oven for 5½–6 hours (approximately). Serve garnished with pineapple rings or maraschino cheeries. Serves 12.

The Cuban Flavor

Sweet and Sour Pork Chops

2 pounds pork chops
1 tablespoon steak sauce
2 tablespoons wine or sherry
½ tablespoon salt

1 tablespoon sugar
½ tablespoon pepper
2 cups water
1 large can crushed pineapple

Marinate the pork chops for 1–4 hours in the steak sauce, wine, salt, sugar, and pepper. Broil the chops until slightly browned. Place the pork chops in a heavy pan, add the water, cover and cook for 2 hours. Add the pineapple and cook for 5 more minutes. Serve immediately.

A Pinch of Sunshine

Festive Baked Ham

1 cup apple cider	1 cup firmly-packed brown sugar
½ cup water	1 (21-ounce) can cherry pie filling
1 (5-pound) uncooked ham half	½ cup raisins
12 whole cloves	½ cup orange juice

Combine apple cider and water in a saucepan; bring to a boil. Set aside. Remove skin from ham. Place ham, fat side up, on a cutting board; score fat in a diamond design, and stud with cloves. Place ham in a shallow baking pan, fat side up; coat top with brown sugar.

Insert meat thermometer, making sure it does not touch fat or bone. Bake, uncovered, at 325° for about 2 hours (22–25 minutes per pound) or until meat thermometer registers 160°, basting every 30 minutes with cider mixture.

Combine remaining ingredients in a saucepan; bring to a boil. Serve sauce with sliced ham. Serves 10.

Sawgrass and Pines

Marinated Ham Steak

Center cut, tenderized ham steak, 1½-inch thick	Garlic powder
½ cup melted butter	2 teaspoons dry mustard
1 cup sherry and/or white wine	1 tablespoon brown sugar
2 teaspoons powdered cloves	2 teaspoons paprika

Combine marinade ingredients. Pour over ham and let stand for four hours, turning occasionally. Brown over charcoal.

Secrets from the Galley

Lat's Gourmet Sauce for Beef
Crowning glory

3 tablespoons butter, melted
3 tablespoons flour
2 teaspoons prepared mustard or
   ½ teaspoon dry mustard
2 teaspoons Worcestershire sauce
1¼ cups beef broth

1 cup Burgundy
4 scallions, thinly sliced
1 (3-ounce) can mushrooms,
   drained and sliced
Arrowroot

Over low heat, blend butter with flour. Stir in mustard and Worcestershire sauce. Add beef broth, a small amount at a time, blending well after each addition. Stir in Burgundy. Cook, stirring constantly until thickened. Add scallions and mushrooms. If more thickening is desired, add small amount of arrowroot. If too thick, add small amount of Burgundy. Serve over beef tenderloin slices. Yields 2 cups.

Fare by the Sea

Kelly's Barbecue Sauce

2–3 cups tomato paste
⅓ cup vinegar
¾ cup oil, butter, or oleo
2 tablespoons pickle relish
½ teaspoon cloves
¼ teaspoon nutmeg
1 bay leaf

1 onion, finely chopped
1 garlic bud, finely chopped
3 teaspoons prepared mustard
4 teaspoons Worcestershire sauce
1 teaspoon sugar
Salt, red and black pepper to taste

Mix all ingredients and boil slowly for about 20 minutes. Add Tabasco sauce or red pepper as desired for "hot" barbecue sauce. Makes approximately 1 quart sauce for beef, pork or chicken.

Apalachicola Cookbook

Vegetables

Marjorie Kinnan Rawlings' home near Gainesville was the setting for her book, Cross Creek, *later made into a movie.*

Artichoke Casserole

2 (14-ounce) cans artichokes,
   drained
4 tablespoons butter or margarine
4 tablespoons flour

½ cup milk
½ cup Parmesan cheese
½ teaspoon celery salt
4 tablespoons bread crumbs

Cut artichokes in quarters; place in greased casserole. Reserve. Melt butter, stir in flour, and mix well over heat. Add milk, cheese, and celery salt, stirring and cooking until thick. Pour over artichokes and mix; sprinkle bread crumbs on top. Bake 30 minutes at 350°. Serves 4–6.

The Prima Diner

Broccoli Puffs

1 (10-ounce) package broccoli cuts
1 (10¾-ounce) can cream of
   mushroom soup
½ cup shredded cheese
¼ cup milk

¼ cup mayonnaise
1 egg, beaten
¼ cup bread crumbs
1 tablespoon melted butter

Cook broccoli and drain well. Put in baking dish. Mix together soup, cheese, milk, mayonnaise and egg; pour over broccoli. Brown bread crumbs in butter; sprinkle on top. Bake at 350° for 45 minutes.

Through Our Kitchen Windows

Broccoli Casserole

1 (10-ounce) package frozen chopped broccoli, thawed
1 (10¾-ounce) can cream of celery soup
1 cup instant rice, uncooked
1 (4-ounce) jar pasteurized process cheese spread
¾ cup chopped celery
¾ cup chopped onion
¼ cup butter, melted
1 (8-ounce) can sliced water chestnuts or 1 cup toasted almonds

Combine all the ingredients. Turn into a greased casserole dish. Bake at 350° for 1 hour. Serves 6.

Variation: For regular, cooked rice (1 cup), cook the broccoli, celery, and onion in ½ cup water about 5 minutes. Combine with the remaining ingredients. Bake until hot.

A Pinch of Sunshine

Broccoli and Bleu Cheese Casserole

2 (10-ounce) packages frozen broccoli, chopped
2 tablespoons butter
2 tablespoons all-purpose flour
1 (3-ounce) package cream cheese, softened
2 tablespoons bleu cheese, crumbled
1 cup milk
½ cup rich, round crackers, crushed
2 tablespoons butter, melted

Cook broccoli according to package directions; drain well. In saucepan melt 2 tablespoons butter; stir in flour, cream cheese and bleu cheese. Add milk; cook and stir until bubbly. Stir in broccoli and pour into a 1-quart casserole. Crush crackers and toss with 2 tablespoons melted butter. Place on top of broccoli. Bake covered at 350° for 45 minutes. Uncover and bake 5–10 minutes more. Serves 6.

Seminole Savorings

Tomatoes Stuffed With Summer Squash

1 pound yellow squash, grated
1 pound zucchini, grated
2 teaspoons salt
8 small tomatoes
Salt and pepper to taste
Olive oil as needed
1 onion, chopped
2 tablespoons butter

2 tablespoons olive oil
1 cup heavy cream
Salt and pepper to taste
½ cup grated Swiss cheese
¼ cup grated Parmesan cheese
4 tablespoons grated Parmesan
cheese

Spread squash and zucchini in a large colander. Sprinkle with salt, toss and let drain for 30 minutes. Transfer vegetables to a tea towel and squeeze out remaining moisture.

Preheat oven to 325°. Slice tops off tomatoes and scoop out seeds. Sprinkle insides with salt and pepper. Brush with olive oil. Bake, cut side up, on a baking sheet for 10 minutes. When done, remove tomatoes and invert on a rack to drain for 30 minutes.

Sauté onion in butter and olive oil until soft. Add squash and zucchini. Cook for 2 minutes. Stir in cream, salt and pepper. Cook until cream is absorbed. Remove pan from heat. Stir in Swiss cheese and ¼ cup Parmesan cheese. Stuff tomatoes with mixture and sprinkle tops with 4 tablespoons Parmesan cheese. Broil for 3–4 minutes until tops are bubbly and golden. If prepared ahead and refrigerated, cook, covered, at 300° for 15 minutes before putting under broiler. Servings: 8. Preparation time: 45 minutes. Baking time: 15 minutes.

Variation: Line bottom of a casserole with sliced tomatoes, cover with squash mixture, sprinkle with Parmesan and proceed as usual.

Jacksonville & Company

Seaside Stuffed Squash
An attractive way to serve squash—and good.

1 pound summer squash
½ cup green pepper, chopped
½ cup Cheddar cheese, grated
½ cup sour cream

½ cup onion, minced
4 slices bacon, cooked and
    crumbled

Boil squash 10–12 minutes. Slice lengthwise. Scoop out pulp. Add remaining ingredients to pulp and mix well. Fill squash with mixture, placing each in a baking dish. Bake 20 minutes in a 350° preheated oven. May be prepared ahead of time and refrigerated until ready to bake. Serves 6.

Sugar Beach

Spinach on Artichoke Bottoms Hollandaise

2 (10-ounce) packages frozen
   chopped spinach
½ pound fresh mushrooms
6 tablespoons butter
1 tablespoon flour
½ cup milk

½ teaspoon salt
⅛ teaspoon garlic powder
⅛ teaspoon ground black pepper
⅛ teaspoon freshly grated nutmeg
1 (14-ounce) can artichoke
   bottoms (7 to a can)

Cook spinach according to package directions. Drain. Reserve 7 mushroom caps and sauté in 2 tablespoons butter. Chop remaining mushrooms and stems and sauté in another 2 tablespoons butter. Set aside.

Make a cream sauce by melting 2 tablespoons butter in heavy saucepan; add flour and cook until bubbly. Add milk, stirring constantly over low heat until smooth. Add seasonings; then add spinach and chopped mushrooms. Remove from heat.

Drain artichoke bottoms and slice a small piece off the bottom so they will sit flat in a buttered baking dish. Cover artichoke bottom with a mound of creamed spinach.

HOLLANDAISE:
1 cup sour cream
1 cup mayonnaise (Hellmann's)

¼ cup lemon juice

Combine ingredients and blend thoroughly. Cover spinach with a generous spoonful of hollandaise. Top with a mushroom cap. Bake in 375° oven for 15–18 minutes. This dish can be prepared in advance and heated in oven right before serving. Yield: 7 servings.

Note: This is a pretty dish that is wonderful for a buffet dinner or brunch.

Some Like It South!

Delicious Company Potatoes

1 (2-pound) bag frozen hash
browns (in cubes)
½ cup melted butter
1 can cream of chicken soup,
undiluted

½ cup onion, finely chopped
10 ounces Cheddar cheese, grated
16 ounces sour cream

Combine all ingredients together. Spread evenly in 9 × 13-inch pan. Bake for 45 minutes in 350° oven. This dish works well for barbecue or brunch.

Variation: For topping combine ¼ cup melted butter and 2 cups crushed corn flakes. Spread over potato mixture. Yield: at least 12 servings.

Florida Flavors

Potato-Onion Crowns

Fluffs of creamy yellow potatoes ringed with buttery broiled onion crown.

ONION CROWNS:

2–3 large Bermuda onions	*Potatoes and Carrots Duchesse*
4 tablespoons butter, melted	(recipe below)

Cut onions into thick slices, about ⅓-inch for 12 slices. Handle gently so the rings do not come apart. Place onion slices in a single layer on rack in broiler pan; brush with melted butter. Broil without turning, 8–10 minutes, or until tender and lightly browned. Make *Potatoes and Carrots Duchesse*.

POTATOES AND CARROTS DUCHESSE:

1½ pounds potatoes, peeled	¼ cup butter
1 pound carrots, scraped	1 teaspoon prepared mustard
½ cup light cream	Salt and pepper to taste
1 egg yolk	

Cook separately in boiling salted water the potatoes and carrots, until the vegetables are tender. Drain the vegetables and put them separately through a fine sieve or puree them in a blender or food processor. Combine the purees and beat in the cream, egg yolk and butter. Season with prepared mustard and salt and pepper to taste. Whip until light and fluffy.

Spoon hot mashed potatoes in 12 even mounds around roast on serving platter. Top each with an onion slice. (Rings will separate enough to make a "cap.") Garnish on top with a small star cut from pimiento. Serves 6.

The Orange Bowl Cookbook

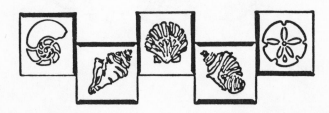

Sweet Potato and Pineapple
(Casserole De Patates Et Ananas)

Sweet potatoes team with pineapple for a good old Southern flavor.

3 pounds sweet potatoes	Pepper
1 stick butter	⅓ cup brown sugar
1½ teaspoons cinnamon	1 large can crushed pineapple
1 teaspoon nutmeg	3 eggs
Salt	Small marshmallows

Boil sweet potatoes in skins. Peel while warm. Beat with electric beater (do not pull strings from beater blades). Add butter. Add eggs, cinnamon, nutmeg, salt and pepper. Add brown sugar. Lift beater and remove strings. Add crushed pineapple (including juices). Pour into buttered casserole. Cover with small marshmallows. Bake at 350° for 5 minutes.

Gourmet Cooking

Mandarin Orange and Sweet Potatoes
(Microwave)

10 medium-size sweet potatoes, scrubbed and dried	2 cans mandarin orange slices
¼ cup butter or oleo	6 tablespoons dark brown sugar
3 tablespoons rum	½ teaspoon salt
	2 tablespoons chopped pecans

Place potatoes on paper towels and bake on HIGH, 16–18 minutes. Remove and wrap in foil for 5 minutes. Mix mashed sweet potatoes with 2 tablespoons butter, 4 tablespoons sugar, rum, salt and 1 can of mandarin orange slices. Combine remaining butter, sugar, nuts with the other can of mandarin orange slices. Put on top of potato mixture, which you have placed in a casserole. Bake uncovered at #7 POWER, for 8–10 minutes or until warmed through. Let stand 5 minutes, covered. You may use canned sweet potatoes if in a real hurry.

Lost Tree Cook Book

Sweet Potato Soufflé
Side dish or dessert

POTATOES:

3 cups sweet potatoes, cooked and
    mashed or 29-ounce can of
    sweet potatoes, drained
1 cup sugar
2 eggs, well beaten

1 teaspoon vanilla
½ cup milk
½ cup butter, melted
1 teaspoon vanilla (optional)

Mix potato ingredients together until well-blended and spread in a 13 × 9-inch pan.

TOPPING:

1 cup light brown sugar
½ cup flour

1 cup pecans, chopped
⅓ cup butter

Mix well. Ingredients will be stiff and crumbly. Crumble over top of sweet potatoes. Bake in 350° oven for 30 minutes.

Note: This may also be put into 2 pie shells and served as a dessert. Preparation: 45 minutes. Easy. Serves: 8. Baking: 30 minutes.

Culinary Arts & Crafts

Brussels Sprouts With Curry Sauce

1 quart Brussels sprouts
¼ cup butter
1 clove garlic, minced
½ teaspoon curry powder

1 teaspoon sugar
½ cup mayonnaise
2 tablespoons lemon juice

Cook sprouts in lightly salted water until tender. Drain well and keep hot. In double boiler, melt butter. Add garlic, curry powder and sugar. Blend thoroughly and cook for 5 minutes, stirring constantly. Beat in mayonnaise with fork or whisk. Add lemon juice slowly while beating vigorously. Spoon over hot Brussels sprouts and serve immediately. Yield: 4 servings.

Friendly Feasts Act II

Onions Braised in Red Wine
(Oignons Bourguignon)

A favorite of the students in my cooking classes is this onion dish in which the onions, cut in rings, absorb the wine and become beautifully glazed. An onion lover's delight.

6 large yellow onions
3 tablespoons butter
2 whole cloves

Salt
Pepper
1 cup Burgundy wine

Cut onions into ¼-inch slices. Separate into rings. Melt butter in a skillet. Add onions. Cook until well coated. Add cloves, salt and pepper. Sauté until golden brown. Add burgundy. Cover and simmer about 15 minutes. Discard cloves. Remove cover and cook until wine is reduced almost to a glaze.

Gourmet Cooking

Eggplant Casserole

1 large eggplant, peeled, sliced
1 large onion, sliced
½ pound mushrooms, sliced
Parsley
Oregano
Garlic powder

Sea salt
Spaghetti sauce
1 pound cheddar cheese, grated
2 zucchini squash, sliced
1 green pepper, chopped

This mouth watering dish will always bring people back for seconds. They will not realize that there is eggplant in this. If you need more vegetables to fill up your 9 × 13-inch glass baking dish, just slice summer squash. Make layers of eggplant, onions and mushrooms. Lightly sprinkle the parsley, oregano, garlic and sea salt. Pour sauce over this layer. Now, grate the cheese (any natural hard cheese will be fine) and sprinkle that on top of the sauce. Next, make a layer of zucchini, onions, mushrooms and pepper. Lightly sprinkle the herbs over this layer. Pour more juice and sprinkle more cheese. Make 2 or 3 layers. Make sure you have enough cheese for the top.

Try to get all layers moistened good, but be careful because the vegetables tend to shrink and the juice bubbles over. Try to keep the level of liquid about 1 inch from the top. Bake about 45 minutes in an oven 350°.

If you want this casserole to be a protein balanced meal, add ½ cup uncooked bulgar.

Step-By-Step to Natural Food

Long Pond Eggplant

1 large eggplant	6 slices bacon, cut in half
4 tablespoons butter or ¼ cup olive oil	Accent
	Salt
6 slices Swiss, American, or mozzarella cheese	Pepper
	Parmesan cheese
6 (½-inch thick) slices tomato	1 tablespoon salt

Peel and cut eggplant in ¾-inch slices. Soak eggplant slices 3–4 hours in salty water, then drain and place on paper towels. Sauté eggplant in butter or olive oil until slightly brown, but not completely done. Place on cookie sheet. Fry bacon slightly and drain. On each slice of eggplant place 1 slice of tomato and sprinkle each with Accent, salt, pepper and Parmesan. Then place 1 slice bacon and 1 slice Swiss, American, or mozzarella cheese on top of tomatoes. Place cookie sheet on bottom rack in oven. Broil until cheese is melted and bacon is cooked. Serves 6.

Gator Country Cooks

Sunshine Carrots
(Microwave)

5 medium carrots	¼ teaspoon salt
2 tablespoons water	¼ teaspoon ginger
1 tablespoon sugar	¼ cup orange juice
1 teaspoon cornstarch	2 tablespoons butter

Slice carrots diagonally, about 1-inch thick. Place in covered 1½-quart glass casserole with water. Cook on HIGH in microwave for 8 minutes. Stir halfway through cooking time. Drain.

Meanwhile, combine sugar, cornstarch, salt and ginger in a small saucepan. Add orange juice; cook, stirring constantly, until mixture thickens and bubbles. Boil 1 minute. Stir in butter. Pour over hot carrots, tossing to coat evenly.

If you do not have a microwave, cook carrots covered in a small amount of boiling salted water until just tender, about 20 minutes. Drain. Serves 4.

Gulfshore Delights

Potato and Carrot Mash

6 medium potatoes, peeled and
cut
1 large onion, peeled and
chopped
6 large carrots, scraped and cut
1 stick butter or margarine

½ cup milk
1 cup grated, sharp cheddar
cheese
1 teaspoon salt
Dash of pepper

Boil potatoes, onions, carrots with salt until tender, about 30 minutes. Drain water and whip with electric beater, adding the butter and the milk. Place in a buttered baking dish and top with cheese. Serve or keep warm in oven.

Alone at the Range

Carrots and Red Grapes
(Carottes Et Raisins)

Vodka or white wine substitute for water as our cooking liquid and bring out the flavor of the carrots. When joined with grapes they form a dish of jewel-like quality. Green seedless grapes can be substituted for red.

2 pounds carrots
2 tablespoons butter
⅛ teaspoon sugar
½ cup vodka or white wine

1 cup red grapes, halved and
seeded
Salt and pepper

Slice carrots into ½-inch diagonal slices. Sauté in butter for 2 minutes. Sprinkle with sugar. Add vodka or wine. Cook until carrots are tender, about 15 minutes. Add grapes. Salt and pepper to taste. Turn into a serving dish.

Gourmet Cooking

Spanish Corn
(Mais Espagnole)

Kernels of corn are cooked in a tomato sauce and seasoned with bacon for a very flavorful dish.

1 dozen ears corn	1 pound bacon
1 large can tomato sauce	1½ teaspoons baking soda
3 large onions, chopped	Salt and pepper

Remove corn kernels from cobs. Fry bacon crisp; save. Add corn and tomato sauce to bacon drippings and cook slowly 45–60 minutes (stir frequently, it burns easily). Add additional bacon drippings if necessary. Add salt and pepper and baking soda. Remove from heat. Crumble bacon over top before serving.

Gourmet Cooking II

Corn Bubble
(Microwave)

2 tablespoons butter or margarine	1 small onion, finely chopped
1 teaspoon salt	2 tablespoons flour
¼ teaspoon dry mustard	½ teaspoon paprika
¾ cup milk	Pepper to taste
1 (16-ounce) can whole kernel corn, drained	1 egg, slightly beaten with milk

Place butter and onion in 1-quart casserole. Microwave 1–2 minutes on HIGH, or until onion is transparent. Add flour, salt, paprika, mustard and pepper. Blend well. Add milk and egg mixture slowly, stirring until smooth. Stir in corn. Cover. Microwave 8–10 minutes on #8 POWER, or until bubbly. Let stand 3–5 minutes, covered. Serves 4–6.

Lost Tree Cook Book

Party Cabbage

5 cups finely shredded cabbage	½ teaspoon salt
1 cup shredded carrot	Pepper to taste
¼ cup chopped green onions with tops	1 beef bouillon cube
	¼ cup boiling water

Dissolve the bouillon cube in the ¼ cup boiling water in a large skillet. Toss remaining ingredients together to blend. Put into skillet with liquid, cover tightly and cook over low heat for five minutes, stirring and turning once. Turn onto warm serving dish and cover with sauce.

SAUCE:

¼ cup butter	⅓ cup chopped pecans
1 teaspoon prepared mustard	⅛ teaspoon paprika

Melt butter; stir in mustard and pecans. Pour over cabbage and sprinkle with paprika. Serves 6–8.

Apalachicola Cookbook

Vegetable Rainbow Platter

2 packages frozen baby lima beans
½ teaspoon dill
Wishbone Italian dressing
3–4 sliced tomatoes
Tomato French dressing
8 small zucchini squash
½ cup Parmesan cheese

2 packages frozen sugar-glazed
  carrots
½ cup wine vinegar
2 packages frozen asparagus
  spears
½ cup capers and liquid

Cook lima beans as directed and drain. Cover with dill and Italian dressing, cover and refrigerate overnight.

Slice tomatoes, place in bowl and cover with French dressing. Cover and refrigerate overnight.

Slice zucchinis thin and cook 5 minutes in salted water. Drain and toss with Parmesan cheese. Cover and refrigerate overnight.

Cook carrots as directed and drain. Toss with wine vinegar. Cover and refrigerate overight.

Cook asparagus as directed and drain. Sprinkle with capers and liquid. Cover and refrigerate overnight.

SAUCE:

1 cup sour cream
1 cup mayonnaise
2 tablespoons lemon juice

Salt and pepper
Lots of chopped parsley

Arrange vegetables on large platter and place bowl of sauce in center. This is a very attractive dish which can be used as a salad or a vegetable with dinner.

Cypress Gardens Cookbook

Steamy Summer Vegetables

My "long hungry" friend Sean brought me a beautiful little fat-lighter'd pine spoon he had carved. Though the summer evening was hot and steamy, I was glad to cook this quick "beat the heat" meal in return for such a fine gift. The spoon was perfect for ladling the lemon-butter sauce over the steamed vegetables.

2 cups sliced yellow squash (½-inch rounds)	1 cup chopped green pepper
	1 cup sliced onion
2 cups sliced zucchini squash (½-inch rounds)	1 cup fresh corn
	1 cup sliced tofu

LEMON-BUTTER SAUCE:
¼ cup melted butter, mixed with	2 tablespoons lemon juice

Place squash, green pepper, and onion on steaming basket in large saucepan. Add 1 inch of water to saucepan and bring to boil. Turn heat to low, cover pan, and simmer for 10 minutes or until squash is nearly tender. Cut corn off cob and add to other vegetables. Cook briefly until vegetables are tender, but still crisp.

Toss tofu with vegetables and pour lemon-butter sauce over them. Serve over brown rice or millet. Good with soy sauce. Serves 4–6.

Variations: 1. Instead of lemon-butter sauce, substitute ½ pound of grated sharp Cheddar cheese. Grate over hot vegetables and allow to melt. 2. Omit lemon-butter sauce and substitute butter pecan rice recipe for plain rice.

Cross Creek Kitchens

 Tofu—Rich in protein and a good substitute for cream cheese, tofu is a bland cheese-like substance made from soy beans.

Black Beans
(Frijoles Negros)

1 pound black beans	½ teaspoon pepper
10 cups water	¼ teaspoon oregano
1 green pepper	1 bay leaf
⅔ cup olive oil	2 tablespoons sugar
1 large onion	2 tablespoons vinegar
4 cloves garlic	2 tablespoons dry wine
1 green pepper	2 tablespoons olive oil
4 teaspoons salt	

Wash the beans and soak in water with the green pepper. When the beans swell, cook in the same water until soft. (45 minutes approximately). Heat the oil in a frying pan and add onion, garlic, followed by ground green pepper. Add 1 cup of the beans to the pan and mash. Add this to the remaining beans together with the salt, pepper, oregano, bay leaf and sugar. Allow to boil for a further hour and add the vinegar and wine, cooking slowly for another hour. If there is still too much liquid, cook uncovered for a while. Add 2 tablespoons of oil just before serving. Serves 8 approximately.

The Cuban Flavor

Bollos
(Pronounced Boy-os)

1 pound black-eyed peas	2 small hot bird peppers
3 cloves garlic, crushed	1 teaspoon salt

Cover peas with water and soak overnight. Remove skins by rubbing peas between hands. Cover peas again with water and skins will rise to the surface. Drain. Combine peas and garlic in food processor and process to a paste-like consistency. Add hot peppers and salt and blend until mixture resembles cake batter. Drop by teaspoon into hot deep fryer. Turn to brown on both sides. Drain on absorbent paper.

Margaritaville Cookbook

Pasta, Rice, Quiche, Dressing, Crepes

Kennedy Space Center at Cape Canaveral.

Noodle and Hamburger Casserole

1 (8-ounce) package noodles
1 pound ground beef
1 tablespoon margarine
2 (8-ounce) cans tomato sauce

1 cup cottage cheese
8 ounces cream cheese
⅓ cup onion, chopped fine
½ cup thick sour cream

Cook noodles according to package, drain. Skillet-brown hamburger in 1 tablespoon margarine. Stir in tomato sauce, remove from heat. Combine cottage cheese, cream cheese, sour cream and onions. In a buttered 3-quart casserole, spread half the noodles, cover with cheese mixture, then cover this with the remaining noodles. Pour hamburger sauce mixture on top. Bake at 350° for 30 minutes, or until hot. Serves 6–8.

Cypress Gardens Cookbook

Tarragon Shrimp Spaghetti

¼ clove garlic
1½ tablespoons olive oil
½ cup white wine
½ cup chicken broth
½ teaspoon lemon juice

¼ teaspoon tarragon
1 cup uncooked shrimp
2 teaspoons butter
Cooked spaghetti noodles

Sauté garlic in olive oil. Add wine, broth, lemon juice and tarragon. Blend together, then add butter and shrimp. Cover and cook for about three minutes or until shrimp have just turned pink. Do not overcook or the delicate flavor will be lost. Serve shrimp sauce over spaghetti or linguini noodles. Serves 2.

Apalachicola Cookbook

Fettuccini Carbonara

½ pound fettuccini
3 ounces cream cheese
¼ pound grated parmesan and romano cheese, mixed
Dash of garlic and pepper
½ pint Half & Half or non-dairy creamer (additional milk, if needed)

1 (¼-inch) slice boiled ham, julienned
½ pound sliced fresh mushrooms or 1 (6½-ounce) can sliced mushrooms, drained
2 tablespoons oil or butter

Place cream cheese softened to room temperature in medium saucepan. Blend in grated cheeses and seasonings. Over medium-low heat, gradually stir in enough Half & Half so that consistency is about that of a medium-light cream sauce. Stir constantly; do not leave unattended. When cheeses are melted, set aside. In small skillet, sauté ham and mushrooms in butter until slightly golden. Also set aside.

Cook fettuccini "al dente," drain and stir in butter or oil. Reheat cheese mixture, stirring constantly, but do not boil. Add more cream or milk if needed to maintain consistency. Toss with fettuccini and serve with ham and mushrooms on top.

Galley Gourmet III

Hogwild Macaroni and Cheese

This dish is so named because it generally causes the menfolk to lose all control. The addition of herbs to the basic macaroni and cheese makes a new experience out of an old favorite.

2 cups elbow macaroni,
    preferably whole wheat
2 tablespoons butter
1 medium onion, finely chopped
1 tablespoon flour
1 teaspoon Dijon mustard
1 teaspoon fresh basil or ½
    teaspoon dried
1 teaspoon fresh thyme or ½
    teaspoon dried

1 teaspoon fresh oregano or ½
    teaspoon dried
1 large clove fresh garlic, minced,
    or ½ teaspoon garlic powder
¼ teaspoon freshly ground black
    pepper
2 cups milk
8 ounces sharp Cheddar cheese,
    grated

TOPPING:
½ cup butter   1 cup bread crumbs

Cook macaroni until just tender. Do not overcook. Drain and keep warm.

Preheat oven to 400° and grease a 2-quart casserole.

In a heavy, medium saucepan, melt butter and sauté onion until transparent. Stir in the flour, mustard, herbs, garlic, and pepper. Stir in the milk and heat, stirring constantly until hot and smooth; do not boil. Remove from heat and stir in three-quarters of the cheese until melted.

Turn macaroni into casserole. Pour on the cheese sauce and stir until well coated. Top with rest of cheese. In a small pan, melt butter and add bread crumbs. Stir until crumbs are coated. Sprinkle crumbs over casserole. Bake, uncovered, for 20 minutes or until bubbly and brown.

Serves 6 to 9 as a side dish or 4 as a main dish.

Cross Creek Kitchens

Crêpes Elegant

CRÊPES:

1 cup all purpose flour
1 tablespoon sugar
1 teaspoon baking powder
½ teaspoon salt

2 eggs, slightly beaten
1 cup milk
1 teaspoon oil
Crabmeat Filling (recipe below)

Combine flour, sugar, baking powder and salt in mixing bowl. Combine eggs, milk and oil; add to flour mixture and beat with rotary beater until smooth. Pour about 2 tablespoons batter into greased 6-inch crêpe pan or skillet, and tilt pan until batter covers pan in thin layer. Cook over medium heat until lightly browned; turn and cook other side. Continue, making 14–16 crêpes. Make Crabmeat Filling.

CRABMEAT FILLING:

1 envelope French's hollandaise
  sauce mix
1 cup dairy sour cream

2 cups crabmeat or diced cooked
  chicken
½ cup thinly sliced water
  chestnuts

Prepare hollandaise sauce as directed on envelope; stir in sour cream. Set aside ¾ cup sauce; combine remaining sauce with crabmeat and water chestnuts. Place 2 tablespoons filling in each crêpe; roll up and place, seam-side down, in a 9 × 13-inch baking dish. Bake at 325° for 20 minutes. Remove from oven and spread with reserved ¾ cup hollandaise sauce. Return to oven and bake 8–10 minutes longer, until bubbling hot.

The Orange Bowl Cookbook

Key West Fried Rice

1 medium onion, minced
4 tablespoons butter
2 cups cooked brown rice, cold
½ teaspoon paprika
1 teaspoon celery seed
¼ teaspoon ginger
1 tablespoon brown sugar
½ teaspoon Accent
½ teaspoon allspice

2 tablespoons soy sauce
¾ pound ham, cubed
1 pound shrimp, cooked and
 deveined
½ cup nuts (peanuts or almonds)
1 egg, well beaten
Parsley
Pineapple (optional)

Sauté onion in 2 tablespoons butter until limp. Add cold rice and 2 tablespoons more butter. Fry gently over low heat. Add the seasonings and the soy sauce. Add the ham, shrimp, nuts and the beaten egg. Stir until warm. Garnish with parsley and pineapple. Serves 6 for main course.

Seasons in the Sun

Consommé Rice

1 cup uncooked rice
1 (10¾-ounce) can condensed
 consommé soup
1 (10¾-ounce) can condensed beef
 bouillon soup

½ stick butter or oleo
2 (4-ounce) cans mushrooms
1 small onion, minced
Dash of Worcestershire

Place butter and onion in an uncovered 2-quart casserole dish. Put this in a 350° oven for 10 minutes, or until onion is transparent. When done, add the consommé, bouillon, mushrooms, rice, and Worcestershire. Bake uncovered for 1 hour. Serves 4–8.

Canopy Roads

Shrimp and Rice Casserole

½ pound cheese
½ cup evaporated milk
½ teaspoon salt
Dash pepper

2½ cups cooked rice
1½ pounds shrimp, cooked and
  peeled
1 cup buttered bread crumbs

Cut cheese in small pieces; melt over hot water. Gradually stir in milk, beating until smooth; then add salt and pepper. Pour half of the cheese sauce into greased casserole; place half of rice over sauce, cover with shrimp and top with remaining rice. Pour remaining cheese sauce over all and top with crumbs; bake in 350° oven for 20–30 minutes. Serves 6–8.

Through Our Kitchen Windows

Wild Rice and Mushroom Stuffing

2 cups wild rice
2 large onions, chopped
1 cup chopped celery and leaves
½ teaspoon poultry seasoning
½ cup butter

4 cups chicken broth
1 cup chopped pecans
2 (3-ounce) cans chopped
  mushrooms
Salt and pepper to taste

Cook rice, onions and celery in butter 5 minutes. Add chicken broth and bring to boil. Cover and simmer 30 minutes or until liquid is absorbed and rice is tender. Add all remaining ingredients, then mix together thoroughly. Use as stuffing for poultry or game birds. Makes about 6 cups.

Apalachicola Cookbook

Paella
Extravagant, but well worth the effort

4 skinless, boneless chicken breasts
1 pound lobster tails, removed from shell, or 8 stone crab claws
1 cup olive oil, divided
½ pound Chorizo or Kielbasa sausage, sliced into ¼-inch pieces
½ pound mushrooms, halved
2 green peppers, cut into eighths
2 red peppers, cut into eighths or pimentos
1 medium zucchini, halved lengthwise and cut into 1-inch pieces
3 large garlic cloves, minced
1 large Spanish onion, minced
1 (8-ounce) can plum tomatoes, drained and finely chopped
2 cups long grain raw rice
¼ cup finely chopped parsley
¼ teaspoon saffron powder
½ teaspoon paprika
3½ cups chicken broth
1 pound shrimp, peeled and deveined, leaving tails intact
2 dozen littleneck clams, scrubbed well
1 pound grouper, cut into ¾-inch chunks
½ pound red snapper, cut into ¾-inch chunks

Cut chicken and lobster crosswise into 1-inch chunks. (If using stone crab claws, carefully crack each section of the claw so that it will not be necessary to crack them while eating. Be sure to remove all loose pieces of shell after cracking.) Set aside.

Heat ½ cup olive oil in paella pan (large shallow pan). Sauté chicken and sliced sausage until light streaky brown; remove from pan. Sauté mushrooms, green and red peppers and zucchini until just barely tender; remove from pan. Wash and dry pan.

Add ½ cup olive oil to pan. Heat 1 minute over low flame. Add garlic, onion, tomatoes, rice, parsley, saffron and paprika; stir well. Sauté, stirring constantly, 5 minutes. Add chicken broth, chicken, sausage, peppers, zucchini and mushrooms. Bring to a boil; reduce heat so that liquid merely simmers. Place lobster pieces, shrimp, clams and fish into pan. Simmer slowly, uncovered, tending pan frequently and stirring gently from time to time. Cook until rice is tender and has absorbed all liquid, about 30–35 minutes. Serves 8.

Traditionally served with green salad, crusty bread, sangría and, for dessert, flan.

Gulfshore Delights

Red Beans and Rice

1 pound dried red beans (about
  2½ cups)
Meaty ham bone or smoked ham
  hock
½ pound salt pork
1 cup chopped onions
½ cup chopped celery
2 garlic cloves, crushed

1 bay leaf
¼ teaspoon basil
¼ teaspoon thyme
¼ teaspoon pepper
½ teaspoon bottled red pepper
  sauce
1 cup long-grained rice

Wash beans: Discard any stones or shriveled beans. Drain and place in large heavy saucepan or Dutch oven. Soak. (For quick-soak method, combine beans and 6 cups water. Heat to boiling: Boil 2 minutes. Remove from heat; cover and let stand 1 hour. Or cover beans with water and soak overnight.)

Drain off soaking liquid. Add 6 cups water and remaining ingredients except rice. Bring to boil. Reduce heat; cover and simmer 1½ hours. Uncover and simmer 1 hour. Remove from heat. Discard salt pork. Remove ham bone; trim meat from bone and cut into bite-size pieces. Strain beans, reserving liquid. Add water if necessary to make 3 cups. Return liquid to saucepot with beans and ham. Add rice; bring to boil. Reduce heat; cover and simmer until rice is tender, about 20 minutes. Makes about 10 servings. About 300 calories per cup.

Fiesta

Tiropita
Greek Cheese Pie

10 sheets fillo dough
½ cup butter, melted
2 (16-ounce) cartons small curd cottage cheese, or ricotta cheese, drained

1 (8-ounce) package cream cheese, softened
4 eggs, beaten
¼ pound feta cheese, crumbled

Thaw fillo according to package directions. Layer a 15 × 11 × 1-inch pan, or equivalent, with 5 sheets fillo. Butter between each sheet. Mix remaining ingredients; pour mixture on fillo. Top with remaining 5 sheets of fillo, buttering between sheets and top layer. With a sharp knife, score top layer only into 3-inch squares. Bake at 350° for 30 minutes. Cut into squares; serve at once. Serves 15.

Suncoast Seasons

Italian Spinach Pie

1 (9-inch) pastry shell
1½ cups cooked and chopped fresh spinach, or 2 (10-ounce) boxes frozen chopped spinach, cooked
4 tablespoons butter
Salt and freshly ground pepper

½ pound ricotta cheese
½ cup freshly grated Parmesan cheese
3 eggs, slightly beaten
½ cup heavy cream
Grated nutmeg

Preheat oven to 450°. Chill pie shell. Prick bottom with fork and bake for 10–15 minutes, being sure not to brown crust. Cool. Reset oven to 375°. Drain and squeeze the cooked chopped spinach. Stir in butter, salt, and pepper to taste. In a large mixing bowl place the ricotta and Parmesan cheese, eggs, cream, and nutmeg. Beat with an electric mixer 2–3 minutes. Stir in the cooked spinach and combine well. Pour into baked shell and bake 30 minutes. Serves 6–8.

Note: The pastry and filling may be prepared early in the day and refrigerated separately. Remove filling from refrigerator 1 hour before assembling.

Palm Beach Entertains

Exceptional Quiche

3 (9-inch) pie shells
1 pound hot bulk sausage
1 cup chopped green pepper
1 cup green onions, chopped (tops and all)
2 packages frozen chopped spinach or frozen chopped broccoli

12 ounces grated Monterey Jack cheese
12 eggs, beaten
2 tablespoons seasoned salt
1 teaspoon white pepper
½ cup half and half
1 teaspoon cumin
1 teaspoon summer savory

Prick pie shells and bake for 5 minutes. Sauté sausage, green pepper and onions; drain well. In same pan, cook spinach until water is gone. Layer each ingredient, ending with eggs and half and half mixed with seasonings poured over it all. These freeze well after baking. Bake 30–40 minutes at 425°.

Sawgrass and Pines

Crab Quiche

1 egg
4 teaspoons all-purpose flour
½ cup light cream
8 ounces crab meat

8 ounces grated Swiss cheese
1 tablespoon green onion, chopped
1 unbaked pastry shell

Preheat oven to 350°. Beat egg with a wire whisk; blend in flour. Add cream and blend well. Fold in crab, cheese, and onion. Fill pie shell and bake for 45 minutes or until toothpick inserted in center comes out clean.

Apalachicola Cookbook

Southern Corn Bread Dressing

3 cups crumbled corn bread
2–2½ cups crumbled day-old
  bread (be sure it is dry)
2–3 eggs
4–5 cups turkey or chicken broth

1 cup chopped celery
⅓ cup oleo or butter
½ teaspoon pepper
½ teaspoon salt
1 large onion, chopped

Sauté onion and celery in butter. Preheat oven to 400°. Mix bread; add eggs and other ingredients and mix well. Have dressing soft, about the consistency of cake batter or thick soup. (The secret of good dressing is to have it really soupy as it will cook dry.)

Bake in greased baking dish, 13 × 9 inches, for about 40 minutes. Serves 10–12. If you wish, you may stuff your bird with this dressing. If bird is stuffed, allow 5 minutes more cooking per pound.

Note: You may make Chestnut Dressing by adding 1 cup chopped, cooked chestnuts; or make Oyster Dressing with the addition of 1 cup chopped oysters.

Sawgrass and Pines

Fruits

Citrus products are Florida's principal agricultural product. The state leads the nation in production of oranges, grapefruit, and tangerines.

Apple Fritter Rings

4 (medium-size) tart cooking
apples, cored and peeled
Sugar
½ teaspoon nutmeg
2 tablespoons lemon juice

Fat for deep frying
1 cup all-purpose flour
½ teaspoon salt
1 cup milk

Slice apples in ½-inch rings. Sprinkle with sugar and nutmeg; pour lemon juice over top. Let stand 1 hour. Heat fat in suitable frying container. Mix flour, salt and ½ .cup milk. Then add remaining milk, beating until smooth. Dip apple slices in batter and fry a few at a time until well browned and puffy. Drain on absorbent paper. Sprinkle with more sugar. Serve warm. Yummy! Yield: Approximately 16 rings.

Seasoned with Sunshine

Peppered Apples
(Pommes au Poivrées)

Three kinds of pepper are combined with green onions and butter to sauté apples for an excellent accompaniment to pork or chicken dishes. Unusual and delicious.

6 apples, peeled and cored
4 ounces butter, clarified
6 green onions, chopped
⅛ teaspoon white pepper

⅛ teaspoon black pepper
⅛ teaspoon cayenne pepper
½ teaspoon salt

Cut each apple into 8 slices. Sauté apple slices in butter for two minutes. Add green onions. Mix well. Lower heat to simmer. Cook for 5 minutes. Add peppers and salt. Cook 2 or 3 minutes or until apples are tender.

Gourmet Cooking II

Swedish Baked Apples With Vanilla Sauce

1 cup ground almonds	6 baking apples
¼ cup sugar	2 tablespoons margarine
¼ cup water	½ cup dry bread crumbs
2 egg whites	

In a blender, combine the first 4 ingredients to a smooth paste. Set aside; peel apples and core almost to bottom. Brush apples with melted butter and roll in bread crumbs. Fill cored apples with almond paste. Place apples with sides just touching in a 9-inch pan. Bake at 350° 30–40 minutes or until fork tender. Serve with Vanilla Sauce.

VANILLA SAUCE:

3 egg yolks	1½ cups heavy cream
¼ cup sugar	1 teaspoon vanilla

In top of double boiler, combine all ingredients, except ½ cup heavy cream. Cook until thickened, beating constantly. Remove from heat, stirring vigorously until custard is cool. Whip remaining ½ cup cream and fold into the cooled custard. Chill and serve over apples. Serves 6.

Seminole Savorings

Holiday Cran-Apples

3 cups apples, peeled and chopped	⅓ cup white sugar
2 cups fresh cranberries	⅓ cup brown sugar

TOPPING:

1 stick margarine, melted	⅓ cup flour
1 cup brown sugar	⅓ cup nuts, chopped
1 cup oatmeal	

Combine apples, cranberries and sugars; pour into a greased 9 × 13-inch Pyrex dish. Combine topping ingredients and pour over cranberry-apple mixture. Bake in a 350° oven for 45 minutes. Delicious with turkey and ham. Serves 8–10.

Seasoned with Sunshine

Escalloped Pineapple

1½ cups granulated sugar
½ cup butter
3 eggs
½ cup milk

2 (9-ounce) cans undrained
   crushed pineapple
4 cups bread cubes
3 tablespoons brown sugar
½ teaspoon nutmeg

Cream granulated sugar and butter. Add eggs and mix. Add milk, pineapple and bread cubes. Pour in buttered 9 × 12-inch casserole and sprinkle top with brown sugar and nutmeg. Bake uncovered for one hour at 350°. Serves 8–10.

The Orange Bowl Cookbook

Baked Apricots

¾–1 pound butter, divided in
   thirds
2 (28-ounce) cans apricot halves,
   peeled and drained

2 boxes light brown sugar
1 (1-pound) box Ritz Crackers,
   crushed

Melt butter. Layer ingredients in a 3-quart casserole dish as follows: ⅓ of melted butter, 1 can apricots, 1 box sugar, ½ of crackers. Repeat, ending with crackers and butter. Bake uncovered at 300° for 1 hour. Serves 12.

A Taste of Tampa

Curried Fruit

⅓ cup butter
¾ cup brown sugar
4 teaspoons curry powder
1 tall can pear halves
1 tall can apricot halves, peeled

1 tall can pineapple chunks
1 tall can peach halves and other
   fruits such as kumquats or
   cherries may be added

Mix butter, sugar and curry powder. Drain the canned fruits and place in baking dish. Spread sugar mixture over fruits and bake for 1 hour at 325°. Can be baked once and reheated and it's even better! Serves 6–8.

Gator Country Cooks

Sun Ray Compote

1 cup watermelon balls	8 grapefruit sections
8 slices cantaloupe	16 orange sections
8 slices Cranshaw melon	

Mound watermelon balls in center of serving platter. Arrange the remaining fruit around the center like rays of sun. Serve with *Banana Dressing*. Serves 6–8.

BANANA DRESSING:

2 ripe bananas	¼ cup honey
2 tablespoons lemon juice	1 cup heavy cream, whipped
¼ cup brown sugar	

Using a blender, combine bananas, lemon juice, sugar, and honey until smooth. Fold into whipped cream.

Palm Beach Entertains

Fresh Fruit With Whipped Rum Sauce

Wash and slice fresh fruits and dip in ascorbic acid (vitamin C) solution to keep from turning brown. You may use fresh pears, apples, bananas, pineapple and strawberries.

WHIPPED RUM SAUCE:

2 eggs, separated
½ cup brown sugar, firmly
  packed, divided

2 tablespoons rum or ½ teaspoon
  rum flavoring
1 cup heavy cream, whipped
⅛ teaspoon nutmeg

In a small bowl of an electric mixer, beat egg yolks until thick and light and gradually beat in ¼ cup of the brown sugar and rum. Beat egg whites until soft peaks form and gradually beat in the remaining ¼ cup sugar. Fold the yolk mixture into the meringue. Stir rum into the whipped cream and fold into the egg mixture. Turn into a sauce bowl and dust the top with nutmeg. Chill. Serve with fresh sliced fruit (marinated in rum, if desired). Yields 3 cups.

The Orange Bowl Cookbook

Sensational Strawberries

¾ cup sugar
½ cup heavy cream
¼ cup light corn syrup
2 tablespoons butter

½ cup Heath Toffee candy bars,
  chopped
1 quart fresh strawberries,
  washed and hulled
Sour cream

Combine sugar, cream, corn syrup and butter in a saucepan. Bring to a boil and cook for 3 minutes. Stir occasionally. Remove from heat and add candy. Stir until most of the candy is dissolved. Cool. Serve strawberries topped with a dollop of sour cream and drizzle with sauce. Serves: 6.

Sugar Beach

Fried Green Plantains
(Tostones o Chatinos de Platano Verde)

Peel the plaintains and cut into 1″ thick pieces. Fry at 365° for 5 minutes or until they begin to brown. Drain on kitchen paper. Flatten and fry again at 385° for approximately 3 minutes. Drain again and sprinkle with salt. For softer fried plantains, soak for a few minutes in salted water after the first fry, drain and fry again.

The Cuban Flavor

Queen of Scots Marmalade

6 large thick-skinned oranges	6 cups water
2 lemons, sliced as thinly as possible	6 cups sugar

Peel oranges close to flesh; slice peel into thin strips about ¾-inch long. Dice orange flesh, discarding seeds. Place orange peel, flesh, lemon and water into a large thick-bottomed saucepan. *Do not use cast iron as this will discolor fruit.* Simmer over low heat until peel is soft and white part is almost clear (about 1 hour); remove from heat. Allow mixture to rest in a cool place for about 12 hours to blend flavors. Measure fruit mixture, (should be about 6 cups) return to saucepan. Stir in 1 cup of sugar for each cup of fruit mixture, be sure to blend well. Over a low heat bring very, very slowly to boil, stirring with a wooden spoon. When mixture boils, raise heat to medium; stir constantly until all sugar is dissolved; taste to be sure marmalade is not gritty. Continue to boil rapidly to jellying point; this should take about 25 minutes; test set.on a plate. Pour marlamade into hot sterilized jars; seal with paraffin then cap. Store in a cool dark place; refrigerate after opening. Makes 6–8 pints.

Note: When Mary Queen of Scots was a girl, she was ill and was sent to France to recover. Her future father-in-law told his cook to make something to tempt her appetite. The cook picked some oranges from the castle grove and combined the citrus with sugar in a sort of jam. She liked it and it was named Mariemalade.

Suncoast Seasons

Mango Chutney

1 quart sliced green mangoes
2 or 3 green peppers, chopped
1 large onion, chopped
2 hot peppers, cut very fine,
  (remove seeds unless very hot
  flavor is desired)
1 clove of garlic, sliced
1 tablespoon salt
1 cup grapefruit juice
1 cup cider vinegar

1 pound brown sugar
1 pound seedless raisins
1 tablespoon white mustard seed
2 teaspoons each of allspice,
  cinnamon and cloves
1 (3-ounce) package sliced
  almonds (optional)
1 or 2 tablespoons finely chopped
  crystallized ginger (optional)

Combine first 6 ingredients. Let stand for 1 hour. Drain. Heat the grapefruit juice, vinegar, sugar, raisins, mustard seed and spices. Add mango mixture. Boil 30 minutes (if pressure cooker is used, cook 15 minutes). Seal while hot. Yields 4 pints.

The Gasparilla Cookbook

Seagrape Jelly

Only those seagrape bushes growing by the sea produce good jelly-making grapes. The leaf of the seagrape was used by early Spanish pioneers as stationery for their 16th century letters home. It still works. Try it some time, using a ball point pen. You can make very original greeting cards.

Use mostly purple grapes but add a few not-so-ripe ones. Wash in soda water. In twice the amount of water, bring to boil and then simmer until grapes are soft and can be mashed off the seeds with a potato masher. Pour cooked jelly into bag, drain and measure juice so rendered. Measure out an equal amount of sugar, bring juice to boil and add sugar gradually, stirring constantly. Boil vigorously until mixture begins to thicken. Pour into clean, hot jars and process by water bath method.

Maurice's Tropical Fruit Cook Book

Bread
and Breakfast

Florida produces graceful thoroughbred horses on its many beautiful horse farms, like this one near Ocala.

Company's Coming for Breakfast

This may be prepared in advance and frozen. Thaw before baking. For easy clean-up afterwards, pour into individual-size, disposable, foil loaf pans. Serve with scrambled eggs.

1 pound mild ground pork sausage
1 pound hot or spicy ground pork
  sausage
½ cup onion, chopped
½ cup apple, peeled and chopped

2 eggs, beaten
½ cup milk
1½ cups Saltine cracker crumbs
1 (17-ounce) can apricot halves,
  drained and chopped

Preheat oven to 350°. Brown sausage in skillet. Add onion and apple and sauté. Drain well. Mix sausage mixture with remaining ingredients in a medium bowl. Pour into greased and floured casserole. Bake 45 minutes. Serves 10–12.

Sugar Beach

Overnight Brunch Main Dish
Prepare the night before

1 dozen eggs
1½ cups milk
¼ cup parsley flakes
1 loaf cubed French bread
2 cups diced ham, turkey, or
  mushrooms

1½ cups grated cheddar cheese
½ cup grated onion (optional)
1 cup sliced mushrooms (optional)
1 cup diced green pepper
  (optional)
Paprika (optional)

Lightly beat eggs, milk, and parsley as for scrambled eggs. Combine all other ingredients. Toss to mix and pour egg mixture over and mix again. Pour into lightly greased casserole pan. Refrigerate overnight. Bake at 350° for 35–40 minutes before serving. Sprinkle with paprika.

Note: A layer of cooked broccoli or spinach may be placed in the middle of casserole. Preparation: 20 minutes. Easy. Serves: 6–8. Cooking: 40 minutes. Must do ahead. Can freeze.

Culinary Arts & Crafts

Cheese Strata
A Christmas morning favorite

8 slices buttered white bread,
  crusts removed
¼ cup butter or margarine,
  softened
4 eggs, slightly beaten

2½ cups milk
1 teaspoon salt
¼ teaspoon dry mustard
3 cups shredded cheddar cheese

Cut bread slices into quarters. Alternate layers of bread and cheese in greased 7 × 11-inch baking dish, ending with cheese. Mix eggs, milk, salt and mustard. Pour over cheese and bread layers. Cover. Chill 6 hours or overnight.

Bake uncovered in a preheated 325° oven 45 minutes or until firm. Let stand a few minutes and cut into squares.

May be frozen after baking. Defrost before reheating. Serves 6–8.

Gulfshore Delights

Eggsistentialist Stuffed Eggs With Hollandaise

6 hard-boiled eggs, halved
3 green onions, diced
½ stick butter
¼ pound mushrooms, minced
½ cup light cream

¼ cup white wine
¼ cup chopped parsley
1 cup prepared Hollandaise
Salt and pepper to taste
½ cup Swiss cheese

Remove yolks from eggs, Chop fine.

In a saucepan, cook green onions in ½ stick butter over medium heat. Add mushrooms, light cream and white wine. Cook mixture for 15 minutes until liquid is reduced. Remove from heat and let cool. Stir in egg yolks and parsley and blend until smooth. Season to taste.

Pour enough Hollandaise sauce in the bottom of a flat casserole to keep eggs from sticking to pan. Fill egg whites with mushroom-yolk mixture and place in casserole dish. Pour remaining Hollandaise over eggs to cover. Sprinkle top with grated cheese. Place casserole on the bottom rack of the oven, and broil eggs 15 minutes or until golden brown. Serves: 4–6. Preparation: 20 minutes. Cooking: 15 minutes. Difficulty: Average.

Juicy Miss Lucy Cookbook

Brunch Eggs

2 (10¾-ounce) cans cream of
  mushroom soup
½ cup sherry
1 (4-ounce) can mushrooms,
  drained

3 dozen eggs
¼ cup milk
½ cup butter
½ pound grated Cheddar cheese
Paprika to taste

Heat soup just enough to stir smooth. Add sherry and mushrooms.

Beat eggs and milk together. Melt butter in a pan and scramble egg mixture until just soft.

Pour a layer of eggs into a casserole. Add a layer of soup mixture and a layer of cheese. Repeat. Sprinkle with paprika. Place dish into a cold oven and turn temperature to 250°. Bake for 1 hour, or until thoroughly heated. Serves 12–14.

Heart of the Palms

Monterey Jack Eggs

12 slices bacon, coarsely chopped
6 scallions, thinly sliced
¾ pound fresh mushrooms, sliced
12 eggs

1½ cups milk
¾ teaspoon seasoned salt
3¾ cups shredded Monterey Jack
  cheese

Preheat oven to 350°. Fry bacon until browned. Drain, reserving 2 tablespoons of drippings. In large, heavy pan, sauté scallions and mushrooms in drippings until limp. Beat eggs with milk and seasoned salt. Stir in bacon, onions, mushrooms, and 3 cups of cheese. Pour mixture into a greased shallow 2-quart baking dish. Bake uncovered for 35–40 minutes until mixture is set and top is lightly browned. When almost done, sprinkle with remaining ¾ cup of cheese. Return to oven until cheese melts. Serve immediately. Serves 6–8.

Note: This may be prepared a day in advance up to the baking point and refrigerated. Bring to room temperature and bake as directed. It's an unusual breakfast to serve house guests.

Palm Beach Entertains

Poached Eggs Élégants

1 cup milk
1 cup heavy cream
1 cup sharp cheddar cheese,
  shredded
½ cup stuffed olives, sliced
1 tablespoon chives, chopped
1 tablespoon butter

⅛ teaspoon salt
Dash Tabasco
1 cup sour cream
8 eggs
4 English muffins, halved, toasted
  and buttered
Chopped parsley

Combine first eight ingredients in large skillet. Simmer gently, stirring until cheese is melted. Stir in sour cream, blending well. Bring sauce to a gentle simmer. Break in eggs, one at a time. Cover and simmer gently 3–5 minutes or until egg whites are set. Serve over muffins and with grilled sausage. Garnish with parsley.

The Prima Diner

Popover Pancake
It's fun to watch it pop and it's mighty good, too!

½ cup all-purpose flour
½ cup milk
2 eggs, slightly beaten

¼ cup butter
2 tablespoons confectioners' sugar
Juice of ½ lemon

Preheat oven to 425°. In mixing bowl combine flour, milk and eggs. Beat lightly. The batter will be slightly lumpy. Put butter into a 12-inch round frying pan with heatproof handle. Place in oven until very hot. Pour in the batter, return to oven, and bake 20 minutes or until pancake is puffed all around sides of the pan and golden brown. Remove from oven and sprinkle with confectioners' sugar and lemon juice. Serve immediately. Serves 2–3.

Cook and Deal

Patsy's Waffles

2 cups sifted flour
2 cups milk
2 eggs
2 tablespoons sugar

4 teaspoons baking powder
1 teaspoon salt
6–7 tablespoons shortening or
    margarine

Sift flour, sugar, baking powder and salt together. Beat yolks of eggs, add milk and flour alternately and beat again. Add melted butter and mix well. Add beaten egg whites. Put in pitcher and pour on hot waffle iron, enough to cover about half. (Recipe is over 25 years old.)

Secrets from the Galley

Orange French Toast

2 eggs, beaten
½ cup freshly squeezed orange
   juice
¼ teaspoon salt

8 slices day-old bread
2 tablespoons butter or
   margarine, divided
Glazed Apple Slices (recipe below)

In shallow bowl combine eggs, orange juice and salt; mix well. Dip bread slices in egg mixture, turning to coat both sides. In large skillet, melt a small amount of butter; brown bread on both sides. Repeat until all bread is used. Serve with *Glazed Apple Slices*.

GLAZED APPLE SLICES:

½ cup freshly squeezed orange
   juice
⅓ cup light brown sugar
⅛ teaspoon ground allspice

3 large apples, cored and thinly
   sliced
Orange French Toast

In large skillet combine orange juice, brown sugar and allspice. Stir over low heat until sugar dissolves and mixture boils. Add apple slices. Simmer, uncovered, over low heat 8–10 minutes, or until apples are tender. Spoon syrup over apples during cooking. Serve hot with *Orange French Toast*. Serves 4.

The Orange Bowl Cookbook

Kitty's Biscuits

2 cups sifted Gold Medal self-
  rising flour
½ cup plus 1 rounded tablespoon
  Crisco

1 teaspoon sugar
¾ cup very cold milk (buttermilk
  may be substituted, adding ⅛
  teaspoon baking soda)

Sift flour and sugar into bowl and work Crisco into flour using hand. Pour milk into mixture, enough to make a soft dough. Handle lightly, using upward motions instead of pressing down. Toss onto floured board and lightly roll out with floured rolling pin to about ½ inch in thickness, for fluffy biscuits, ¼ inch for crusty biscuits. Cut out with a small biscuit cutter. Dip cutter in flour often for easy cutting. Place on greased cookie sheet and bake on top rack in preheated 450° oven for 5–7 minutes until golden brown. To freeze, place pan of unbaked biscuits in freezer until firm, then package in plastic bags. They will keep as long as two weeks. Take out as many as needed and place on greased tin pan and thaw. Follow same baking instructions. Makes approximately 2½ dozen.

Gator Country Cooks

Blueberry-Orange Muffins

3 cups sifted flour
4 teaspoons baking powder
¼ teaspoon soda
¾ cup sugar
1½ teaspoons salt
2 cups blueberries
2 eggs, slightly beaten

¾ cup milk
½ cup butter, melted
1 tablespoon grated orange peel
½ cup plus 4 teaspoons orange
   juice
¼ cup butter, melted
1 cup sugar
2 teaspoons cinnamon

Preheat oven to 425°. Sift together flour, baking powder, soda, sugar and salt. Stir in blueberries, tossing lightly until coated. Beat together eggs, milk, ½ cup melted butter, orange peel and orange juice; pour into dry ingredients and stir just until moistened. Fill greased muffin tins or paper liners ⅔ full. Bake for 25 minutes. Remove from tins while hot and brush tops with melted butter; then sprinkle with a mixture of 1 cup sugar and cinnamon. Yield: 2 dozen.

Some Like It South!

Bourbon Sticky Buns

1 package hot roll mix
¾ cup scalded milk, cooled to
   lukewarm
1 egg
¾ cup bourbon

2¾ cups brown sugar
¼ cup butter or margarine,
   softened
1 cup pecans
2 teaspoons cinnamon

Make dough according to package directions except use milk instead of water and add the egg. Grease 18 muffin cups; into each measure 1½ teaspoons bourbon, 2 tablespoons brown sugar, and 3 or 4 pecans. Roll dough on lightly floured surface in 12 × 18-inch rectangle. Combine remaining bourbon, brown sugar, butter and cinnamon and spread on dough. Roll up jelly-roll fashion, beginning at the narrow end, and cut roll into 18 slices. Place a slice in each muffin cup, cover pans, and let rise about 30 minutes. Bake at 375° for 18–20 minutes or until nicely browned. Cool on rack 5 minutes before turning out of pans. Serve warm. Makes 18 buns.

Cypress Gardens Cookbook

Bran Muffins

We place *Bran Muffins* at the top of the list. They are so good for us and yet easy to make.

1 egg	1 teaspoon baking soda
2 tablespoons safflower oil	¼ teaspoon sea salt
2 tablespoons honey	1 cup bran
2 tablespoons molasses	¾ cup whole wheat flour
¾ cup yogurt	¼ cup water

Mix the first column of ingredients together. Add the second column. Butter and flour a muffin tin or use paper muffin holders. Bake for 30 minutes at 350°. Cool before serving

Variations:

Add ½ cup raisins or sunflower seeds

Bake in 8 × 10-inch glass pan, cut into squares

Add 1 cup mashed ripe banana

Add 1 cup fresh or frozen blueberries

Add 1 cup finely chopped apples

Add ¼ teaspoon nutmeg, ½ teaspoon cinnamon and ½ cup chopped apples

Step-By-Step to Natural Food

Banana Bread

The easiest of all banana breads. You don't need to beat the eggs. Nor add ingredients in any particular order. Just toss it all together, stir it to mix, and bake.

2 cups flour	4 large bananas, mashed
1 cup sugar	½ cup black walnuts
½ cup shortening	1 teaspoon baking soda
2 eggs	½ teaspoon salt
Juice and grated rind of 1 orange	

Mix all ingredients and bake in loaf pan for 1 hour at 350°.

Maurice's Tropical Fruit Cook Book

Sweet Lemon Bread

1 cup butter, softened	1 cup buttermilk
2 cups sugar	1 lemon rind, grated
4 eggs	1 cup chopped pecans
½ teaspoon salt	Juice of 3 lemons
½ teaspoon baking soda	1 cup sugar
3 cups all-purpose flour	

Preheat oven to 325°. Cream butter and sugar. Add eggs, one at a time, beating after each addition. Sift together salt, soda and flour. Add to sugar mixture alternating with buttermilk. Stir in lemon rind and pecans. Pour into 2 greased and floured loaf pans. Bake for 1 hour.

While bread bakes, mix lemon juice and sugar. Stir until sugar is dissolved, making a glaze. After bread has baked, turn onto waxed paper and spoon glaze over top while bread is still hot. Servings: 2 loaves. Preparation time: 30 minutes. Baking time: 1 hour.

Jacksonville & Company

Mango Bread

2 eggs
1¼ cups sugar
½ cup vegetable oil
¼ cup honey
2 cups mango, slightly mashed
2 cups all-purpose flour

2 teaspoons cinnamon
2 teaspoons baking soda
½ teaspoon salt
½ teaspoon vanilla
½ cup walnuts, chopped
½ cup raisins

Beat eggs until fluffy. Beat in sugar, oil, and gradually add honey. Blend in mango. Combine dry ingredients and add very gradually to the mixture. Stir in vanilla, walnuts, and raisins. Pour into greased and floured bread pans. Let stand for 20 minutes. Bake at 350° for 50–60 minutes. Frozen mango can be used. Makes 2 loaves.

Seasons in the Sun

Onion Herb Bread
Absolutely delicious!

1 package dry yeast	1 tablespoon butter, softened
¼ cup warm water	¼ teaspoon baking soda
1 cup cottage cheese, heated to lukewarm	1 teaspoon salt
	1 egg
2 tablespoons sugar	2¼–2½ cups flour, sifted
1 tablespoon dry onion	½ cup butter, melted
2 teaspoons dill seed	1½ teaspoons celery seed

Preheat oven 350°. Dissolve yeast in warm water. In large bowl, combine cottage cheese, sugar, onion, dill seed, butter, soda, salt and egg. Add yeast. Gradually add flour, enough to make a stiff dough. Mix well. Cover and let rise until double. Punch down. Turn dough into greased 9 × 5-inch loaf pan. Let rise until double. Bake 40–50 minutes. When bread is removed from oven, pour mixture of melted butter and celery seed over top. Yields 1 loaf.

Fare by the Sea

Stuffed French Bread

1 loaf French bread	Mayonnaise to moisten
8 ounces Cheese Spread or 8 ounces commercial spread	6 ounces crab meat
	3 tablespoons chopped parsley

Pre-heat oven to 350°. Cut French bread in half lengthwise and remove some of the bread to make a shallow trench in each half. Cover with cheese spread. Add mayonnaise to the crab and spread over cheese. Bake for 20 minutes or till bubbly. Sprinkle with chopped parsley. Cut into serving pieces and serve.

CHEESE SPREAD:

8 ounces sharp Cheddar cheese	1 tablespoon butter, softened

Place in processor or blender and blend until smooth.

Secrets from the Galley

Gourmet French Bread

1 thin loaf French bread, sliced
  lengthwise
Margarine
1 cup mayonnaise
½ cup green onions, finely
  chopped

½ cup Monterey Jack cheese,
  grated
½ teaspoon Worcestershire sauce
Paprika
Parmesan cheese

Spread margarine on both lengths of bread. Mix mayonnaise, onions, cheese and Worcestershire sauce. Spread mixture on bread. Sprinkle with paprika and Parmesan cheese and bake at 350° for 15–20 minutes.

Sugar Beach

Bread Sticks

1 package wiener buns
1 stick margarine

1 tablespoon Beau Monde
  seasoning (Lawry's Seasoned
  Salt will do as substitute)
Sesame seeds

Slice buns longway into 4 pieces. Melt margarine and mix with seasoning. Pour down center of each stick of bread. Sprinkle with sesame seed. Bake on cookie sheet in 250° oven for 2 hours to dry completely.

Cut in smaller pieces, these make good cocktail snacks.

Cypress Gardens Cookbook

Cornbread

¾ cup yellow cornmeal
¾ cup flour
1 teaspoon salt
3 teaspoons baking powder
2 eggs

½ cup oil
1 cup sour cream
1 cup fresh corn, off cob
¼ pound butter

Mix dry ingredients. Add eggs, oil, sour cream, and corn. Bake at 400° until done. Melt butter and pour over top when done.

The Colonel's Inn Caterers'—Tallahassee Historical Cookbook

Cakes

Thousands of tourists each year pass through Palm Beach's ornate Henry Flagler
Museum, built in 1902 at a cost of over $4 million.

Orange Cream Almond Meringue Layer Cake

ORANGE CREAM FILLING FOR CAKE:

1½ cups pure orange juice	Pinch of salt
½ cup granulated sugar	1 tablespoon cornstarch or instant
Drop of lemon juice	cooking starch

Thicken in double boiler with cornstarch or instant cooking starch. Cool before using. (Instant starch must be mixed with a little sugar first.)

BOTTOM (CAKE):

1 cup butter	½ teaspoon salt
2 cups sifted confectioners' sugar	6 tablespoons milk
8 egg yolks	1 teaspoon each of almond and
2 cups sifted cake flour	vanilla extract
2 teaspoons baking powder	

Cream butter until light and fluffy. Add sugar gradually, cream until smooth. Add well-beaten yolks and blend thoroughly. Sift dry ingredients together and blend into butter mixture. Combine milk with flavoring and add to mixture. Pour into greased cake pans.

TOP (MERINGUE):

8 egg whites	Pinch of powdered ginger
2 cups granulated sugar	1 cup chopped almonds
Few grains salt	

Beat egg whites until stiff and sift in, gradually, the sugar with salt and ginger. Dip spatula in cold water and spread meringue over cake batter. Sprinkle each layer with chopped toasted almonds. Bake cake topped with meringue at 300° until tan colored, then at 250° for a total baking time of 50–60 minutes. Remove from pan and spread with orange cream filling. Top with **whipped cream.**

The Orange Bowl Cookbook

You can get more juice from a lemon, lime, orange, or grapefruit by microwaving it on HIGH for 10–20 seconds. If a microwave isn't available, drop the fruit in boiling water for 10 minutes.

Case's Orange Pound Cake
First to sell at any bake sale

CAKE:

1 cup butter, softened
2 cups sugar
6 eggs
2 cups all-purpose flour

½ teaspoon orange extract
3 tablespoons orange juice
1 tablespoon lemon juice
Zest of 2 oranges*

Preheat oven to 350°. Cream butter and sugar. Add eggs, one at a time, and beat well after each. Gently beat in remaining ingredients. Bake in a greased and floured tube pan 45 minutes or until tester comes out clean. Cool in pan 10 minutes, turn out, and place top side up. Pour glaze over warm cake, if desired.

ORANGE GLAZE, OPTIONAL:

2 cups confectioners' sugar
4 tablespoons orange juice

½ teaspoon orange extract

Combine all ingredients and pour over warm cake. As cake cools, occasionally spoon glaze over the top and sides. Serves 16.

*The term "zest" refers to finely grating the outer layer of a whole orange, lemon or lime.

Gulfshore Delights

Apricot Rum Cake

4 eggs
¾ cup vegetable oil
¾ cup apricot nectar (canned)
1 box yellow cake mix

5 ounces margarine
¾ cup sugar
½ cup rum
Confectioners' sugar

In a large bowl, beat eggs lightly and combine with oil, apricot nectar and cake mix. Beat at medium speed for 4 or 5 minutes until smooth. Pour into large greased and floured bundt or deep cake pan. Bake at 350° for 50 minutes. Melt margarine and sugar in pan over low heat and stir in rum. As soon as cake is done, place pan on cooling rack and pour rum mixture over cake, allowing it to soak in well. Cool for 1 hour before removing from pan. Sift confectioners' sugar over top. Yield: 12–16 servings.

Friendly Feasts Act II

Apple Cake

The following cake is easy to make and can be whipped up in 20 minutes with a little help from a husband. Most of the time we eat it plain without icing.

1 cup butter
1 cup honey
3 eggs
2 teaspoons vanilla
½ teaspoon sea salt
1 teaspoon cinnamon

2 teaspoons baking soda
2 cups whole wheat flour
3 cups diced apples, peeled or
  unpeeled
2 cups walnuts, chopped

Mix together the butter, honey and eggs. Add vanilla, salt, cinnamon, and soda. Beat until smooth. Gradually add the flour. Apples can be peeled or unpeeled. Fold in the apples and walnut pieces and place in a buttered and floured 13 × 9-inch glass baking dish. Bake at 350° for 25–30 minutes. If icing is desired, use *Spice Icing*.

SPICE ICING:

⅓ cup honey
4 tablespoons melted butter
1 cup non-instant dry powdered
  milk
1½ teaspoons cinnamon

1 teaspoon allspice
1 teaspoon carob powder
4 tablespoons water
1 teaspoon vanilla

Mix all the ingredients together. Use the milk as a dry powder. Beat until smooth.

Step-By-Step to Natural Food

Carrot Cake
Pineapple and coconut make this an outstanding cake

2 cups sifted flour
2 teaspoons baking powder
1½ teaspoons baking soda
1 teaspoon salt
2½ teaspoons cinnamon
2 cups sugar
4 eggs

1½ cups oil
2 cups finely grated carrots
⅓ cup chopped pecans
1 (8-ounce) can crushed
    pineapple, drained
1 (3½-ounce) can flaked coconut

Sift together first five ingredients. Add sugar, eggs, and oil; mix well. Stir in carrots, pecans, pineapple, and coconut; blend thoroughly. Pour into three greased and floured 9-inch cake pans. Bake at 350° for 35–40 minutes. Cool briefly in pans, then turn onto racks. Cool completely. Combine frosting ingredients. If frosting is too thick, add small amount of milk. Spread frosting between layers and on top of cake. Serves 10.

CREAM CHEESE FROSTING:
¼ pound butter or margarine,
    softened
1 (8-ounce) package cream cheese,
    softened

1¼ teaspoons vanilla
1 box (1-pound) confectioners
    sugar

What would Florida be without Coconut Palms?—So useful, too (practically all parts are usable)—Thrives on wind and water from the sea—Nothing is as satisfying as cracking the hairy, brown husk of the coconut and exposing the sweet white meat and translucent milk. But climbing 100 feet to get the nut—that's the truly hard part!

Sunny Side Up

Sunshine Island
(Second prize winner, Second All-Florida Orange Dessert Contest)

⅓ cup butter
⅓ cup Crisco
1½ cups sugar
3 eggs
2¼ cups sifted flour
2½ teaspoons baking powder

1 teaspoon salt
½ cup milk
½ cup orange juice
1 cup coconut flakes
1½ teaspoons grated orange rind

Cream together butter, Crisco and sugar until fluffy. Beat in thoroughly the eggs. Sift together flour, baking powder, salt. Stir in, alternating with milk and orange juice. Add coconut and rind. Bake in greased and floured 9-inch pans for 25–30 minutes at 350°. Put cooled layers together with *Clear Orange Filling*. Frost top and sides with *Orange Mountain Icing*. Decorate with fresh orange sections (membranes removed) nestled in coconut.

CLEAR ORANGE FILLING:

1 cup sugar
4 tablespoons cornstarch
½ teaspoon salt
2 tablespoons butter

1 cup orange juice
2 tablespoons grated orange rind
1½ tablespoons lemon juice

Mix together in saucepan and bring to rolling boil and boil 1 minute, stirring constantly. Cool.

ORANGE MOUNTAIN ICING:

2 egg whites
1 cup sugar
⅛ teaspoon cream of tartar

¼ cup orange juice
Dash of salt
2 tablespoons light corn syrup

Combine all ingredients in top of double boiler. Place over boiling water stirring occasionally for about 2 minutes. Then with mixer, on high speed, beat until mixture holds its shape.

The Gasparilla Cookbook

Oatmeal Cake

1¼ cups boiling water
1 cup quick oats
½ cup shortening
1 cup brown sugar, firmly packed
1 cup white sugar
2 eggs

1⅓ cups flour
1 teaspoon soda
½ teaspoon salt
½ teaspoon cinnamon
½ teaspoon nutmeg
1 teaspoon vanilla

Grease and flour a 9 × 13-inch pan. Preheat oven to 375°. Pour boiling water over oats. Cream together shortening and sugars until fluffy. Add eggs, one at a time, beating well. Add vanilla. Sift dry ingredients together. Whip up oats and add to creamed mixture. Add flour gradually. Pour into prepared pan. Bake 30–35 minutes. Remove from oven and let stand 5 minutes.

TOPPING:
1 stick margarine
1 cup brown sugar, firmly packed
1 cup chopped nuts

1 cup coconut
2 egg yolks, beaten
Milk

Mix first 5 ingredients together and add enough milk to spread. Spread over cake and return to oven to brown. Serve plain or with whipped cream or ice cream.

(Jack Nicklaus) *Seminole Savorings*

Key Lime Cake

1 package Duncan Hines lemon
  supreme cake mix
½ cup water
½ cup Key lime juice

1 (3-ounce) package lime Jell-O
½ cup Crisco or Puritan oil
4 eggs

ICING:

2 cups *sifted* confectioners' sugar   ¼ cup lime juice

With an electric mixer, blend all ingredients together on medium speed for about 2 minutes. Pour into greased tube pan or 9 × 13 × 2-inch baking pan and bake at 325° for 45 minutes (test by inserting toothpick in center). After removing from oven, use an ice pick and stick through cake, top to bottom, many times. Drizzle with icing while still warm.

Margaritaville Cookbook

Gooey Butter Cake

1 yellow cake mix
4 eggs
1 stick butter, melted

1 box powdered sugar
1 (8-ounce) package of cream
  cheese

Mix together the cake mix, two eggs, and butter. Spread in a 9 × 13-inch greased and floured pan. Batter will be thick. Blend remaining two eggs, powdered sugar and cream cheese. Pour over top of batter. Bake at 350° for 45 minutes or until the top has a brown glaze and pulls from the sides.

A Taste of Tampa

Chocolate Cake
There is no other!

1 cup butter
2 cups sugar
4 eggs
2 cups flour, sifted
¼ teaspoon salt
1½ teaspoons soda

⅔ cup buttermilk
1 teaspoon vanilla extract
3 (1-ounce) squares unsweetened
  chocolate, melted in ⅔ cup
  boiling water

Preheat oven to 325°. Cream butter and sugar with electric beater until light and fluffy. Add eggs, one at a time, and beat well after each addition. Sift flour with salt. Mix soda with buttermilk and add alternately with flour to creamed mixture, starting and ending with flour. Add vanilla and melted chocolate with water; stir until smooth. Grease a 9×13-inch pan. Pour batter into pan and bake 50–55 minutes. Cool in the pan. While slightly warm, frost with chocolate frosting. Makes about 20 (2-inch) squares. The cake freezes well.

CHOCOLATE FROSTING:

½ cup margarine
1½ cups sugar
⅓ cup milk

¾ cup semi-sweet chocolate pieces
1 cup chopped pecans or walnuts
  (optional)

In a heavy saucepan cook margarine, sugar and milk to a full rolling boil. Boil for 2 minutes. Remove from heat; add chocolate pieces and nuts. Blend quickly. Beat until a spreading consistency. (It won't take more than a minute or two.) Spread at once over chocolate cake.

Cook and Deal

Chocolate Cake Roll

5 eggs
¾ cup sugar
¼ cup cocoa
¼ cup flour
½ teaspoon baking powder
½ teaspoon vanilla

Pinch of salt
1 pint whipping cream
1–2 teaspoons instant coffee
2 teaspoons sugar
1–2 tablespoons Creme de Cocoa

Separate egg whites and yolks. Beat yolks until lemony yellow. Blend in sugar and cocoa, then flour, baking powder, vanilla, and salt. With electric or hand beater, beat whites until they stand up in soft peaks. Gently fold whites into chocolate mixture. Pour into greased and floured 11 × 16-inch jelly roll pan. Bake in 350° oven for 15–20 minutes. Allow cake to cool 15–30 minutes, then cover with kitchen towel and turn out of pan. Roll up (with towel) so that roll is 16″ long and wrap in foil for safe carrying.

Take aboard 1 pint of whipping cream, instant coffee and Creme de Cocoa. To serve, fill roll with cream whipped with 1–2 teaspoons of instant coffee, 2 teaspoons sugar and 1–2 tablespoons Creme de Cocoa, leaving enough whipped cream to cover outside of roll. Can be garnished with chopped nuts, chocolate curls or sprinkled with cocoa. (If boat freezer allows, you may prefer to substitute ice cream for the whipped cream.)

Galley Gourmet III

Milky Way Cake
A special occasion treat, rich, and expensive

8 Milky Way bars, regular size
3 sticks butter or margarine
4½ cups sugar
4 eggs, beaten
2½ cups flour
½ teaspoon baking soda

1½ cups buttermilk
1 (8-ounce) can evaporated milk
1 cup chopped pecans
1 (6-ounce) package chocolate
  chips
1 cup marshmallow cream

Combine bars and one stick butter in saucepan. Cook over low heat, stirring constantly until melted. Set aside. Cream 2 cups sugar and 1 stick butter in large bowl. Beat in eggs. Sift flour and soda and add to creamed mixture alternately with buttermilk. Stir in candy mixture. Add nuts and mix well. Pour into greased and floured 13 × 9-inch pan. Bake at 325° for 1 hour and 10 minutes. Combine remaining sugar, milk, and remaining butter in a saucepan and cook to soft ball stage, stirring frequently. Remove from heat and add chocolate chips and marshmallow cream. Cool slightly. Beat until thick and spread over cake. Preparation: 20 minutes. Moderately difficult. Serves: 12. Baking: 1 hour 10 minutes. Can do ahead.

Culinary Arts & Crafts

Patron's Party Chocolate Cake

1 package devil's food cake mix
1 (3-ounce) package chocolate or
  fudge instant pudding
¾ cup water
¾ cup oil

4 large eggs
1 tablespoon instant coffee
1 cup sour cream
6 ounces chocolate semi-sweet
  chips

Combine all ingredients except chips in a large bowl. Beat slowly at first, then at high speed for 2 minutes. Fold in chips. Bake at 350° for 1 hour in greased and floured 10-inch tube or bundt pan or in 10 × 15 × 1-inch pan until done. May be cut in squares, like brownies. Too rich for frosting. Highly successful. Cool completely before removing from pan. Serves 12–16.

The Prima Diner

Hummingbird Cake

3 cups all-purpose flour
2 cups white sugar
1 teaspoon salt
1 teaspoon baking soda
1 teaspoon ground cinnamon
3 eggs, beaten
½ cup salad oil

1½ teaspoons vanilla
1 (8-ounce) can crushed
   pineapple, undrained
1 cup chopped pecans or black
   walnuts
1 cup chopped bananas

Preheat oven 350°. Combine flour, sugar, salt, baking soda and cinnamon in a large mixing bowl. Mix well until all ingredients are thoroughly mixed.

Add eggs, oil and vanilla. Stir until dry ingredients are moistened. DO NOT BEAT.

Stir in pineapple, nuts and bananas. Mix thoroughly, but do not beat batter. Spoon into three well-greased and floured 9-inch cake pans. Bake for 25–30 minutes or until cake tests done. Cool 10 minutes and remove from pan. Cool completely and ice with following frosting.

FROSTING:

2 (8-ounce) packages cream
   cheese, softened
1 cup butter, softened
1 tablespoon cocoa

2 (16-ounce) boxes of
   confectioners' sugar
2 teaspoons vanilla

Combine cream cheese and butter until smooth. Add sifted powdered sugar and cocoa and beat until fluffy. Stir in vanilla. (Sprinkle an additional cup of nuts between layers and on top of frosting.) Makes enough for 3-layer cake. This cake must be refrigerated.

Age only matters in cheese.

Sweet Surrender with Advice á la Carte

Miami Mango Cake

2½ cups diced mangos	½ teaspoon ginger
1 teaspoon lemon juice	½ teaspoon salt
3 eggs	½ teaspoon cloves
¾ cup vegetable oil	½ teaspoon cinnamon
1 teaspoon vanilla	½ cup raisins
1¼ cups sugar	¾ cup chopped nuts
2 cups flour	Icing (recipe below)
1½ teaspoons baking soda	

Marinate mangos in lemon juice. In the bowl of an electric mixer, beat together eggs, vegetable oil, vanilla and sugar. Add mangos. Sift dry ingredients together and mix in lightly and quickly. Gently add raisins and nuts. Pour into greased 13 × 9-inch cake pan. Bake at 325° for 45–60 minutes. Cool.

ICING:

½ cup butter, softened	2 tablespoons milk
Powdered sugar	1 teaspoon vanilla
1 egg	½ cup chopped nuts

Cream the butter. Beat in enough powdered sugar to make stiff. Add the egg, beat and add more sugar. Add milk and vanilla. Spread on cake and top with chopped nuts.

The Orange Bowl Cookbook

Blueberry Cheesecake Macadamia
Superb dessert—guests will call it, divine!

CRUST:

1 (3½-ounce) jar Macadamia nut pieces, crushed in blender
1 cup all-purpose flour
¼ cup brown sugar, firmly packed
½ cup sweet butter, softened

Combine all ingredients. Mix well; press onto bottom of a 10-inch springform pan. Bake in preheated oven at 400° for 10–15 minutes. Reduce oven to 350°.

FIRST LAYER

3 (8-ounce) packages cream cheese, softened
1 teaspoon vanilla extract
1 cup sugar
4 eggs, room temperature

Crumble cheese in large bowl. Add remaining ingredients; beat at high speed with electric mixer until blended and smooth, approximately 5 minutes. (Food processor may be used.) Pour over crust. Bake at 350° for 40 minutes until set (not completely firm). Remove from oven; cool for 10 minutes.

SECOND LAYER:

1 cup sour cream
2 tablespoons sugar
½ teaspoon vanilla extract

Combine sour cream, sugar and vanilla. Spread over top of cheesecake. Bake at 350° for 5 minutes. Cool; spread blueberry topping over. Refrigerate before serving.

TOPPING:

2 cups fresh or frozen blueberries
1 tablespoon cornstarch
2 to 3 tablespoons cold water

Mix cornstarch with cold water to form a smooth paste. Stir in blueberries; cook until thickened. Let cool; spread on cake. Cool 1 hour; then refrigerate. Serves 12.

Suncoast Seasons

Manatee Merry Cheese Cakes

1 cup flour
½ cup butter or margarine,
  softened
½ cup brown sugar, firmly packed
½ cup pecans, chopped
1 (8-ounce) package cream cheese,
  softened

¼ cup sugar
1 egg, beaten
2 tablespoons each: milk and
  lemon juice (or lime juice)
½ teaspoon vanilla

Combine first three ingredients and beat with mixer until particles are fine. Add pecans. Reserving one cup for topping, pat mixture in ungreased 8 × 8-inch pan. Bake at 350° for ten minutes. Remove from oven and spread remaining ingredients, well mixed. Sprinkle with reserved crumbs. Return to oven and bake thirty more minutes or until brown. Cool. Cut into bars and store in refrigerator or freezer. Yields 25–30 small bars.

The Prima Diner

Cheese Cupcakes

3 (8-ounce) packages cream
  cheese, softened
1 cup sugar

5 eggs
1 teaspoon vanilla

TOPPING:
1 cup sour cream
3 tablespoons sugar

½ teaspoon vanilla
24 red or green glazed cherries

Combine cream cheese, sugar, eggs, and vanilla; blend until smooth. Line muffin tins with paper or foil liners. Fill each ⅔ full. Bake at 300° for 40–45 minutes. Remove from oven. When cakes sink, in about 5 minutes, top with 1 tablespoon topping and a cherry. Return to oven for 5–10 minutes. Cool. Freeze if desired. Best made day before serving. Makes 2 dozen.

Variation: A dollop of any preserves may be substituted for the cherries.

Sunny Side Up

Almond Cheesecake

CRUST:

1½ cups graham cracker crumbs
2 tablespoons sugar

1 teaspoon flour
¼ cup melted butter

FILLING:

2 pounds cream cheese, softened
1 cup sugar
2 eggs

½ teaspoon vanilla
½ teaspoon almond extract

TOPPING:

1 pint sour cream
¾ cup sugar

¾ teaspoon almond extract
½ teaspoon lemon juice

Preheat oven to 350°. Combine all ingredients for crust in a medium mixing bowl. Press into a 10-inch springform pan. Bake for 5 minutes. Remove from oven and allow to cool. Turn off oven and open door to cool.

Mix all ingredients for filling in a bowl and pour into the cooled crust. Place in cold oven and turn to 350°. Bake ½ hour.

Combine all topping ingredients and pour over baked cheesecake. Return to oven for 8 minutes longer. Chill overnight. Serves 18–20.

Palm Beach Entertains

Cookies
and Candies

The Magic Castle at Disney World near Orlando still captures the dreams and fancies of
adults and children from all over the world.

Chocolate Mint Squares

CAKE LAYER:

½ cup butter, softened
1 cup sugar
2 eggs
½ cup all-purpose flour

2 (1-ounce) squares unsweetened
   chocolate, melted
½ cup chopped pecans

Cream butter and sugar until light and fluffy. Add eggs and beat thoroughly. Add flour and blend well. Add chocolate, blending thoroughly; stir in pecans. Pour into a greased 9 × 9-inch pan. Bake at 350° for 20 minutes. Cool in pan.

PEPPERMINT FILLING:

1 tablespoon butter, softened
1 cup confectioners' sugar

2 tablespoons crème de menthe

Blend butter and sugar. Stir in crème de menthe until of spreading consistency. Spread filling over cake layer. Refrigerate.

CHOCOLATE GLAZE:

2 (1-ounce) squares semi-sweet
   chocolate

1 tablespoon butter

Melt chocolate and butter, stirring well. Spread glaze over cold peppermint filling. Chill. Cut into 1-inch squares. Store in refrigerator. Makes 4 dozen.

Heart of the Palms

Lemon Squares
Terrific finger dessert

CRUST:

1 stick butter, softened   ¼ cup confectioners' sugar
1 cup flour

Preheat oven to 350°. Melt butter in 8-inch square pan. Mix in flour and sugar, spreading mixture evenly in pan. Bake 20 minutes.

FILLING:

2 eggs, beaten slightly   ¼ teaspoon salt
1 cup sugar   ⅛ cup flour
3 tablespoons lemon juice   Confectioners' sugar
¼ teaspoon baking powder

Mix ingredients and pour over baked crust. Bake 25 minutes at 350°. Dust with confectioners' sugar. Let cool before cutting into squares.

   Note: For thicker dessert, filling portion may be doubled. Preparation: 10 minutes. Easy. Yield: 12. Baking: 55 minutes. Can do ahead. Can freeze.

Culinary Arts & Crafts

Ruby's Date Nut Squares

1½ sticks margarine   2 teaspoons baking powder
1 box light brown sugar   ½ teaspoon salt
2 teaspoons vanilla   ½ teaspoon cinnamon
4 eggs   1 box dates, cut up
2½ cups flour   1½ cup pecan pieces

Melt margarine in saucepan over low heat. Add to brown sugar in mixing bowl. Add vanilla and eggs, one at a time. Beat with electric mixer on low speed. Add dry ingredients; stir in dates and nuts. Pour in large baking pan and bake at 325° for approximately 30 minutes or until toothpick inserted in center comes out clean. Cool and cut into squares; dust with powdered sugar.

Margaritaville Cookbook

Peanut Butter Brownies

1 cup butter	1½ cups flour
⅓ cup cocoa	½ teaspoon salt
2 cups sugar	1 teaspoon vanilla
4 eggs	1 cup crunchy peanut butter

Preheat oven to 350°. Melt 1 cup butter and cocoa in double boiler. Cool. Blend in sugar and eggs. Combine flour, salt and vanilla; to this add first mixture. Bake in greased 13 × 9 × 2-inch pan for 20–30 minutes. Spoon peanut butter over hot cake and spread while melting.

FROSTING:

½ cup butter	¼ teaspoon salt
¼ cup cocoa	1 teaspoon vanilla
⅓ cup milk	1 box confectioners' sugar, sifted
8 large marshmallows	

Melt together ½ cup butter, cocoa, milk, marshmallows, salt and vanilla. Beat in confectioners' sugar. Spread over cooled peanut butter. Yield: 4 dozen 1½-inch squares.

Some Like It South!

Chocolate Chip Cheesecake Brownies

1 (12-ounce) package Nestle's Chocolate Chips	¾ cup sugar
2 (8-ounce) packages cream cheese, softened	2 eggs
	1 cup pecans, chopped

Follow directions on back of Nestle's package to make chocolate chip cookies. Divide chocolate chip batter in half and spread one-half in bottom of lightly greased 12 × 9-inch baking pan. Combine cream cheese with sugar and eggs in mixer or food processor and blend until very creamy. Pour cream cheese batter on top of chocolate chip batter in pan. Sprinkle with nuts. Spread remaining chocolate chip batter carefully over cheese filling. Bake in 350° oven for 45 minutes. Cut into squares. Yields: 36 squares. Preparation: 20 minutes. Cooking: 45 minutes. Difficulty: Easy.

Juicy Miss Lucy Cookbook

Carob Brownies

2 eggs	1 teaspoon baking soda
⅔ cup honey	¾ cup water
½ cup melted butter	⅓ cup carob, sifted
1 teaspoon vanilla	1 cup whole wheat flour
1 banana	1 cup broken walnut pieces
½ teaspoon sea salt	

Beat eggs slightly, add honey, cooled butter, vanilla and banana. Mix well. Then add the dry ingredients alternately with water. Add broken walnut pieces last. Butter and flour a 13×9-inch glass baking dish and bake *exactly* 23 minutes. Do not overbake. The oven should be set at 350°.

CAROB BROWNIE ICING NO. 1:

⅓ cup honey	¼ cup sifted carob powder
4 tablespoons melted butter	4 tablespoons water
1 cup non-instant dry powdered milk	1 teaspoon vanilla

Mix all the ingredients together. Use the milk as a dry powder. Beat until smooth. If more water is needed, add 1 more tablespoon.

Step-by-Step to Natural Food

Heath Bars
Munchy, crunchy good!

2 cups flour	1 cup pecans, chopped
1 cup butter	1 (6-ounce) package semi-sweet
1½ cups brown sugar	chocolate chips

Preheat oven 350°. Mix flour, ⅓ cup butter and 1 cup brown sugar until fine. Spread mixture into 9×13-inch pan. Cover with pecans. In small saucepan, combine ⅔ cup butter and ½ cup brown sugar. Cook over medium heat, stirring constantly until entire surface boils ½–1 minute. Spread over nuts. Bake 18–22 minutes. Remove from oven. Immediately sprinkle chocolate chips over top; spread evenly. Cool. Cut into bars. Yields 32 cookies.

Fare by the Sea

Orange Tea Cookies

½ cup shortening
½ cup sugar
1 egg yolk
½ teaspoon vanilla
⅓ teaspoon salt

1 tablespoon grated orange rind
1 tablespoon grated lemon rind
1 cup flour
2 egg whites, unbeaten
½ cup chopped nuts

In the medium bowl of an electric mixer, cream shortening, sugar, egg yolk, vanilla, salt, grated orange and lemon rind. Work in flour. Shape in balls the size of walnuts. Roll in unbeaten egg whites and chopped nuts. Place on a greased baking sheet and flatten with a spatula. Bake at 350° for 10–12 minutes. Makes 3 dozen.

The Orange Bowl Cookbook

Strawberry Cookies

5 tablespoons butter
1 cup sugar
Pinch of salt
2 eggs
1½ cups chopped dates

1 teaspoon vanilla
1 cup chopped pecans
2½ cups rice cereal
Red sugar crystals

Melt butter in electric skillet at 300°. Combine sugar, salt and eggs. Cook, stirring constantly until mixture thickens. Add dates and continue cooking for several minutes. Cut off heat. Stir in vanilla, pecans, and rice cereal. Pinch off small portions and roll into balls the size of quarters. Form into the shape of a strawberry. Roll into red sugar crystals. Use real strawberry caps for top of strawberries. Makes 5–6 dozen.

The Colonel's Inn Caterers—Tallahassee Historical Cookbook

Lace Cookies

1 cup sifted flour
1 cup chopped flaked coconut (or nuts)
½ cup light syrup

½ cup firmly packed brown sugar
½ cup margarine
1 teaspoon vanilla

Mix flour and coconut. Combine syrup, sugar, and margarine in heavy saucepan. Bring to a boil over medium heat, stirring constantly. Remove from heat; gradually blend in flour mixture, then vanilla. Drop onto foil-covered cookie sheets by scant teaspoonfuls, 3 inches apart. Bake at 350° for 8–10 minutes. Cool on wire racks until foil peels off easily. Place cookies on absorbent paper.

The Prima Diner

Gooies
Seven-Layer Cookies

Wonderful for waterfront outings where your appetite soars and your activities burn up the calories.

1 stick butter
Layer of graham crackers (total 16–18 crackers)
1 (6-ounce) package chocolate chips

1 cup pecans
1 (6-ounce) package butterscotch chips
1 small can Angel Flake coconut
1 can Eagle Brand milk

Preheat oven 350°. Melt stick of butter in 9 × 13-inch Pyrex dish or pan. On top of melted butter place a layer of graham crackers, a layer of chocolate bits, a layer of butterscotch bits, layer of coconut, layer of chopped pecans. Dribble a can of Eagle Brand milk on top and bake until a little brown around the edge (about 30 or 40 minutes). Cut as soon as you remove from oven. Let stand at least 4 hours. Better to let stand overnight.

If at first you don't succeed, you're running about average.
Sweet Surrender with Advice à la Carte

Christmas Cookies

Serve these as you would fruit cake. Most people like them even better.

1 cup butter
1 cup brown sugar, packed (8 ounces)
3 eggs
3 cups flour (plain)
½ teaspoon soda
1½ cups milk

2 tablespoons sherry flavoring
7 cups pecans (broken in large pieces)
1 pound candied pineapple
1 pound candied cherries
¾ pound white raisins

Combine butter and brown sugar and mix well. Add eggs. Combine flour and soda in sifter and add to first mixture alternately with milk and sherry. Add nuts, fruits, and drop by teaspoon onto well greased cookie sheet. Bake 30–35 minutes. Yield: 160 cookies.

A person who is wrapped up in himself makes a very small bundle.

Sweet Surrender with Advice à la Carte

Almond Trifles
Great for the holidays

1 (6-ounce) package semi-sweet chocolate chips
1 (6-ounce) package butterscotch morsels
¾ cup sifted confectioners' sugar

½ cup sour cream
1½ teaspoons grated orange rind
¼ teaspoon salt
2 cups vanilla wafer crumbs
¾ cup chopped almonds, toasted

Melt chocolate and butterscotch together in double boiler over hot, not boiling water. Remove from heat. Add confectioners sugar, sour cream, orange rind, and salt. Mix in crumbs. Chill until firm. Shape into 1-inch balls. Roll in almonds. Store in tightly covered container in refrigerator. Makes 5 dozen.

Sunny Side Up

Florida Sunshine Cookies

2 cups flour	1 cup corn oil
2 cups sugar	2 large eggs
4 teaspoons baking powder	2 tablespoons orange juice
1 teaspoon salt	4 teaspoons grated orange rind
1 teaspoon nutmeg	3 cups uncooked rolled oats

Sift flour, sugar, baking powder, salt and nutmeg together into a large bowl. Add eggs, corn oil, orange juice and orange rind and mix well. Add rolled oats and again mix well. Drop by level tablespoonfuls on greased baking sheet about 2 inches apart. Bake at 375° for 12–15 minutes. Remove from pans as soon as done and allow to cool thoroughly before storing.

Gator Country Cooks

Cinnamon Crispies
Batter to rolls in 1¾ hours

2¼ cups flour
1 package yeast (dry)
⅓ cup sugar
½ teaspoon salt

½ teaspoon nutmeg
¾ cup warm water
3 tablespoons shortening
1 egg

TOPPING:
¾ cup sugar
¼ cup brown sugar

½ cup chopped nuts
1 teaspoon cinnamon

In mixer bowl combine 1 cup flour, yeast, ⅓ cup of sugar, salt and nutmeg, mix well; add warm water, shortening and egg, blend then beat 3 minutes at medium speed. By hand add rest of flour to make a stiff batter. Cover and let rise until doubled about 45 minutes. Punch down batter.

Mix sugar, brown sugar, cinnamon and nuts, mix well. Pour ½ mixture on wax paper. Drop dough by tablespoons into sugar mixture, toss to coat. Pat out to 4–5-inch circles. Pour rest of topping out as needed. Bake on well-greased cookie sheet. Bake at 400° for 12–15 minutes or until golden brown, do not overbake. Remove immediately, cool on cake rack, store loosely covered.

Fiesta

Sandies

1 cup margarine
¼ cup powdered sugar
2 teaspoons vanilla extract
2 teaspoons water
2 cups all-purpose flour

1 (6-ounce) package semi-sweet
  chocolate chips
2 tablespoons water
1 cup chopped nuts

Cream margarine with sugar in medium bowl; blend in vanilla and 2 teaspoons water. Add flour and mix well; chill 1 hour. Shape dough into small fingers; place on cookie sheet. Bake at 325° for 20 minutes or until lightly browned. In top of double boiler melt together chocolate chips and 2 tablespoons water. Dip tips of cookies in chocolate and then in nuts. Makes 6 dozen.

Suncoast Seasons

Mystery Cookies

Everyone loves mystery cookies. The secret is in the melted butter.

2 cups light or dark brown sugar
  (1 [16-ounce] box)
1¼ cups flour
1 teaspoon baking powder
2 eggs
1 cup melted butter

Pinch of salt
1 teaspoon vanilla
1 cup chopped pecans (peanuts or
  M & M's may be substituted but
  use 2 cups)
Powdered sugar (optional)

Preheat oven to 300° and grease a 9 × 13-inch Pyrex baking dish. Mix sugar, flour and baking powder. Pour into eggs and add other ingredients. Bake in middle of oven for 45 minutes or until batter falls. Cut into squares. Let cool. When absolutely cold, roll in powdered sugar, if desired. Beware of overcooking or cookies will be like bricks!!

Nothing is impossible for those who don't have to do it.
Sweet Surrender with Advice à la Carte

Linzer Tarts
Great at Christmas Time!

¾ pound butter
6 tablespoons sugar
4 egg yolks
4 cups all-purpose flour
1 teaspoon baking powder

1 teaspoon vanilla extract
2 egg whites
½ cup walnuts, finely chopped
1 (12-ounce) jar raspberry
   preserves

In a large bowl cream butter, sugar and egg yolks. Sift flour and baking powder together; blend into butter mixture along with vanilla. Divide dough into 4 pieces. Roll ¼ of dough at a time into ¼-inch thicknesses on a floured board. Cut into rounds using a 2-inch biscuit cutter. Use a thimble to cut holes in center of ½ of the cookies. Combine holes into remaining dough; roll and cut as before. Bake on an ungreased cookie sheet at 350° for 8–9 minutes or until lightly brown. Brush top half of cookies (ones with holes) with egg white; then dip into nuts. Spread raspberry preserves on bottom half of cookies. Put top in place, making a sandwich. Makes 2–3 dozen.

Note: The same dough makes wonderful cut-out cookies for children. Decorate as desired.

Suncoast Seasons

Guess-Again Cookies
The crisp bits in these are potato chips!

1 cup butter, softened (no
   substitutes)
½ cup sugar
1½ cups flour

1 teaspoon vanilla extract
¾ cup finely crushed fresh potato
   chips

Preheat oven to 325°. Mix butter and sugar in electric mixer until fluffy. Add flour and mix until smooth. By hand, add vanilla and potato chips; mix well. Drop on ungreased cookie sheet by small teaspoonfuls. Bake 15–20 minutes, until light brown. Cool and sprinkle with sifted confectioners' sugar. These freeze exceptionally well. Makes 5 dozen.

Cook and Deal

Melting Moments

1 cup butter or margarine,
  softened
½ cup powdered sugar

1¼ cups unsifted all-purpose flour
¾ cup cornstarch

In a large mixing bowl cream butter and sugar until light and fluffy. Beat in flour and cornstarch until well mixed. Wrap and refrigerate dough at least 2 hours or overnight. Roll dough into 1-inch balls. Place on ungreased cookie sheet; bake at 325° for 10 minutes or until firm but golden. Cool slightly and remove from pan; cool completely. Top cookies with glaze; let dry. Makes about 3½ dozen.

GLAZE:
1½ cups powdered sugar, sifted

3 tablespoons orange or lemon
  juice

In a small bowl mix sugar and juice. Frost cookies.

Beyond the Bay

Oatmeal Chip Cookies

1 cup butter
1 cup sugar
1 cup firmly-packed brown sugar
2 eggs
2 cups sifted all-purpose flour
1 teaspoon soda

1 teaspoon salt
2 cups quick-cooking oatmeal
1 cup chopped pecans
1 cup (6-ounces) chocolate chip
  pieces

Cream butter and both sugars together. Add eggs and beat well. Add flour, soda and salt which have been sifted together. Stir in oatmeal, nuts and chocolate pieces. If desired, chill for easier handling. Shape dough into balls, using rounded teaspoonfuls for each. Place on ungreased baking sheets. Bake at 375° for 9–12 minutes, until golden brown. Makes about 8 dozen. This cookie is the Schrenk family's favorite.

Sawgrass and Pines

Incredible Edibles

2 cups graham cracker crumbs
2 cups confectioners' sugar
¾ cup margarine, melted

1 (12-ounce) jar crunchy peanut
butter
1 (12-ounce) package chocolate
chips

Mix cracker crumbs, sugar, margarine and peanut butter with hands. Pat in a greased 11 × 13-inch baking dish. Melt chocolate chips in the top of a double boiler. Spread over cookie mix. Let cool. Cut into squares. Store in refrigerator in an airtight container. Servings: 24 cookies. Preparation time: 20 minutes.

Jacksonville & Company

White Christmas Candy

2 cups sugar
½ cup sour cream
⅓ cup light corn syrup
2 tablespoons butter
¼ teaspoon salt

1 teaspoon vanilla extract
1 teaspoon rum or brandy extract
¼ cup candied cherries,
quartered
1 cup coarsely chopped walnuts
Butter or margarine

Combine first 5 ingredients in a large saucepan; gradually bring to a boil, stirring until sugar is dissolved. Boil (do not stir) over medium heat to soft ball stage (236°) on candy thermometer. Remove from heat; let stand for 15 minutes (do not stir). Add flavorings and beat until it begins to lose its gloss. Add cherries and nuts and pour into a buttered 8-inch square pan. Let harden and cut into squares. Do not double.

Beyond the Bay

Microwave Candy Bark
A great quick gift

¾ cup pecan chips or slivered almonds
1 cup sugar
½ teaspoon salt

1 stick unsalted butter
¼ cup water
1 (4-ounce) Hershey chocolate bar

Butter cookie sheet and sprinkle nuts on sheet. Combine sugar, salt, butter, and water in medium size microwave bowl and cook in microwave for 8–8½ minutes on full power. Pour over nuts. In separate microwave bowl, cook chocolate bar for 2¼ minutes on level 6. Spread melted chocolate over nuts and caramelized sugar. Put in freezer for 20 minutes or refrigerate for 45–60 minutes. Break in pieces, bag, and refrigerate. Preparation: 10 minutes. Easy. Serves: 8. Cooking: 10 minutes. Must do ahead.

Culinary Arts & Crafts

Best Ever Caramels

1 cup light corn syrup
2 cups sugar

3 cups heavy cream

Combine corn syrup, sugar, and 1 cup cream in a heavy saucepan. Insert a candy thermometer and cook, stirring constantly, until mixture reaches 236°. Add 1 more cup of cream and boil to 236°. Add remaining 1 cup cream and boil until thermometer reaches 246°. Pour mixture into a well-buttered 9 × 13-inch pan. Cool.

Cut into bite-size squares and wrap each piece in waxed paper. Keep in a covered container in the refrigerator. Makes 5 dozen pieces candy.

Heart of the Palms

Good and Easy Candy

1 cup peanut butter, creamy or
   crunchy
2 sticks butter or margarine,
   melted

1 pound powdered sugar
2 (8-ounce) Hershey bars

Mix together peanut butter, butter and powdered sugar. Put in 8 × 8-inch pan. Spread evenly. Melt Hershey bars and pour over mixture. Let cool. Cut into squares.

Better to do something imperfectly than to do nothing flawlessly.
Sweet Surrender with Advice à la Carte

Pies
and Desserts

Daytona International Speedway hosts stock car, race car, motorcycle and even go-cart races as well as the prestigious Daytona 500.

Paper Bag Apple Pie

1 unbaked (9-inch) pie shell
6 large cooking apples (York, Granny Smith, Golden Delicious or any firm tart apple)

1¼ cups sugar
2 tablespoons flour
½ teaspoon cinnamon
2 tablespoons lemon juice
1 tablespoon butter

Peel and thinly slice the apples. Combine the sugar, flour and cinnamon. Sprinkle over apples. Arrange in the prepared pie shell. Sprinkle lemon juice over mixture. Cut butter into small bits and distribute evenly over pie.

TOPPING:

½ cup butter
½ cup sugar

½ cup flour
½ cup chopped pecans

Mix butter, sugar and flour until crumbly, using two knives or fingers. Mix the nuts into crumbled mixture. Place evenly over pie and press with hands to completely cover apple mixture. Place pie in a large brown paper bag. Fold ends of bag and secure with paper clips to seal. Bake in 425° oven for 1 hour. Yield: 8 servings.

Friendly Feasts Act II

How Do You Like Them Apples Apple Pie

6–8 tart green apples, peeled and
    sliced thin
1 egg, lightly beaten
1¼ cups sour cream
½ cup sugar

½ teaspoon salt
2 teaspoons vanilla
¼ cup flour
Pastry for a 10-inch one-crust pie,
    uncooked

Mix together egg, sour cream, sugar, salt, vanilla and flour. Blend together well. Add mixture to sliced apples. Toss lightly. Spoon into pie shell. Bake in a 450° oven for 10 minutes, reduce heat to 350° and bake 45 minutes.

TOPPING:

⅓ cup brown sugar
⅓ cup white sugar
⅛ teaspoon salt
1 teaspoon cinnamon

½ teaspoon nutmeg
½ cup flour
1 cup chopped pecans
6 tablespoons melted butter

Mix all topping ingredients together. Spoon on top of hot pie, mix in lightly with the apples, and bake an additional 10–15 minutes at 350° until golden. Serves: 8. Preparation: 30 minutes. Cooking: 1 hour. Difficulty: Average.

Juicy Miss Lucy Cookbook

Amazing Fruit Cobbler

1 stick margarine, softened
1 cup sugar
1 cup self rising flour

1 cup milk
1 can pie filling (any fruit)

Mix all items together in a baking dish. Bake at 350° for 1 hour. Serve hot. Serves 4–6.

Hint: If you have bananas that are ripening too quickly, peel the skin and discard. Wrap the banana in Saran Wrap, twist ends and freeze. Cut into chunks while still frozen and enjoy. Tastes like ice cream.

Alone at the Range

Angel Pie
Gorgeous looking and a heavenly taste

MERINGUE:

4 egg whites

¼ teaspoon cream of tartar

1 cup sugar

Pinch of salt

1 teaspoon vanilla extract

Preheat oven to 275°. Beat egg whites until frothy. Add cream of tartar and beat until stiff, gradually adding sugar and salt. Fold in vanilla. Spread in a 9-inch buttered pie pan covering bottom and sides; shape with the back of a spoon, making the bottom ¼-inch thick and the sides 1-inch thick. Bake for 1 hour; leave in the oven to cool for 1 hour.

FILLING:

4 egg yolks

½ cup sugar

¼ cup lemon juice

2 tablespoons grated lemon peel

2 cups whipping cream

Toasted almonds, for garnish

Beat egg yolks until lemon-colored, gradually adding sugar, lemon juice and lemon peel. Cook in the top of a double boiler over hot water (not touching pan) until thick, stirring constantly. This will take between 5 and 8 minutes. Cool. Fold in one cup of cream, whipped. Spread over meringue and cover with one cup of cream, whipped. Sprinkle toasted almonds over the top. Refrigerate a minimum of 12 hours. May be made the day before serving. Serves 8.

Cook and Deal

Meringue Torte

6 egg whites
¼ teaspoon salt
½ teaspoon cream of tartar
1½ cups sugar
1 teaspoon vanilla

1 cup heavy cream, whipped or
    Cool Whip
Whole strawberries, fresh or
    frozen

Let egg whites warm to room temperature. Lightly butter the bottom and sides of tube pan or bundt pan. Preheat oven to 450°. Add salt and cream of tartar to egg whites, beat at high speed until stiff. Then add sugar, 2 tablespoons at a time, beating well after each addition. Add vanilla. Mix well. Pour into pan, spreading evenly. Place on middle rack in oven and turn off heat. Let stand three hours or overnight in oven. To serve, turn out on plate, frost with whipped cream, place strawberries in center and along sides.

Canopy Roads

Kolachy
A rich, fancy, finger pastry

1 (3-ounce) package cream cheese,
    softened
½ cup butter, softened
1 cup sifted flour

4 ounces apricot or raspberry
    jam, approximately
Powdered sugar

Combine the cream cheese, butter, and flour. Divide the dough in half. Chill. Roll out half at a time, approximately ¼-inch thick. Cut with a small square-shaped, circular-shaped, or diamond-shaped cookie cutter. Place ½ teaspoon of jam on each cookie. Bring 2 sides of the cookies up to meet in the middle and crimp. Bake on ungreased cookie sheets at 350° for 20 minutes or until lightly browned. Cool on racks. Sprinkle with powdered sugar. Yields 2 dozen.

Variation: Recipe may be doubled using 8 ounces of cream cheese. Add 3 tablespoons sugar and ¼ teaspoon salt.

A Pinch of Sunshine

Green Mango Pie

4 cups sliced green mangos
1 pastry shell, with top crust
1¼ cups sugar

½ teaspoon nutmeg
½ teaspoon cinnamon
1 stick butter

Parboil mangos until slices are limber. Arrange mango slices in pastry shell. Mix sugar and spices and sprinkle over mangos. Dot with butter and cover with top crust, making openings with knife. Bake 45–50 minutes in a 350° oven.

Maurice's Tropical Fruit Cook Book

Calamondin Pie

½ cup calamondin
6 tablespoons sugar
1 can condensed milk
4 eggs
½ teaspoon cream of tartar

12 cinnamon graham crackers, crumbed
1 teaspoon cinnamon
¼ cup sugar
4 tablespoons butter, melted
1 tablespoon flour

Calamondins are small tart oranges resembling kumquats. Seed fruit and pulverize in blender (skin and all) enough to measure ½ cup. Mix with condensed milk, plus 4 beaten egg yolks. Fold 1 stiffly beaten egg white into above mixture. Pour into graham cracker shell made by combining last 5 ingredients (Pat shell into 9-inch pie tin and prebake at 225° for ½ hour before filling). For topping, beat remaining 3 egg whites, adding 6 tablespoons sugar and cream of tartar gradually, until stiff. Decorate pie with meringue and bake at 325° for 15 minutes or until meringue is delicately brown. Serves 8.

Lost Tree Cook Book

Black Bottom Pie
Serve at your next dinner party

1 (9-inch) ready-made graham
　cracker pie crust
1 (3¾-ounce) package of vanilla
　pudding—not instant
2 cups milk

1 (6-ounce) package of Nestle
　Semi-Sweet Chocolate Morsels
1 tablespoon rum extract
8 ounces prepared non-dairy
　topping

Cook pudding and milk according to directions on pudding box for
pie filling. Separate mixture into 2 bowls putting an equal amount
in each. Pour chocolate morsels into 1 bowl and stir until dissolved.
Add rum extract to the other bowl and mix well. Pour chocolate
mixture into pie shell. Ladle vanilla-rum mixture evenly on top.
Chill until firm and spread whipped topping on top before serving.
Preparation: 15 minutes. Easy. Serves: 6. Must do ahead.

Culinary Arts & Crafts

Fudge Pie

2 eggs
1 cup sugar
¼ cup all-purpose flour
⅛ teaspoon salt

2 (1-ounce) squares unsweetened
　chocolate
½ cup butter
1 (8-inch) unbaked pie shell

Beat eggs and sugar together. Add flour and salt and beat well.
　In a saucepan, melt chocolate and butter. Add to flour mixture
and beat well. Pour into pie shell and bake at 350° for 25 minutes.
Makes 1 pie.

Heart of the Palms

French Silk Chocolate Pie

¾ cup margarine
1⅓ cups sugar
2 squares unsweetened chocolate, melted
¼ teaspoon salt

1½ teaspoons vanilla
3 eggs
Whipped cream
1 graham cracker pie shell

Cream margarine and add sugar gradually, creaming well. Blend in cooled chocolate and vanilla; mix well. Add eggs, one at a time, beating 5 minutes after each addition. Turn into pie shell. Chill 2 hours. Top with whipped cream.

Sawgrass and Pines

Rum Cream Pie

CRUST:

1 (6-ounce) package Zwieback
2 tablespoons sugar

½ teaspoon cinnamon
½ cup butter, softened

Mix and press into 10-inch glass serving dish.

FILLING:

1 envelope unflavored gelatin
½ cup cold water
6 egg yolks
1 cup sugar

1 pint heavy cream, whipped
½ cup dark Jamaican rum
Bittersweet chocolate
Additional whipped cream

Place water in a small saucepan and sprinkle gelatin over. Allow to soften. Place saucepan over low heat and dissolve gelatin. Beat eggs with sugar until light and fluffy. Pour hot gelatin over egg mixture, stirring constantly. Fold whipped cream into egg mixture and add rum. Chill until firm. Shave bittersweet chocolate on top. Garnish with whipped cream, if desired.

The Orange Bowl Cookbook

Coffee Toffee Pie

CRUST:

1½ cups finely crushed Nabisco Chocolate Wafers

¼ cup butter, melted

Preheat oven to 325°. Combine crumbs and butter with fork and press gently into 10-inch pie plate. Bake for 10 minutes and cool.

FILLING:

¾ cup butter, softened
1 cup sugar
1½ ounces unsweetened chocolate

1 tablespoon instant coffee
1 tablespoon boiling water
3 eggs

Beat butter until creamy. Gradually add sugar, beating until light and lemon-colored. Melt chocolate over hot water; cool slightly and add to butter mixture. Add instant coffee to boiling water and stir into mixture. Add eggs one at a time, beating well after each addition. Pour filling into cooled pie shell and refrigerate overnight, covered.

TOPPING:

2 cups whipping cream
½ cup confectioners' sugar
2 tablespoons instant coffee

2 tablespoons coffee liqueur
Chocolate curls for garnish

Beat cream until stiff. Add confectioners' sugar, coffee and coffee liqueur. Spread over filling and garnish with chocolate curls. Refrigerate at least two hours before serving. Yield: 8 servings.

Some Like It South!

Margarita Pie
Tastes just like its namesake.

CRUST:

1½ cups crushed pretzel sticks
¼ cup sugar

¼ pound butter, melted

Combine crushed pretzels and sugar. Add melted butter. Press into 9-inch buttered pie plate and chill.

FILLING:

1 (14-ounce) can sweetened
  condensed milk
⅓ cup fresh lime juice
2 tablespoons tequila

2 tablespoons Triple Sec
1–2 drops green food coloring
1 cup heavy cream, whipped

Combine sweetened condensed milk, lime juice, tequila, and Triple Sec. Add food coloring, if desired. Fold whipped cream into mixture. Pour into chilled crust and freeze for 3–4 hours or until firm. (Can be stored in freezer for several days.) Before serving, garnish each piece with thin slice of lime. Serves 8–10.

Sunny Side Up

Impossible Pie
Makes its own crust

4 eggs
1¾ cups sugar
½ cup flour
1 (7-ounce) can coconut

2 cups milk
1 teaspoon vanilla
½ stick oleo, melted

Butter two 9-inch pie pans. Combine ingredients in order listed. Pour into pie pans and bake at 350° for 30 minutes.

Bay Leaves

Wild Orange Pie

The wild orange pie is North Florida's answer to South Florida's key lime pie.

⅔ cup juice from wild oranges
1 tablespoon unflavored gelatin
½ cup hot water
½ cup orange blossom honey (or any mild honey)

1 cup lowfat cottage cheese
1 (9-inch) graham cracker pie crust

Mix wild orange juice and gelatin in blender and allow to stand a few minutes. Dissolve honey in hot water and add to juice. Blend until gelatin is dissolved. Add cottage cheese and blend until smooth and creamy.

Pour into crust. Refrigerate until firm. Serves 6–8.

Note: Lemon, lime, or calamondin juice may be substituted for equally good pies.

Cross Creek Kitchens

Oranges

Oranges were introduced to Florida by the Spanish, who planted groves of sour or wild orange trees around Orange and Lochloosa Lakes. The Indians may have roasted the sour oranges over their outdoor fires. Southern ladies gathered the oranges to make a refreshing drink for the soldiers during the Civil War. In the 1870s when "orange fever" came to this area, early settlers developed groves of sweet oranges using the sour orange rootstock. The Rawlings grove is one of these; it was probably established in the 1880s. Some of the sweet trees have reverted to their sour rootstock after being frozen below the graft during a cold winter. We leave the sour oranges interspersed among the sweet because they are so hardy and beautiful and also because they are surprisingly useful.

Cross Creek Kitchens

Frosted Daiquiri Pie

1 envelope unflavored gelatin	1 teaspoon grated lime or lemon
1 cup sugar, divided	rind
½ teaspoon salt	Few drops green food coloring
3 eggs, separated	⅓ cup light rum
¼ cup cold water	1 (9-inch) baked pastry shell
½ cup fresh lime or lemon juice	Whipped cream

In top of a double boiler combine gelatin with ⅔ cup sugar, salt, egg yolks, water and lime juice. With rotary beater beat until blended. Cook over boiling water, stirring until mixture coats a spoon. Remove from heat; add rind and food coloring to a pale green tint. Cool mixture; stir in rum. Refrigerate mixture until slightly thicker than unbeaten egg whites. In large bowl beat egg whites until they form soft peaks; add remaining ⅓ cup sugar, 1 tablespoon at a time, beating until stiff. Fold in gelatin mixture. Turn mixture into baked pastry shell; refrigerate several hours. Top with whipped cream before serving.

Beyond the Bay

Chocolate Coronet
Lovely at Christmas

18 Ladyfingers (split)	3 eggs, separated
½ cup orange juice	3 (4-ounce) packages chocolate
1 pound cream cheese, softened	pieces, melted and cooled
¾ cup granulated sugar	2 cups heavy cream, whipped
½ teaspoon salt	½ cup chopped nuts (optional)
2 teaspoons vanilla	

Stand Ladyfingers in a 9 × 3-inch springform pan. Arrange remaining Ladyfingers on bottom of the pan. Combine orange juice, cream cheese, sugar, salt and vanilla. Beat until well blended and smooth. Add egg yolks and beat until smooth. Blend in melted chocolate. Beat egg whites until stiff and fold them in along with whipped cream. Pour mixture into pan over Ladyfingers. Put in freezer. Prior to serving, set out a few minutes until soft enough to cut.

Canopy Roads

Fresh Strawberry Pie
To celebrate Florida's strawberry season

CRUST:

1½ cups flour
½ teaspoon salt
1 tablespoon sugar

½ cup shortening
1 egg
1 tablespoon water (optional)

Preheat oven 450°. Place flour, salt and sugar in mixing bowl. Cut in shortening with pastry blender until mixture resembles crumbs. Stir in egg. Add water. Form a ball and roll on floured board into a thick crust. Ease into 9-inch pie pan without stretching dough. Prick evenly with fork. Bake 10 minutes or until light brown. Serves 8.

FILLING:

4 cups strawberries, hulled
¾ cup water
¾ cup sugar
¼ teaspoon salt

3 tablespoons cornstarch
Cream cheese (optional)
Whipped cream

Crush 1 cup strawberries. Add water and bring to boil. Simmer 3 minutes. Strain juice; add enough water to make 1 cup. Combine sugar, salt and cornstarch in saucepan. Slowly add juice, stirring until smooth. Bring to boil, stirring constantly. Cook 3 minutes or until thick and clear. Cool slightly. Place thin layer of cream cheese on crust. Add strawberries. Cover with glaze. Chill. Serve with whipped cream.

Tip: Substitute fresh peaches for strawberries.

Fare by the Sea

Frozen Key Lime Pie

This pie was chosen as the Best Key Lime Pie in Florida by Burton Wolf (James Beard's Associate) in a 1977 cooking competition.

CRUST:

1¼ cups graham cracker crumbs
¼ cup softened butter or margarine
¼ cup firmly packed dark brown sugar

1 teaspoon cinnamon
¼ teaspoon fresh ground nutmeg

Combine ingredients for crust. Spray pie plate with Pam Spray and "tamp" crumbs into pan, gently (do not pack firmly). Reserve 2 tablespoons crumbs for topping. Bake at 350°, 10 minutes.

FILLING:

1 can sweetened condensed milk
2 eggs, separated
½ cup (generous) Key lime juice

Grated peel of 2 lemons (coarse grated)

Beat yolks until thick and lemon-colored. Add milk and blend. Add juice, 2 tablespoons at a time. Blend well after each addition. Add one-half of grated lemon peel and blend again.

Beat whites stiff. Fold one-half of whites into milk-juice mixture. (Discard remaining whites or use to make meringue cookies). Pour into prepared curst.

Sprinkle reserved crumbs and remaining half of lemon peel over top. Freeze until firm. Then cover with aluminum foil and keep frozen until ready to use.

Remove from freezer about 5 minutes before serving. After 10 minutes, pie will no longer seem "frozen." Serves 6–8.

Seasons in the Sun

Key Lime Pie
The tart and the sweet alternate
on the tongue to delight and refresh.

1 can sweetened condensed milk	3 egg whites
3 egg yolks	¼ teaspoon cream of tartar
½ cup fresh key lime juice	½ teaspoon vanilla
1 baked pie shell	6 tablespoons superfine sugar

Beat first three ingredients together until thick and smooth. Pour mixture in pie shell. Make meringue and spread over pie filling. Bake to brown, then chill before serving.

A key lime pie that is green is not a key lime pie. The Florida Cracker purist insists on the yellow pie made from true key limes. The trick is to squeeze them while they're in season, freeze the juice in ice cube trays, store them in freezer bags, and you'll have *Key Lime Pie* all year round.

Maurice's Tropical Fruit Cook Book

Frozen Lemon Tarts

3 eggs, separated	1 teaspoon vanilla
¼ cup fresh lemon juice	1 cup heavy cream, whipped
⅔ cup granulated sugar	½ cup fine vanilla wafer crumbs
¼ teaspoon salt	
1 teaspoon grated lemon rind	

In double boiler, combine well-beaten egg yolks, lemon juice, sugar and salt. Cook over hot water until custard coats metal spoon. Chill. Stir in rind and vanilla. Beat egg whites stiff; fold into custard. Fold in whipped cream.

Place a couple of fluted baking cups in each of twelve 2½-inch muffin tins. Sprinkle bottom of each with 1 teaspoon crumbs. Fill with lemon mixture. Sprinkle remaining crumbs over top. Freeze until firm.

Sawgrass and Pines

Chocolate Mousse Pie
Absolutely Luscious!

CRUST:

3 cups chocolate wafer crumbs   ½ cup unsweetened butter, melted

Combine crumbs and butter. Press on the bottom and completely up sides of a 10-inch springform pan. Refrigerate for 30 minutes or chill in freezer. A wide flat-bottomed glass is good to compress crumbs.

FILLING:

1 pound semi-sweet dark
  chocolate
2 eggs
4 egg yolks

2 cups whipping cream
6 tablespoons powdered sugar
4 egg whites, room temperature

Soften chocolate in top of double boiler (or in bowl over simmering water). Let cool until lukewarm. Add 2 eggs and mix well; then add 4 egg yolks and mix until thoroughly blended. Whip cream with powdered sugar until soft peaks form. Beat egg whites until stiff but not dry. Stir a little of the cream and egg white into chocolate mixture to lighten; then fold in remaining cream and egg whites until thoroughly mixed. Pour into crust and chill at least 6 hours, or preferably overnight.

CHOCOLATE LEAVES:

4 ounces (approximately) semi-
  sweet chocolate

1 teaspoon vegetable shortening
Camelia or other waxy leaves

Melt chocolate and shortening in top of a double boiler. Using a spoon generously coat underside of 10 or 12 leaves. Place on waxed paper and chill or freeze until firm.

TOPPING:

2 cups whipping cream   2 tablespoons powdered sugar

Whip remaining 2 cups of cream with sugar until quite stiff. Loosen crust on all sides of pie, using sharp knife. Remove springform. Spread whipped cream over top of mousse. Peel leaves away from chocolate starting at stem end of leaf and decorate top of mousse.

CONTINUED

CONTINUED

Cut pie into wedges with a thin, sharp knife. *A delicious and impressive dessert!* Serves 12–15.

Note: This dessert can be prepared ahead and frozen. Thaw overnight in the refrigerator.

Suncoast Seasons

Lemon Pie With Blueberry Sauce
Light and simple to prepare

CRUST:

1 cup all-purpose flour
½ cup butter

2 tablespoons sugar
¼ teaspoon salt

Preheat oven to 375°. In a food processor mix flour, butter, sugar and salt until crumbly. Place ⅓ cup of the crumb mixture in a small baking dish; press remaining mixture into a greased and floured 9-inch pie plate. Bake both 12–15 minutes; cool.

FILLING:

2 egg whites
⅔ cup sugar
¼ cup fresh lemon juice

2 teaspoons grated lemon peel
1 cup heavy cream, whipped

Combine egg whites, sugar and lemon juice; beat to stiff peaks. Fold lemon peel and whipped cream into egg white mixture. Turn entire mixture into pie shell. Top with baked crumbs. Chill. Serve with blueberry sauce.

SAUCE:

⅔ cup sugar
1 tablespoon cornstarch

⅔ cup cold water
2 cups fresh blueberries

In a saucepan combine sugar and cornstarch. Add water; cook and stir until thick. Cook 2 minutes more. Add blueberries. Return mixture to boiling. Remove from heat. Chill.

The pie freezes well. Do not freeze sauce. Serves 8.

Gulfshore Delights

Extra Special Banana Cream Pie

1 tablespoon unflavored gelatin (1 envelope)
¼ cup cold water
6 egg yolks
1 cup sugar
2 cups heavy cream, whipped

2 tablespoons banana-flavored liqueur *or* 1 teaspoon banana extract
1 (9-inch) graham cracker pie crust, baked and cooled

Make graham cracker crust as instructed on graham cracker box. (Do not use less than a 9-inch size.) Let cool.

In a small saucepan sprinkle 1 tablespoon gelatin over ¼ cup cold water to soften for 5 minutes. Then stir it over a pan of simmering water until it is dissolved; let cool. Beat 6 egg yolks at high speed until frothy. Gradually add 1 cup sugar. Continue to beat the mixture for several minutes or until it ribbons when beater is lifted. Pour gelatin in a thin stream into the egg yolk mixture, beating constantly. Fold the whipped cream into the mixture; add the banana liqueur *or* extract. Mound the filling into the graham cracker crust. Chill pie for 30 minutes or until set. Add glaze.

GLAZE:

⅓ cup apricot preserves
½ teaspoon lemon juice

2 or 3 bananas

Bring apricot preserves to a boil; stir in the lemon juice and strain mixture into a bowl, if necessary. Slice bananas over pie surface (⅛-inch thick). Brush warm apricot glaze over bananas and chill. Serves 8.

Apalachicola Cookbook

Four Layer Delight

FIRST LAYER:

1 stick butter or margarine,
  melted
1 cup plain flour

1 cup chopped nuts

Mix well and pat into a 9×13-inch baking dish. Bake for 15–20 minutes at 325°. Cool.

SECOND LAYER:

8 ounces cream cheese, softened
1 cup powdered sugar

1 cup Cool Whip

Mix together cream cheese and powdered sugar, add Cool Whip. Spread over first layer.

THIRD LAYER:

Is Your choice:
  2 packages each chocolate,
  lemon or vanilla instant
  pudding, using 3 cups of milk

Or 1 can cherry or blueberry
pie filling

Spread over cream cheese layer.

FOURTH LAYER:

Place remaining Cool Whip on top. Nuts or strawberries may be sprinkled on top. Chill 2–3 hours or overnight.

Fiesta

Mini Blinis
For party hors d'oeuvres dessert table

1 (2-pound) loaf thin-sliced bread   1 pound cream cheese, softened
2 egg yolks   ½ cup sugar

Cut crust from bread and roll with rolling pin to flatten. In a medium-sized bowl, cream together egg yolks, cream cheese, and sugar. Spread mixture on bread and roll up.

TOPPING:

1 teaspoon cinnamon   1 stick margarine, melted
1 cup sugar

Dip bread rolls in melted margarine and then in sugar and cinnamon mixture. Freeze for 2 hours on cookie sheet and cut each in half. Bake at 400° for 10–15 minutes. These store in freezer until ready to use. Preparation: 30 minutes. Baking: 10–15 minutes. Easy. Must do ahead. Can freeze. Yield: 5 dozen.

Culinary Arts & Crafts

Girdle Buster
Coffee-Fudge Pie

Graham cracker crust   1 can chocolate frosting
3 cups coffee ice cream   1 cup pecans

Let ice cream soften. Fill graham cracker crust with softened ice cream. Return to freezer to harden and then spread on fudge frosting. Decorate with pecans and freeze. Remove from freezer 10–15 minutes before serving.

One can never catch up with good intentions.

Sweet Surrender with Advice à la Carte

Miniature Cream Cheese Tarts With Cherry Sauce

PASTRY:

2 (3-ounce) packages cream
  cheese, softened

1 cup butter, softened
2 cups all-purpose flour

Mix cream cheese, butter and flour by hand. Form into a ball. Cover and chill for 1 hour. Form dough into 1-inch balls and press to fit in ungreased miniature muffin tins.

FILLING:

1 pint sour cream
5 tablespoons sugar

2 teaspoons vanilla extract

Preheat oven to 350°. Blend all ingredients. Fill each muffin cup with a heaping teaspoon of filling. Bake for 15–20 minutes, or until pastry is light brown and filling bubbles. Cool slightly in tins. Then remove to cooling racks.

CHERRY SAUCE:

1½ tablespoons cornstarch
⅛ teaspoon ground cinnamon
1 (16-ounce) can pitted dark sweet
  cherries

2 tablespoons brandy
½ teaspoon lemon juice

Combine cornstarch and cinnamon in a small saucepan. Drain cherries, reserving liquid. Gradually add cherry liquid to cornstarch mixture. Cook over medium heat, stirring constantly, until mixture thickens. Remove from heat and stir in brandy, lemon juice and cherries. Cool. Spoon a little sauce into each tart. Servings: 4 dozen tarts. Preparation time: 1 hour. Baking time: 15–20 minutes. Chilling time: 1 hour.

Jacksonville & Company

White Chocolate Mousse With Strawberry Sauce

MOUSSE:

1 cup heavy cream
½ cup sugar (¼ pound)
¼ cup water
¼ cup egg whites
½ pound white chocolate, cut into
small cubes

1. Whip cream until stiff and refrigerate. 2. Heat water and sugar to 250°. 3. Meanwhile, when sugar reaches about 240°, beat egg whites until they form soft peaks. When sugar reaches 250° add to whites in a slow, steady stream and blend for 3 minutes. 4. Add chocolate cubes and beat for 1 minute more. 5. Fold in whipped cream and chill several hours. 6. When chilled, put a little strawberry sauce onto each dessert plate and then spoon mousse onto sauce.

Suggested garnishes: candied violets, chocolate leaves, grated dark chocolate, amaretti or amarettini cookies.

STRAWBERRY SAUCE:

2 (10-ounce) packages frozen
strawberries and/or raspberries
¼ cup sugar
2 tablespoons cornstarch
¼ teaspoon almond extract (I use
3 tablespoons Grand Marnier at
restaurant)

Thaw berries, drain and reserve syrup, add water to make 1½ cups of liquid. Mix sugar and cornstarch in saucepan and gradually add syrup/water mixture. Cook and stir until simmers, 2 minutes, remove from heat and add berries and flavoring. Chill well. Berries may be puréed before adding to sauce.

(Jamie's French Restaurant—Seville) Fiesta

Brandied Pumpkin Flan

¾ cup sugar
1 cup canned pumpkin
1 cup milk
1 cup light cream
6 eggs

½ cup sugar
½ teaspoon salt
2 teaspoons vanilla
⅓ cup brandy
2 tablespoons brandy for flaming

In a large heavy skillet, over medium heat, cook ¾ cup sugar until it melts to a golden syrup. Immediately pour syrup into a heated 8½-inch baking dish or mold. Quickly rotate mold to cover bottom and sides completely. Set aside to cool.

Combine pumpkin, milk, and cream in medium saucepan. Heat over low heat until bubbles form around edge of pan. In large bowl, beat eggs slightly. Add sugar, salt and vanilla. Gradually stir in hot pumpkin mixture and ⅓ cup brandy. Pour into prepared baking dish. Set dish in shallow pan; pour boiling water to ½ inch level around dish. Bake 50–60 minutes in 325° oven or until silver knife inserted in center comes out clean. Let custard cool and refrigerate overnight.

To serve: Run small spatula around edge of dish to loosen custard. Invert on shallow serving dish; shake gently to release. The caramel acts as sauce. At the table, warm 2 tablespoons brandy slightly; ignite and quickly pour over flan. Yield: 8 servings.

Friendly Feasts Act II

Bread Pudding

1 quart milk (scalded)	½ teaspoon salt
2 cups bread cubes	1 teaspoon vanilla
¼ cup butter	1 cup raisins
2 eggs, beaten	Dash nutmeg
⅓ cup sugar	

Add bread cubes and butter to scalded milk. Add eggs and mix well. Add sugar, salt and vanilla. Stir in raisins (optional) and pour into well-greased baking dish. Sprinkle with nutmeg and place entire dish in pan of hot water that goes halfway up. Bake at 350° for 1 hour and 15 minutes. Cool and serve with whiskey sauce. Serves 8.

WHISKEY SAUCE:

8 tablespoons butter	1 egg, beaten
1 cup sugar	¼–½ cup bourbon whiskey

Melt butter in top of double boiler. In a separate bowl combine eggs and sugar. When butter is melted, add egg-sugar mixture. Stir 2–3 minutes until sugar and egg are incorporated. Do not let it boil! Remove from heat; cool; stir in bourbon whiskey.

Fiesta

Caramel Egg Custard
(Crème Renversée au Caramel)

This recipe is probably my most favorite dessert and is always a hit with my students.

½ cup sugar   2 tablespoons water

Cook sugar and water in a small heavy saucepan (slowly) without stirring. The sugar will caramelize. When good and brown, pour immediately all at once into a mold turning around to coat the sides. Place in cold water. Repeat turning and cooling until the caramel is no longer liquid. Set aside.

CREME:

3 whole eggs   3 cups milk
6 egg yellows   1 teaspoon vanilla
¾ cup sugar

Blend first three ingredients in a mixing bowl. Scald milk and pour all at once into mixture while stirring. Strain into caramel mold. Bake in a bain-marie in the bottom third of oven at 325° for 40 minutes. Remove and chill mold in refrigerator. Unmold on a serving platter.

Gourmet Cooking

Custard
(Natilla)

1 liter milk   1½ cups sugar
1 small stick cinnamon   4 tablespoons cornflour
1 piece lemon peel   ¼ cup water
¼ teaspoon salt   1 teaspoon vanilla
8 egg yolks

Boil milk with cinnamon, lemon peel and salt. Allow to cool. Beat egg yolks with sugar and the cornflour dissolved in water. Add the milk. Strain and cook in a double boiler or over medium heat, stirring constantly until thickened. Add the vanilla, pour into dish and allow to cool well. Sprinkle with cinnamon. Serves 6.

The Cuban Flavor

Frozen Amaretto Parfaits

1 package macaroon cookies
6 egg yolks
2 eggs
¾ cup sugar
¾ cup Amaretto liqueur

2 cups heavy cream, whipped
Crushed macaroons
Additional whipped cream
Toasted almonds

Crumble macaroons coarsely and toast at 300° for 20 minutes until brown and crunchy but not too hard. Stir occasionally during baking; set aside. In a large bowl, combine egg yolks, eggs and sugar. Beat on high speed of electric mixer until thick and fluffy and sugar is dissolved, about 6 minutes. Continue beating and gradually add liqueur. By hand fold in whipped cream and ¾ of macaroon crumbs. Gently spoon ½ mixture into parfait glasses. Layer a thin layer of crumbs and spoon remaining soufflé. Freeze 4–6 hours (cover with foil if longer). To serve, top with whipped cream and toasted almonds. Serves 4–6.

Beyond the Bay

Blueberry Supreme

1 (12-ounce) box vanilla wafers
1 cup butter (not margarine),
    softened
2 cups powdered sugar
3 whole eggs

2 (21-ounce) cans blueberry pie
    filling
2 cups whipping cream, whipped
1 cup chopped pecans

Crush the vanilla wafers. Line a buttered square layer cake pan with ⅔ of the crumbs. Cream the butter, sugar, and eggs; beat well. Spread the egg mixture over the vanilla wafers. Cover with the blueberry pie filling. Cover the blueberry mixture with the whipped cream. Top with the remainder of the crumbs, then sprinkle the top with the pecans. Refrigerate 24 hours. Cut into squares to serve.

A Pinch of Sunshine

Peach Freeze
Cool and refreshing

FIRST LAYER:
¾ cup vanilla wafer crumbs

Spread ¾ cup vanilla wafer crumbs over bottom of an 8-inch square pan.

SECOND LAYER:

1 cup dairy sour cream   1 cup fresh puréed peaches
½ cup sugar

Beat sour cream until fluffy, about 5 minutes. Continue to beat and add ½ cup sugar. Fold peaches into sour cream. Pour peach mixture over crumbs. Freeze until firm.

THIRD LAYER:

1 stick margarine   2 eggs
2 cups confectioners' sugar   2 tablespoons vanilla wafer
        crumbs

Cream butter. Add confectioners' sugar and beat until fluffy. Add eggs one at a time and beat. Spread over frozen peach layer and sprinkle with 2 tablespoons crumbs. Return to freezer. Preparation: 30 minutes. Easy. Must do ahead. Can freeze. Serves: 6–8.

Culinary Arts & Crafts

Cold Lime Soufflé
Light treat

1 envelope unflavored gelatin
¼ cup cold water
4 egg yolks
1 cup sugar
½ cup lime juice
½ teaspoon salt
1 tablespoon lime rind, grated

2 drops green food coloring
  (optional)
6 egg whites
1 cup heavy cream, whipped
Coconut, grated (optional)
Lime slices (optional)

Wrap waxed paper around top of 1½-quart soufflé dish, extending 4 inches above rim. Brush inside paper with oil. Sprinkle gelatin over water. In top of double boiler, mix egg yolks, ½ cup sugar, lime juice and salt. Cook over simmering water, stirring constantly until slightly thickened. Remove from heat. Add gelatin and stir until completely dissolved. Add lime rind and food coloring. Cool. Beat egg whites until stiff, gradually adding remaining sugar. Fold into lime mixture. Fold whipped cream into mixture. Spoon into prepared dish. Chill until firm. Remove paper to serve. Garnish with coconut and lime slices. Serves 6–8.

Fare by the Sea

Buttermilk Ice Cream
(Glace au Petit-Lait)

Mrs. Sis Lipson provided me with this very old recipe for buttermilk ice cream as it was served by a now closed Pensacola ice cream parlor.

1 quart buttermilk
½ pint cream
1 (15-ounce) can condensed milk

1 (13-ounce) can evaporated milk
½ cup lemon juice
½ cup sugar

Combine buttermilk, cream, milks, vanilla, lemon juice and sugar. Place in ice cream freezer can and freeze according to directions.

Optional: Replace part or all the lemon juice with 1 cup crushed pineapple.

Gourmet Cooking II

Vanilla Sunshine Ice Cream

For old-fashioned family fun, make home-made ice cream. This is our family's favorite—unbeatable!

5 eggs
2 cups sugar
1½ pints light cream

1 (13-ounce) can Carnation
 evaporated milk
5 cups milk
3 tablespoons vanilla

Mix eggs and sugar thoroughly. Add cream and evaporated milk. Mix well. Add milk and vanilla and stir. Pour into freezer and churn or plug in. Makes one gallon of happy Florida ice cream. To make peach ice cream add 2–3 cups peaches which have been put in blender for 45 seconds.

If it will brighten someone's day—say it.

Sweet Surrender with Advice à la Carte

Steve's Three-Cupper Ice Cream
This ice cream is very creamy and never gets icy.

3 bananas, mashed
Juice of 3 lemons (approximately 6
  tablespoons)
Juice of 3 oranges (approximately
  1½ cups)

3 cups sugar
3 cups milk
3 cups Half and Half

Combine the ingredients in an ice cream freezer and follow freezer
directions. Yields 3 quarts.

Note: This recipe seems to be even better if it is allowed to sit
overnight in the refrigerator before freezing.

A Pinch of Sunshine

Gold Brick

1 stick margarine
1 (12-ounce) package chocolate
  chips

⅓ cup evaporated milk
1 cup chopped walnuts, pecans, or
  peanuts (optional)

Melt margarine, chocolate and milk in double boiler. Stir until
chocolate is melted. Remove from heat and add nuts. Serve over
ice cream (it will harden). Store in glass jar in refrigerator. Reheat
in pan of warm water.

Lost Tree Cook Book

INDEX

A

Ajiaco 38
Almond Trifles 222
Amazing Fruit Cobbler 233
Angel Pie 234
Appetizers:
  Baked Brie 26
  Black Bean Dip 18
  Broccoli Dip 19
  Cheese and Mushroom Cups 21
  Crystallized Orange Nuts 27
  Curry Dip 16
  Frosted Artichokes With Caviar 22
  Hot Beef Dip 17
  Layered Crab or Shrimp Cocktail Spread 25
  Mystery Dip 16
  Pickled Okra 28
  Reuben Dip 19
  Sherry Cheese Pate 26
  Shrimp and Clam Mousse 24
  Shrimp Butter 24
  Shrimp Marinade 24
  Smoked Oyster Dip 16
  Spinach Cheese Squares 20
  Spinach in a Bread Bowl 20
  Springtime Filling for Cocktail Sandwiches 23
  Stuffed Mushrooms 21
  Stuffed Raw Cabbage 23
  You'd Never Guess It's Spinach Dip 19
Apple:
  Cake 202
  Fritter Rings 178
  Holiday Cran- 179
  How Do You Like Them Apples Apple Pie 233
  Paper Bag Apple Pie 232
  Peppered 178
  Swedish Baked Apples With Vanilla Sauce 179
Apricot Rum Cake 201
Artichokes:
  Bottoms Hollandaise, Spinach on 150
  Casserole 146
  Crab-Stuffed Artichoke Entree 98
  Frosted Artichokes With Caviar 22
  Mystery Dip 16
  –Rice Salad 54
Aspic, Tomato Ring 61
Aunt Alice's Grapefruit and Avocado Salad Dressing 67
Aunt Carrie's Eggnog 15
Avocado:
  Crabmeat Stuffed Baked 95

  Spinach Salad 46
  Tomato Aspic Topping 61

B

Baja Bowl 39
Baked Apricots 180
Baked Brie 26
Baked Chicken and Brown Rice 112
Baked Chicken Breasts Supreme 108
Baked Fish With Sour Cream 77
Baked "Fried" Chicken 106
Banana:
  Bread 194
  Dressing 181
  Punch 13
  Strawberry Shake 12
Barbecued Fish 76
Bastille Day Salad 57
Beans:
  Black 164
  Black Bean Dip 18
  Red Beans and Rice 173
  Spanish Bean Soup 35
Beef:
  Ajiaco 38
  and Vegetable Stir-Fry 126
  Boeuf aux Champignons a la Creme 125
  Brisket in Beer 123
  Burt's Beef Stew 133
  Elegant Spicy Meat Balls 131
  Empanada 132
  Father's Day Steak 122
  Hot Beef Dip 17
  Hamburger-Spinach Casserole 128
  Lucy's Spaghetti Meat Sauce 134
  Male Chauvinist Chili 135
  Noodle and Hamburger Casserole 166
  Picadillo II 131
  Reuben Dip 19
  Steak au Poivre 123
  Stuffed Burger Bundles 129
  Stuffed Sirloin Roast 127
  Swedish Meat Balls 130
  Tomatoes Yemistes 129
  Wellington 124
  With Cashews 127
  Veal or Round Steak Lausanne 136
  Zucchini Casserole With Ground 128
Best Even Caramels 230
Beverages:
  Aunt Carrie's Eggnog 14
  Banana Punch 13
  Banana Strawberry Shake 12
  Champagne Punch 15
  Cross Creek Tea Blend 12

Hot Cranberry Tea 12
Lime Luscious 14
Vodka Slush 15
Whisper 15
Biscuits, Kitty's 192
Black Bart's Seafood Ambrosia 60
Black Bean Dip 18
Black Beans 164
Black Bottom Pie 237
Blender Mayonnaise 68
Blueberry Cheesecake Macadamia 212
Blueberry-Orange Muffins 193
Blueberry Supreme 256
Boeuf aux Champignons a la Creme 125
Boiled Shrimp With Butter Sauce 89
Bollos 164
Bourbon Sticky Buns 193
Bran Muffins 194
Brandied Pumpkin Flan 253
Bread:
  Banana 194
  Blueberry-Orange Muffins 193
  Bourbon Sticky Buns 193
  Bran Muffins 194
  Cornbread 198
  Gourmet French 198
  Mango 196
  Onion Herb 197
  Pudding 154
  Spinach in a Bread Bowl 20
  Sticks 198
  Stuffed French 197
  Sweet Lemon
Brisket in Beer 123
Broccoli:
  and Bleu Cheese Casserole 147
  Casserole 147
  Chicken and Cheese Soup 33
  Cream of Broccoli Soup 33
  Dip 19
  Puffs 146
Brunch Eggs 188
Brussel Sprouts With Curry Sauce 155
Burt's Beef Stew 133
Buttermilk Ice Cream 258

C

Cabbage, Party 161
Cabbage, Stuffed Raw 23
Cakes:
  Almond Cheesecake 214
  Apple 202
  Apricot Rum 201
  Blueberry Cheesecake Macadamia 212
  Carrot 203
  Case's Orange Pound 201
  Cheese Cupcakes 213
  Chocolate 207

Chocolate Cake Roll 208
Gooey Butter 206
Hummingbird 210
Key Lime 206
Manatee Merry Cheesecakes 213
Miami Mango 211
Milky Way 209
Patron's Party Chocolate 209
Oatmeal 205
Orange Cream Almond Meringue Layer
  200
Sunshine Island 204
Calamondin Pie 236
Candy:
  Best Ever Caramels 230
  Good and Easy 230
  Microwave Candy Bark 229
  White Christmas 228
Caramel Egg Custard 255
Carob Brownies 219
Carrots:
  and Red Grapes 159
  Cake 203
  Cashew and Carrot Soup 34
  Duchesse, Potatoes and 152
  Mash, Potato and 159
  Sunshine 158
Case's Orange Pound Cake 201
Cashew and Carrot Soup 34
Cauliflower Potato Salad 48
Cauliflower Soup 32
Caviar, Frosted Artichokes With 22
Celestial Golden Salad 63
Champagne Punch 15
Cheese Strata 187
Cherry Mold 65
Chicken:
  Ajiaco 38
  a la Grecque 105
  Alma Peyroux 107
  and New Potato Salad 49
  and Pasta Salad 53
  Asparagus Casserole 110
  Baked Chicken and Brown Rice 112
  Baked Chicken Breasts Supreme 108
  Baked "Fried" 106
  Breast Baked in Wine 105
  Breast Mediterranean 111
  Breast Parmesan 109
  Breast With Orange Sauce 104
  Chinese Chicken Cashew 114
  Coco-Cola 106
  Committee's Choice Salad 50
  Hot Chicken Salad 51
  Hot Chicken Sandwich 115
  Key West 109
  Rice With 112
  Sweet and Sour 110
  Tallahassee Chicken Salad 52

Tetrazzini 113
  With Garlic 115
Chili, Male Chauvinist 135
Chinese Chicken Cashew 114
Chocolate:
  Cake 207
  Cake, Patron's Party 209
  Cake Roll 208
  Chip Cheesecake Brownies 218
  Coronet 242
  French Silk Pie 238
  Fudge Pie 237
  Mint Squares 216
  Mousse Pie 246
  Oatmeal Chip Cookies 227
  White Chocolate Mousse With Straw-
    berry Sauce 252
Chowder, Conch 37
Chowder, Pat's Corn 36
Chowder, Seacloud 37
Chow Shia 82
Christmas Cookies 222
Chutney, Mango 184
Cinnamon Crispies 224
Clam and Shrimp Mousse 24
Coco-Cola Chicken 106
Coffee Toffee Pie 239
Cold Lime Souffle 258
Cold Seafood and Pasta Salad 56
Cole Slaw, Fruited 47
Cole Slaw, Garden Fresh 47
Committee's Choice Chicken Salad 50
Company's Coming for Breakfast 186
Conch Chowder 37
Conch Fritters 101
Consumme Rice 170
Cookies:
  Almond Trifles 222
  Carob Brownies 219
  Chocolate Chip Cheesecake Brownies
    218
  Chocolate Mint Squares 216
  Christmas 222
  Cinnamon Crispies 224
  Florida Sunshine 223
  Gooies 221
  Guess-Again 226
  Heath Bars 219
  Incredible Edibles 228
  Lace 221
  Lemon Squares 217
  Linzer Tarts 226
  Melting Moments 227
  Mystery 225
  Oatmeal Chip 227
  Orange Tea 220
  Peanut Butter Brownies 218
  Ruby's Date Nut Squares 217
  Sandies 225

Strawberry 220
Cornbread 198
Corn Bubble 160
Corn Chowder, Pat's 36
Cornish Game Hen Tropical 117
Cornish Game Hens, Mary Ann's 116
Corn, Spanish 160
Crab:
  and Shrimp Hot Dish 94
  Bastille Day Salad 57
  Burgers 97
  Crepes Elegant 169
  Deviled 94
  Florida Crab Mold 59
  Layered Crab or Shrimp Cocktail Spread
    25
  Louis Salad 58
  Meeting Street 96
  Ollie's Crab Cakes 95
  Quiche 175
  Shrimp and Crabmeat au Gratin 89
  Shrimp and Crab Stuffing 80
  Stone 97
  Stuffed 96
  –Stuffed Artichoke Entree 98
  Stuffed Baked Avocado 95
  Yummies 94
Crawfish Enchilado 97
Cream of Broccoli Soup 33
Creole Gumbo Apalachicola 40
Crepes Elegant 169
Cross Creek Tea Blend 12
Crystallized Orange Nuts 27
Cucumber Soup 31
Curry Dip 16
Custard:
  Brandied Pumpkin Flan 153
  Bread Pudding 154
  Caramel Egg Custard 155
  Custard (Natilla) 255
Curried Fruit 180

D

Delicious Company Potatoes 151
Desserts (See Cakes, Candy, Cookies,
  Custard, Fruit, Ice Cream, Pies)
Deviled Crab 94
Deviled Eggs 85
Dips (See Appetizers)
Dolphin Pot Pie 73
Dolphin Street Broiled Oysters 91
Doves With Rice 118
Dressing, Southern Cornbread 176
Duck Casserole 119
Duck, Orange and Wine Roasted 119

E

Eggnog, Aunt Carrie's 14

Eggplant Casserole 156
Eggplant, Long Pond 157
Eggs:
    Brunch 188
    Cheese Strata 187
    Company's Coming for Breakfast 186
    Eggsistentialist Stuffed Eggs With Hollandaise 188
    Monterey Jack 189
    Overnight Brunch Main Dish 187
    Poached Eggs Elegants 189
    Shrimp and Deviled 85
Elegant Spicy Meat Balls 131
Empanada 132
Escalloped Pineapple 180
Exceptional Quiche 175
Extra Special Banana Cream Pie 148

F

Fantastic Fruit Salad With Banana Sauce 64
Fantastic 24-Hour Salad 44
Fast and Easy Scalloped Scallops 100
Father's Day Steak 122
Festive Baked Ham 143
Fettucini Carbonara 167
Fillet of Sole, Florentine 76
Fillets de Yellowtail aux Bananas 79
Fish:
    Baked Fish With Sour Cream 77
    Barbecued 76
    Black Bart's Seafood Ambrosia 60
    Dolphin Pot Pie 73
    Fillet of Sole, Florentine 76
    Fillets de Yellowtail aux Bananas 79
    Florida Lime Seviche 100
    Heavenly Broiled 78
    Red Snapper With Avocado Sauce 74
    Seacloud Chowder 37
    Seafood Casserole 71
    Seafood Gumbo 41
    Snapper in Foil 74
    Snapper With Sour Cream Stuffing 75
Florida Crab Mold 59
Florida Lime Seviche 100
Florida Sunshine Cookies 222
Florida Sunshine Salad 63
For People Who Aren't Afraid of Their Shell Beef With Cashews 127
Four Layer Delight 249
French Silk Chocolate Pie 238
French Toast, Orange 191
Fresh Fruit With Whipped Rum Sauce 182
Fresh Strawberry Pie 243
Fried Green Plantains 183
Frosted Artichokes With Caviar 22
Frosted Daiquiri Pie 242
Frosting:
    Carob Brownie Icing 219
    Chocolate 207

Cream Cheese 203
Hummingbird 210
Miami Mango Icing 206
Oatmeal Cake Topping 205
Orange Mountain Icing 204
Peanut Butter Brownies 218
Spice Icing 202
Frozen Amaretto Parfaits 256
Frozen Key Lime Pie 244
Frozen Lemon Tarts 245
Frozen Strawberry Salad 65
Fruit:
    Apple Fritter Rings 178
    Baked Apricots 180
    Carrots and Red Grapes 159
    Curried Fruit 180
    Escalloped Pineapple 180
    Fresh Fruit With Whipped Sauce 182
    Fried Green Plantains 183
    Glazed Apple Slices 191
    Holiday Cran-Apples 179
    Mango Chutney 184
    Peppered Apples 178
    Queen of Scots Marmalade 183
    Seagrape Jelly 184
    Sensational Strawberries 182
    Sun Ray Compote 181
    Swedish Baked Apples 179
Fruited Cole Slaw 47
Fruited Pork 138
Fudge Pie 237

G

Game (See Doves, Duck, Venison)
Garden Fresh Slaw 47
Gazpacho 30
Girdle Buster 250
Glazed Apple Slices 191
Gold Brick 260
Good and Easy Candy 230
Good-Bye Turkey Casserole 120
Gooey Butter Cake 206
Gooies 221
Gourmet French Bread 198
Grapefruit Shrimp Salad 55
Green Mango Pie 236
Guess-Again Cookies 226
Gulf Shrimp Divine 86
Gumbo Apalachicola, Creole 40
Gumbo, Seafood 41

H

Ham and Rice Salad 55
Ham, Festive Baked 143
Ham Steak, Marinated 143
Hamburger-Spinach Casserole 128
Heath Bars 219
Heavenly Broiled Fish 78

Hogwild Macaroni and Cheese 168
Holiday Cran-Apples 179
Hors D'Oeuvres (See Appetizers)
Horseradish Salad 62
Hot Beef Dip 17
Hot Chicken Salad 51
Hot Chicken Sandwich 115
Hot Cranberry Tea 12
How Do You Like Them Apples Pie 233
Hummingbird Cake 210

I

Ice Cream:
  Buttermilk 258
  Steve's Three-Cupper 260
  Vanilla Sunshine 259
Icing (See Frosting)
Impossible Pie 240
Incredible Edibles 228
Italian Spinach Pie 174

J

Jelly, Seagrape 184

K

Kelly's Barbecue Sauce 144
Key Lime Cake, 206
Key Lime Pie, 245
Key Lime Pie, Frozen 244
Key West Fried Rice 170
Kitty's Biscuits 192
Kolachy 235

L

Lace Cookies 221
Lat's Gourmet Sauce for Beef 144
Layered Crab or Shrimp Cocktail Spread 25
Lemon Bread, Sweet 195
Lemon Pie With Blueberry Sauce 247
Lemon Squares 217
Lemon Tarts, Frozen 245
Lime Luscious 14
Linzer Tarts 226
Lobster Thermidor 99
Long Pond Eggplant 157
Lucy's Spaghetti Meat Sauce 134

M

Male Chauvinist Chili 135
Manatee Merry Cheesecakes 213
Mandarin Orange and Sweet Potatoes 153
Mango Bread 196
Mango Chutney 184
Mango Pie, Green 236
Margarita Pie 240

Marinated Ham Steak 143
Marinated Squash 45
Marmalade, Queen of Scots 183
Marty's Stew 39
Mary Ann's Cornish Game Hens 116
Meat (See Beef, Pork, Veal, Venison)
Melting Moments 227
Memree's Soppin Shrimp 86
Meringue Torte 235
Miami Mango Cake 211
Milky Way Cake 209
Miniature Cream Cheese Tarts With Cherry
  Sauce 251
Mini Blinis 250
Mixed Seafood Lasagna 72
Monterey Jack Eggs 189
Mushrooms:
  Cheese and Mushroom Cups 21
  Stuffed 21
  Stuffing, Wild Rice and 171
  –Walnut Salad 45
Mystery Cookies 225
Mystery Dip 16

N

Noodle and Hamburger Casserole 166
Nuts, Crystallized Orange 27

O

Oatmeal Cake 205
Oatmeal Chip Cookies 227
Okra, Pickled 28
Ollie's Crab Cakes 95
Onion Crowns, Potato- 152
Onion Herb Bread 197
Onions Braised in Red Wine 155
Orange:
  and Wine Roasted Duck 119
  Cream Almond Meringue Layer Cake 200
  French Toast 191
  Pork Chops 139
  Pound Cake, Case's 201
  Tea Cookies 220
Overnight Brunch Main Dish 187
Oysters:
  Club Sandwich 92
  Dolphin Street Broiled 91
  Golden Rod 93
  Lydia 92
  Marty's Stew 39
  Rockefeller V 91
  Salad 58
  Smoked Oyster Dip 16

P

Paella 172
Pancake, Popover 190

Papaya Seed Salad Dressing 66
Paper Bag Apple Pie 232
Party Cabbage 161
Pasta Salad 54
Patron's Party Chocolate Cake 209
Pat's Corn Chowder 36
Patsy's Waffles 190
Peach Freeze 257
Peanut Butter Brownies 218
Peppered Apples 178
Perkie's Salad 44
Picadillo II 131
"Pickin' Pork" 140
Pickled Okra 28
Pies:
  Amazing Fruit Cobbler 233
  Angel 234
  Black Bottom 237
  Calamondin 236
  Chocolate Mousse 246
  Coffee Toffee 239
  Extra Special Banana Cream 248
  French Silk Chocolate 238
  Fresh Strawberry 243
  Frosted Daiquiri 242
  Frozen Key Lime 244
  Fudge 237
  Green Mango 236
  How Do You Like Them Apples 233
  Impossible 240
  Key Lime 245
  Lemon Pie With Blueberry Sauce 247
  Margarita 240
  Miniature Cream Cheese Tarts 251
  Paper Bag Apple 232
  Rum Cream 238
  Wild Orange 241
Plantains, Fried Green 183
Pleasure Island Shrimp 83
Poached Eggs Elegants 189
Popover Pancake 190
Pork:
  Chops, Sarasota 141
  Chops, Sweet and Sour 142
  Chops With Beer 139
  Company's Coming for Breakfast 186
  Festive Baked Ham 143
  Fruited 138
  Marinated Ham Steak 143
  Orange Pork Chops 139
  "Pickin'" 140
  Southern Shredded 140
  Stuffed Leg of 142
Potatoes:
  and Carrots Duchesse 152
  and Carrot Mash 159
  Chicken and New Potato Salad 49
  Delicious Company 151
  —Orange Crowns 152
  Salad, Sour Cream 48

Swiss Potato and Cheese Soup 35
Poultry (See Chicken)
Pudding (See Custard)
Punch (See Beverages)

Q

Queen of Scots Marmalade 184
Quiche, Crab 175
Quiche, Exceptional 175

R

Red Beans and Rice 173
Red Snapper With Avocado Sauce 74
Reuben Dip 19
Rice:
  Artichoke-Rice Salad 54
  Consumme 170
  Doves With 118
  Ham and Rice Salad 55
  Key West Fried 170
  Paella 172
  Red Beans and 173
  Shrimp and Rice Casserole 171
  Wild Rice and Mushroom Stuffing 171
  With Chicken 112
Ruby's Date Nut Squares 217
Rum Cream Pie 238

S

Salads:
  Artichoke-Rice 54
  Avocado Spinach 46
  Bastille Day 57
  Black Bart's Seafood Ambrosia 60
  Cauliflower Potato 48
  Celestial Golden 63
  Cherry Mold 65
  Chicken and New Potato 49
  Chicken and Pasta 53
  Cold Seafood and Pasta 56
  Committee's Choice Chicken 50
  Crab Louis 58
  Fantastic Fruit Salad With Banana Sauce 64
  Fantastic 24-Hour 44
  Florida Crab Mold 59
  Florida Sunshine 63
  Frozen Strawberry 65
  Fruited Cole Slaw 47
  Garden Fresh Slaw 47
  Grapefruit Shrimp 55
  Ham and Rice 55
  Horseradish 62
  Hot Chicken 51
  Marinated Squash 45
  Mushroom-Walnut 45
  Oyster 58
  Pasta 54

Perkie's 44 ·
Sauerkraut 46
Sour Cream Potato 48
Tallahassee Chicken 52
Tart and Sweet 62
Tomato Aspic Ring 61
Tuna and Salmon Mold 57
Salad Dressings:
Aunt Alice's Grapefruit and Avocado 67
Blender Mayonnaise 68
Bleu Cheese 50
Mayonnaise 56
Papaya Seed 66
Tarragon French 58
Salmon Salad Mold, Tuna and 57
Sandies 225
Sandwiches:
Hot Chicken 115
Oyster Club 92
Springtime Filling for Cocktail 23
Sauces:
Gold Brick 260
Hollandaise 150
Kelly's Barbecue 144
Lat's Gourmet Sauce for Beef 144
Tartar 102
Sausage Stuffed Rigatoni 138
Sauerkraut Salad 46
Scallops, Fast and Easy Scalloped 100
Scampi With Mustard Sauce 87
Seacloud Chowder 37
Seafood (See also Clam, Conch, Crab,
Crawfish, Fish, Lobster, Oyster, Scallops,
Shrimp)
Bastille Day Salad 57
Casserole 71
Cold Seafood and Pasta Salad 56
Gumbo 41
Medley 70
Mixed Seafood Lasagna 72
Paella 174
Treasure 71
Tuna and Salmon Salad Mold 57
Seagrape Jelly 184
Seaside Stuffed Squash 149
Sensational Strawberries 182
Seviche, Florida Lime 100
Sherry Cheese Pate 26
Shrimp (See also Seafood)
and Clam Mousse 24
and Crabmeat au Gratin 89
and Crab Stuffing for Flounder, Bass, etc.
80
and Deviled Eggs 85
and Rice Casserole 171
Bisque 42
Boats 84
Boiled Shrimp With Butter Sauce 89
Butter 24
Chow Shia 82

Crab and Shrimp Hot Dish 98
Florentine 88
Grapefruit Shrimp Salad 55
Gulf Shrimp Divine 86
Layered Crab or Shrimp Cocktail Spread
25
Marinade 24
Memree's Soppin 86
Pleasure Island 83
Scampi With Mustard Sauce 87
Shrimply Delicious 90
Soy 82
Spaghetti, Tarragon 166
Sweet and Sour 81
Smoked Oyster Dip 16
Snapper in Foil 74
Snapper With Sour Cream Stuffing 75
Soups:
Ajiaco 38
Baja Bowl 39
Broccoli, Chicken and Cheese 33
Cashew and Carrot 34
Cauliflower 32
Conch Chowder 37
Cream of Broccoli 33
Creole Gumbo Apalachicola 40
Cucumber 31
Gazpacho 30
Marty's Stew 39
Pat's Corn Chowder 36
Seacloud Chowder 37
Seafood Gumbo 41
Shrimp Bisque 42
Spanish Bean 35
Strawberry 31
Swiss Potato and Cheese 35
What a Crock Cream of Almond and Zuc-
chini 32
Sour Cream Potato Salad 48
Sour Cream Venison and Noodle Bake 117
Southern Corn Bread Dressing 176
Southern Shredded Pork 140
Spaghetti Meat Sauce, Lucy's 134
Spaghetti, Tarragon Shrimp 166
Soy Shrimp 82
Spanish Bean Soup 35
Spanish Corn 160
Spinach:
Avocado Spinach Salad 46
Cheese Squares 20
Hamburger-Spinach Casserole 128
in a Bread Bowl 20
Italian Spinach Pie 174
on Artichoke Bottoms Hollandaise 150
You'd-Never-Guess-It's-Spinach Dip 19
Springtime Filling for Cocktail Sandwiches
23
Spreads (See Appetizers)
Squash, Marinated 45
Squash, Seaside Stuffed 149

Squash, Tomatoes Stuffed With Summer 148
Steak (See Beef)
Steamy Summer Vegetables 163
Steve's Three-Cupper Ice Cream 260
Strawberries:
Banana Strawberry Shake 12
Cookies 220
Frozen Strawberry Salad 65
Pie, Fresh 243
Sensational 182
Soup 31
Stone Crabs 96
Stuffed Burger Bundles 129
Stuffed Crab 96
Stuffed French Bread 197
Stuffed Leg of Pork 142
Stuffed Mushrooms 21
Stuffed Raw Cabbage 23
Stuffed Sirloin Roast 127
Stuffing, Shrimp and Crab 80
Stuffing, Wild Rice and Mushroom 171
Sun Ray Compote 181
Sunshine Carrots 158
Sunshine Island 204
Swedish Meat Balls 130
Swedish Baked Apples With Vanilla Sauce 179
Sweet and Sour Chicken 110
Sweet and Sour Shrimp 81
Sweet and Sour Pork Chops 142
Sweet Lemon Bread 195
Sweet Potato and Pineapple 153
Sweet Potatoes, Mandarin Orange and 153
Sweet Potato Souffle 154
Swiss Potato and Cheese Soup 35

T

Tallahassee Chicken Salad 52
Tarragon Shrimp Spaghetti 166
Tart and Sweet Salad 62
Tartar Sauce 102
Tiropita 174
Tomato Aspic Ring 61
Tomatoes Stuffed With Summer Squash 148
Tomatoes Yemistes 129
Tuna and Salmon Salad Mold 57
Tuna Burgers 97
Turkey, Good-Bye Casserole 120

V

Vanilla Sunshine Ice Cream 259

Veal:
Meat Balls Italian Style 137
or Round Steak Lausanne 136
Victory Skillet 136
Vegetables: (See also Appetizers, Salads, Soups)
Artichoke (See Artichokes)
Beans (See Beans)
Bollos 164
Broccoli (See Broccoli)
Brussel Sprouts With Curry Sauce 155
Cabbage, Party 161
Cabbage, Stuffed Raw 23
Carrots (See Carrots)
Corn Bubble 160
Corn, Spanish 160
Eggplant Casserole 156
Eggplant, Long Pond 157
Onions Braised in Red Wine 155
Potatoes (See Potatoes, Sweet Potatoes)
Spinach (See Spinach)
Squash (See Squash)
Tomatoes (See Tomatoes)
Vegetable Rainbow Platter 162
Zucchini (See Zucchini)
Venison Bake, Sour Cream Noodle and 117
Venison Swiss Steak 118
Vodka Slush 15

W

Waffles, Patsy's 190
What a Crock Cream of Almond and Zucchini Soup 32
Whisper 15
White Chocolate Mousse With Strawberry Sauce 252
White Christmas Candy 228
Wild Orange Pie 241
Wild Rice and Mushroom Stuffing 171

Y

You'd-Never-Guess-It's-Spinach Dip 19

Z

Zucchini Casserole With Ground Beef 128
Zucchini Soup, What a Crock Cream of Almond and 32

Catalog of Contributing Cookbooks

Sunlight over the ocean creates a silhouette of sabal palms, the state tree of Florida.

CATALOG OF CONTRIBUTING COOKBOOKS

All recipes in this book have been submitted from the Florida cookbooks shown on the following pages. Individuals who wish to obtain a copy of any particular book can do so by sending a check or money order to the addresses listed. Prices are subject to change. Please note the postage and handling charges that are required. Florida residents add tax only when requested. Retailers are invited to call or write to same address for wholesale information.

ALONE AT THE RANGE
by Mary Lou Freeman
Team Cookbooks
P. O. Box 6082
Fernandina Beach, FL 32034   904/261-6161

A cooking guide for the novice and directed at the single person (also for couples), this book of cooking hints and varied recipes will appeal to all levels of cooking skills. A chapter of 21 recipes is devoted to microwave cooking in smaller amounts. There are 53 conventional recipes in the 70-page book.
$6.50 Retail price
$ .33 Tax for Florida residents
$1.00 Postage and handling
Make check payable to Team Cookbooks

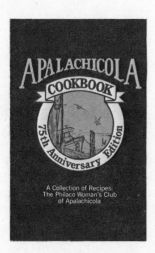

APALACHICOLA COOKBOOK
Philaco Woman's Club
P. O. Box 895
Apalachicola, FL 32320   904/653-8676

Apalachicola, known for generations as having a bay that produces quality oysters, has a rich history as well. Both of these aspects are emphasized in these 341 pages. Some of the recipes have been passed down from generation to generation. Sketches and histories of our churches and old homes are scattered throughout the book.

$11.95 Retail price
$ .60 Tax for Florida residents
$ 1.50 Postage and handling
Make check payable to Philaco Woman's Club
ISBN 0-9614600-0-8 (spiral bound); 0-9614600-1-6
   (case bound)

BAY LEAVES
Panama City Junior Service League
P. O. Box 404
Panama City, FL 32402   904/785-7870

A collection of recipes for the gourmet and novice cook. There are 325 spiral-bound pages filled with 800 tested recipes featuring an excellent seafood section. The book is enhanced by original pen and ink drawings by a regional award-winning artist.

$9.95 Retail price
$ .50 Tax for Florida residents
$1.55 Postage and handling
Make check payable to Bay Publications
ISBN 0-9615014-0-5

BEYOND THE BAY
Panama City Junior Service League
P. O. Box 404
Panama City, FL 32402   904/785-7870

An elegant sequel to the award-winning *Bay Leaves*. There are 316 spiral-bound pages filled with 700 tested recipes reflecting the Southern charm of this coastal community. The book features original artwork evocative of Panama City, commissioned by a well-known local artist.

$13.95 Retail price
$ .70 Tax for Florida residents
$ 1.55 Postage and handling
Make check payable to Bay Publications
ISBN 0-9615014-1-3

CANOPY ROADS
Tallahassee Junior Woman's Club
P. O. Box 944
Tallahassee, FL 32302   904/576-5134 or 222-4787

Canopy Roads is a 352-page collection of recipes which includes everything from appetizers to vegetables. The book is a souvenir cookbook which is full of historical information on Tallahassee. There are sections on international cooking, microwave and an extra special dessert section featuring local cake recipes.

$9.95 Retail price
$ .50 Tax for Florida residents
$1.50 Postage and handling
Make check payable to Tallahassee Junior Woman's Club
ISBN 0-918544-85-8

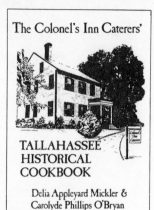

The Colonel's Inn Caterers'

TALLAHASSEE
HISTORICAL
COOKBOOK

Delia Appleyard Mickler &
Carolyde Phillips O'Bryan

THE COLONEL'S INN CATERERS'—
TALLAHASSEE HISTORICAL
COOKBOOK
by Delia Appleyard Mickler & Carolyde Phillips O'Bryan
1508 Cristobal Drive
Tallahassee, FL 32303   904/222-1290

This is a book about the families who came and settled
in Tallahassee over a hundred-year period from 1824 to
1924. The 195 pictures in the book are mostly of houses
which are no longer standing, with recipes, information
and quotes from their owners and descendants.

$20.00 Retail price
$ 1.00 Tax for Florida residents
$ 3.00 Postage and handling
Make check payable to Delia A. Mickler

COOK AND DEAL
by D. J. Cook
P. O. Box 3238 Beach Station
Vero Beach, FL 32964   305/231-1996

Nominee for 1982 R. T. French Tastemaker Award and
reviewed in over 300 national newspapers, *Cook and
Deal* features "Four Decks" of carefully tested recipes,
and "One Deck" of challenging and instructive bridge
hands. The author is Life Master #236 and past
president of the American Bridge Teachers' Association.
210 pages.

$10.95 Retail price
$ .55 Tax for Florida residents
$ 1.50 Postage and handling
Make check payable to *Cook and Deal*
ISBN 0-939114-53-4

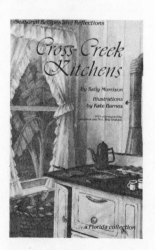

CROSS CREEK KITCHENS
by Sally Morrison
Triad Publishing Co., Inc.
1110 N.W. 8th Avenue
Gainesville, FL 32601   904/373-5308 or 5800

Filled with delightful tales of life today in Cross Creek.
The recipes, many original, blend traditional southern
style with contemporary flair. An American treasure,
lavishly illustrated. The author is caretaker of the
Marjorie Kinnan Rawlings home where she has created
many of the recipes on the original woodstove. 224
pages. 175 recipes.

$11.95 Retail price comb-bound; $8.95 paper; $19.95
     deluxe hardcover
5% Tax for Florida residents
$ 2.00 Postage and handling
Make check payable to Triad Publishing Co., Inc.
ISBN 0-937404-25X (comb); 0-937404-063 (paper);
     0-937404-500 (hard)

272

THE CUBAN FLAVOR
by Raquel Rabade (Roque)
Downtown Book Center, Inc.
247 S.E. First Street
Miama, FL 33131 305/377-9939

Like its passionate people, Cuban food is alive with color and excitement. Raquel Roque is a Miamian with a colorful Cuban heritage—many of these recipes have been handed down from generations of successful cooks. With the ongoing popularity of regional foods, this is a *must* for collectors. 240 pages.

$8.95 Retail price
$ .45 Tax for Florida residents
$1.25 Postage and handling
Make check payable to Downtown Book Center
ISBN 0-941010-00-7

CULINARY ARTS & CRAFTS
The Park Maitland School
1450 S. Orlando Avenue
Maitland, FL 32751 305/647-3038

A collection of the best of parents, teachers and students, ranging from punches, eggs and cheese, main dishes, desserts, lunch box ideas, and children's parties. Each recipe gives preparation time and difficulty level; freezability, microwave suggestions and serving suggestions are also provided for many recipes.

$12.00 Retail price
$ .60 Tax for Florida residents
$ 1.20 Postage and handling
Make check payable to The Park Maitland School
ISBN 0-9613532-0-1

CYPRESS GARDENS COOKBOOK
St. Agnes Guild—St. Paul's Episcopal Church
P. O. Box 373
Winter Haven, FL 33882-0373 813/294-8887 or 293-8252

Compiled as a fund-raiser for guild welfare projects, this book, now in its 6th printing, has sold 30,000 copies and was selected in 1974 by *Ladies' Home Journal* for its continuing series on community cookbooks. All recipes, thoroughly tested, were selected for great taste and easy availability of ingredients.

$7.95 Retail price
$ .40 Tax for Florida residents
$1.25 Postage and handling
Make check payable to *Cypress Gardens Cookbook*

FARE BY THE SEA

Junior League of Sarasota
P. O. Box 25074
Sarasota, FL 34277   813/922-8430

Over 500 delicious recipes are included in this elegant
and tasteful collection of recipes from the Sarasota coastal
area. A "Pinch of History" and beautiful drawings
depicting the cultural history of Sarasota are additional
features in this 319-page book. The diverse recipes will
delight all cooks.

$10.95 Retail price
$ .55 Tax for Florida residents
$ 1.50 Postage and handling
Make check payable to *Fare by the Sea*
ISBN 0-9611186-0-1

FIESTA

Pensacola Junior Woman's Club, Inc.
P. O. Box 9215
Pensacola, FL 32513   904/477-5544

In recognition of the many festivals which celebrate
Pensacola's past and present, *Fiesta* offers a delectable
array of irresistible Gulf Coast culinary delights.
Illustrated by local artists and cross-referenced for easy
accessibility, these twice-tested 500 recipes offer you the
best in traditional and contemporary recipes.

$11.95 Retail price
$ .60 Tax for Florida residents
$ 1.50 Postage and handling
Make check payable to Pensacola Junior Woman's Club

FLORIDA FLAVORS

Environmental Studies Council, Inc.
2900 N.E. Indian River Drive
Jensen Beach, FL 33457   305/334-1262

Serving recipes and helpful advice, *Florida Flavors*
makes fascinating reading—and cooking—for natives and
newcomers alike. The full-color cover was painted by
well-known Florida artist James Hutchinson. Florida
conservation writer, Ernest Lyons, contributed the
foreword and quotes from his book, *My Florida*. 365
pages. Spiral-bound. Beautiful!

$12.95 Retail price
$ .75 Tax for Florida residents
$ 2.00 Postage and handling
Make check payable to Environmental Studies Council,
Inc.
ISBN 0-916629-00-7

FRIENDLY FEASTS ACT II

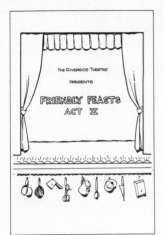

Friends of Riverside Theatre
P. O. Box 3788
Vero Beach, FL 32963   305/231-5860

Three years after its appearance, not a copy of our first cookbook remained unsold and the applause given to *Friendly Feasts* encouraged the editors to try again. Here in *Act II* are 241 dramatically successful recipes, collected, concocted, and kitchen-tested by the Friends of Riverside Theatre. 110 pages.

$8.50 Retail price
$ .43 Tax for Florida residents
$1.50 Postage and handling
Make check payable to Friends of Riverside Theatre

GALLEY GOURMET III

by Ferne Raveson
811 Gloucester Street
Boca Raton, FL 33431   305/997-5656

Simplified recipes using few but choice ingredients for tasteful, attractive food prepared with a minimum amount of time and effort. Contents include packaged food recipes, fresh, quick and easy foods, elegant main dishes, appetizers, soups, desserts, tips for wonderful sandwiches, and general improvement of meals. Written for home and boat.

$7.95 Retail price
$ .40 Tax for Florida residents
Make check payable to Ferne Raveson
ISBN 0-396-06828-6

THE GASPARILLA COOKBOOK

The Junior League of Tampa, Inc.
P. O. Box 10223
Tampa, FL 33679   813/254-1734

Gourmet cooking with recipes from famous West Coast Florida restaurants and hostesses, features Spanish, French, English, Greek, Italian, Southern and Yankee recipes. Hardbound, illustrated, 712 recipes, 309 pages. Has been reprinted 15 times, over 200,000 copies sold.

$11.95 Retail price
$ .63 Tax for Florida residents
$ 1.50 Postage and handling
Make check payable to The Junior League of Tampa, Inc.
ISBN 0-9609556-0-7

GATOR COUNTRY COOKS
Junior League of Gainesville, Florida, Inc.
P. O. Box 422
Gainesville, FL 32602   904/376-3805

Gator Country Cooks represents a long and proud
tradition of some of the best cooks around. Few visitors
to Gator Country forget the dinner parties, luncheons,
buffets, and brunches of a social life that largely centers
around food. 387 pages. Approximately 1,000 recipes.
Washable cover. Cross-index. A taste of Southern
hospitality and good eating.

$9.95 Retail price
$ .50 Tax for Florida residents
$1.50 Postage and handling
Make check payable to Junior League of Gainesville
ISBN 0-9606616-0-3

GOURMET COOKING
Peyroux Enterprises, Inc.
P. O. Box 1026
Pensacola, FL 32595   904/434-3346

Chef Peyroux, a native of New Orleans, first mastered
Creole cooking, then after locating in Pensacola, studied
Gulf Coast cooking and began instructing these and other
styles of cuisine at Pensacola Junior College. After
attending several cooking schools in France, he began his
weekly TV series for PBS called "Gourmet Cooking." 328
pages of recipes from his shows.

$13.95 Retail price (postage included)
$ .70 Tax for Florida residents
Make check payable to *Gourmet Cooking*

GOURMET COOKING II
Peyroux Enterprises, Inc.
P. O. Box 1026
Pensacola, FL 32595   904/434/3346

In this volume, WSRE-TV-23 presents more recipes from
Gourmet Cooking as it enters its ninth year of local
broadcasting and its fourth on National PBS. These
television presentations, which are produced at Pensacola
Junior College, are seen in 55 cities. 224 pages.

$13.95 Retail price ($26.50 Volumes I & II) Postage
   included
$ .70 Tax for Florida residents
Make checks payable to *Gourmet Cooking*

GULFSHORE DELIGHTS
Junior League of Fort Myers, Florida
P. O. Box 6774
Fort Myers, FL 33911-6774   813/275-4336

Gulfshore Delights captures the flavor of Southwest
Florida. It contains featured sections on wines and
favorite Southwest Florida restaurant recipes, cooking
hints, and breathtaking sketches of subtropical flora,
fauna and Southwest Florida area landmarks. 286 pages.
400 recipes. Exquisite 5-color artist-designed hard cover
with durable plastic comb binding.

$11.95 Retail price
$ .60 Tax for Florida residents
$ 1.50 Postage and handling
$ 1.00 Gift wrapping
Make check payable to *Gulfshore Delights*
ISBN 0-9613314-0-2

HEART OF THE PALMS
Junior League of the Palm Beaches, Inc.
P. O. Box 168
Palm Beach, FL 33480   305/655-4802

An artist-designed cover in full color, hard cover with a
plastic comb. 261 pages with over 400 double-tested
recipes. Thirteen sections: Hearts of Palm, Appetizers,
Breads, Soups, Salads and Salad Dressings, Seafood,
Meats, Poultry, Cheese and Eggs, Vegetables, Desserts,
Beverages and Jams, Tropical Fruits. Some microwave
recipes.

$11.95 Retail price
$ .60 Tax for Florida residents
$ 1.50 Postage and handling
Make check payable to Junior League Publications
ISBN 0-9608090-0-7

JACKSONVILLE & COMPANY
Junior League of Jacksonville
2165 Park Street
Jacksonville, FL 32204   904/387-5497

Jacksonville & Company contains 365 pages and over 550
carefully tested recipes. Clear concise directions with
comprehensive index for easy reference. Durable hard
cover with spiral heat-sealed binding. Special
entertainment section and special section on herb
cooking for the health-conscious cook.

$12.00 Retail price
$ .60 Tax for Florida residents
$ 1.55 Postage and handling
Make check payable to *Jacksonville & Company*
ISBN 0-9609338-0-8

JUICY MISS LUCY COOKBOOK
by Nancy Brail and Kathy Kahan
Two Girls from Filly
P. O. Box 3674
Longwood, FL 32779   305/788-2136

Juicy Miss Lucy is a collection and creation of recipes
easy enough to cook for your family and elegant enough
to serve to company. Recipes are quick and easy as well
as unusual. With its red and white cover and unique
colorful heart, spiral-binding and bookmark, it is
entertaining reading with mouthwatering results.

$9.95 Retail price
$ .50 Tax for Florida residents
$1.50 Postage and handling
Make check payable to Two Girls from Filly
ISBN 0-9610406-0-2

LOST TREE COOK BOOK
Lost Tree Chapel
11149 Turtle Beach Road
North Palm Beach, FL 33408   305/626-910C

The *Lost Tree Cook Book* is a collection of the recipe
favorites of 272 Lost Tree Village residents. It contains
360 pages and 832 recipes, and revenues from its sale
benefit Lost Tree Chapel. Compiled by Pan W.
Seastrunk, it is currently in its fifth printing.

$10.00 Retail price
$ 2.50 Postage and handling
Make check payable to Lost Tree Chapel

MARGARITAVILLE COOKBOOK
by Ruth Perez and Brenda Vidal
VIPCO
P. O. Box 2096
Key West, FL 33045   305/294-30č

More than a cookbook, *Margaritaville Cookbook* feature
drawings of historical landmarks and local items of
interest including "Political Potluck." There are meat
charts, conversion tables, a substitution list, handy
kitchen helpers, and 400 indexed household hints. Its
over 400 recipes include "old time" Conch recipes and
traditional Florida Keys favorites.

$11.00 Retail price
$ .50 Tax for Florida residents
$ 1.00 Postage and handling
Make check payable to VIPCO

MAURICE'S TROPICAL FRUIT COOK BOOK

by Maurice de Verteuil
Great Outdoors Publishing Company
4747 28th Street North
St. Petersburg, FL 33714   813/525-6609

Florida is a land of abundance. Two things in abundance are tropical fruits and new residents. This book marries the two, happily. You just moved here and find an avocado tree (mango, carambola?) in the yard? Try Cornish Hen Tropical, Mango Chutney, Seagrape Jelly; you'll learn over 200 exciting ideas for adding exotics to your menus. 80 pages. Paperback.

$2.95 Retail price
$ .15 Tax for Florida residents
$1.00 Postage and handling
Make check payable to Great Outdoors Publishing
  Company
ISBN 0-8200-0806-0

ODE TO THE OYSTERS

by Joan and Doug Adams
Dolphin Street Enterprises
317 Dolphin Street
Gulf Breeze, FL 32561   904/932-3433

In 1776, David Herd noted: "The oysters are a gentle kin. They winna talk unless you sing." *Ode to the Oysters* celebrates the gentle kin by offering 168 outstanding oyster recipes collected from around the world. The versatility of the oyster is seen in this wide variety of recipes.

$6.95 Retail price
$ .35 Tax for Florida residents
$1.00 Postage and handling
Make check payable to Dolphin Street Enterprises

Ode to the Oysters

THE ORANGE BOWL COOKBOOK

The Orange Bowl Committee
P. O. Box 350748
Miami, FL 33135   305/642-1515

This was a team effort of all the wives of Orange Bowl members and the Orange Bowl Staff. Not just another hodgepodge of celebrity recipes, but rather a thoughtful, tested collection of the best recipes submitted by players and coaches and their spouses who have participated in the Orange Bowl Foodball Classic.

$19.95 Retail price
$ .80 Tax for Florida residents
Make check payable to The Orange Bowl Committee
ISBN 0-9610552-0-0

PALM BEACH ENTERTAINS

Junior League of the Palm Beaches, Inc.
P. O. Box 168
Palm Beach, FL 33480   305/655-4802

A unique cookbook and Palm Beach social history.
Recipes tested and edited under guidance of culinary
expert, Maurice Moore-Betty, Director of the Moore-
Betty Cooking School, New York. Over 60 photographs
depicting Palm Beach, then and now. Exciting menus for
all occasions from famous Palm Beach hostesses.
Hardbound. 241 pages.

$10.95 Retail price
$ .55 Tax for Florida residents
$ 1.50 Postage and handling
Make check payable to Junior League Publications
ISBN 698-10748-9

A PINCH OF SUNSHINE

Junior Service League of Brooksville
P. O. Box 936
Brooksville, FL 33512   904/799-3795 or 796-3056

In this collection of 635 favorite recipes in all categories,
there is a special Citrus Showcase which includes recipes
developed by chefs of famous Florida restaurants and
favorite recipes of Florida Citrus Queens, as well as a
Florida Wild section and appetizers for every occasion.
Cover and interior art by wildlife artist Ernest Brundage.
334 pages.

$9.95 Retail price
$ .50 Tax for Florida residents
$1.50 Postage and handling
Make check payable to Brooksville Junior Service League
ISBN 0-939-11463-1

THE PRIMA DINER

Sarasota Opera Society
Box 1393
Sarasota, FL 33578   813/371-2408

The Prima Diner is a collection of recipes from opera
stars and famous musicians, their mothers, grandmothers,
and friends. Spiral-bound, the book is accented by
quotations about food from opera libretti. Directions for
the recipes are concise and uniform. 172 pages. 275
recipes.

$7.95 Retail price
$ .40 Tax for Florida residents
$1.50 Postage and handling
Make check payable to The Prima Diner Sarasota Opera
  Society
ISBN 0-9605844-0-4

SAWGRASS AND PINES
Perry Garden Club
802 W. Bay Street
Perry, FL 32347   904/584-3734

Sawgrass And Pines includes 387 pages and 800 favorite
recipes collected from members and friends. The artwork
on the cover and ten inside divider-page drawings were
done by a talented member and depicts the local history
of Taylor County.

$9.50. Retail price
$ .50 Tax for Florida residents
$1.50 Postage and handling
Make check payable to Perry Garden Club

SEASONED WITH SUNSHINE
P.A.C.E. Grace Lutheran School
P. O. Box 9265
Winter Haven, FL 33880   813/324-1321

An exciting collection of over 800 "hand-picked" recipes
featuring the many flavors of Florida-fresh fruits,
vegetables, seafood, beef, wild game, and much more!
This eye-catching book, with brightly colored laminated
cover, note pages and colored section dividers, has
enjoyed national television coverage. A must from the
sunshine state!

$11.95 Retail price
$ .60 Tax for Florida residents
$ 1.50 Postage and handling
Make check payable to *Seasoned With Sunshine*
ISBN 0-9612728-0-5

SEASONS IN THE SUN
Beaux Arts, Inc.
The Lowe Art Museum
1301 Stanford Drive
Coral Gables, FL 33146   305/284-3535

South Florida's always popular cookbook has 302 pages
full of tropical flavor from "Everglades Caviar" to "Frozen
Key Lime Pie." Beautiful color plates depicting familiar
South Florida scenes, art and menu selections divide
over 600 recipes into 13 sections. An enlarged edition
features exciting ideas for picnics, parties and gifts.

$12.95 Retail price
$ .65 Tax for Florida residents
$ 1.50 Postage and handling
Make check payable to Beaux Arts, Inc.
ISBN 0-9607010-0-1

SECRETS FROM THE GALLEY

The Galley Kitchen Shoppe, Inc.
905 U.S. One
Lake Park, FL 33403   305/844-0378

An old-fashioned cookbook with a new-fashioned twist from one of the S.E.'s largest and most complete kitchen shoppes. Nearly 600 favorite recipes from around the country. A gadget glossary describes the handiest kitchen gadgets. Over 1200 entries in the index under 102 headings, preceded by the Index-at-a-Glance for quick and easy reference.

$12.95 Retail price
$ .65 Tax for Florida residents
$ 1.50 Postage and handling
Make check payable to The Galley Kitchen Shoppe, Inc.
ISBN 0-9612544-0-8

SEMINOLE SAVORINGS

Seminole Productions, Inc.
P. O. Box 957
Tallahassee, FL 32302   904/488-6393

Seminole Savorings is a handsome hardbound collection of over 800 recipes (561 pages) from Florida State University fans and friends as well as some well known alumni—Burt Reynolds, Robert Urich, Rita Coolidge and Sonny "Enos" Shroyer, to name a few. Seventeen sections are preceded by beautiful sketches of historical landmarks in and around Tallahassee, the Capital of Florida.

$15.95 Retail price
$ .80 Tax for Florida residents
$ 2.00 Postage and handling
Make check payable to Seminole Productions, Inc.
ISBN 0-9608942-0-9

SOME LIKE IT SOUTH!

Junior League of Pensacola, Inc.
P. O. Box 87
Pensacola, FL 32591   904/433-4353

Some Like It South! contains 366 pages of over 550 delectable recipes thoroughly tested by discriminating cooks. This attractive, hardcover edition is Smythe-sewn to lie flat. Here is a colorful and appealing entertainment book designed with ideas from some of the best cooks and hostesses on the Gulf Coast.

$12.95 Retail price
$ .65 Tax for Florida residents
$ 1.50 Postage and handling
Make check payable to Julep Publications
ISBN 0-9613622-0-0

STEP-BY-STEP TO NATURAL FOOD
by Diane Campbell
CC Publishers
P. O. Box 4044
Clearwater, FL 33518   813/797-3321

The book contains instructions for the preparation of 97 vegetables, ways to use 38 herbs and spices, how to serve protein balanced meals without costly meat, a complete vitamin and mineral guide, 30 menus, 6 charts, desserts, and complete nut, seed and grain list. Over 760 indexed items make this nutritional guide a necessary book.

$7.95 Retail price
$1.00 Postage and handling
Make check payable to CC Publishers
ISBN 0-9603766-0-7

SUGAR BEACH
Fort Walton Beach Junior Service League
P. O. Box 24
Fort Walton Beach, FL 32549   904/862-6018

Discover the simple elegance of Florida's Emerald Coast with *Sugar Beach*. Dine on our freshest seafood ideas. Over 400 triple tested recipes, 320 pages in 14 sections. Special sections include Restaurants, Greek, Gifts, and Children's Recipes. Colorful hard cover with comb binding.

$11.95 Retail price
$ .60 Tax for Florida residents·
$ 1.75 Postage and handling
Make check payable to Sugar Beach Publications
ISBN 0-961356-0-0

SUNCOAST SEASONS
Dunedin Youth Guild, Inc.
P. O. Box 1453
Dunedin, FL 34296-1453   813/734-0394

With an emphasis on fresh ingredients and detailed instructions, this beautiful cookbook has true Florida pioneer recipes as well as ones from Suncoast restaurants and famous people. Winner of the 1985 Tastemaster Award in the community-service category, the book is now in the Hall of Fame at Syracuse University. 432 pages. 750 recipes.

$13.95 Retail price
$ .70 Tax for Florida residents
$ 1.75 Postage and handling
Make check payable to *Suncoast Seasons*
ISBN 0-9613858-0-4

283

SUNNY SIDE UP

The Junior League of Fort Lauderdale
2510 N.E. 15th Avenue
Fort Lauderdale, FL 33305   305/566-3736

Sunny Side Up offers 336 pages and 570 recipes along
with collector-quality pen and ink drawings. The book
contains both simple and sophisticated recipes for casual
entertaining with family, to elegant evenings with friends.
This new edition contains a very special "Truly Tropical"
section.

$11.95 Retail price
$ .60 Tax for Florida residents
$ 1.50 Postage and handling
Make check payable to *Sunny Side Up*
ISBN 0-9604158-0-7

SWEET SURRENDER WITH ADVICE A LA CARTE

by Jane Warnock McElyea and Pam McElyea Barnard
McElyea Publications
2850 W. Fairbanks Avenue
Winter Park, FL 32789   305/644-4981

Forget the calories! This is definitely *not* a diet book, but
a collection of 111 mouth-watering recipes with 111 bits
of sage advice for your indulgence and enjoyment! These
sweet concoctions provide a treat for every occasion
whether it's a party, a gift, a fund-raiser, or just a plain
old "sweet attack!"

$8.00 Retail price
$ .40 Tax for Florida residents
$1.00 Postage and handling
Make check payable to McElyea Publications
ISBN 0-9615622-0-X

A TASTE OF TAMPA

The Junior League of Tampa, Inc.
P. O. Box 10223
Tampa, FL 33679   813/254-1734

Timely, up-to-date cookbook featuring quick and easy
recipes with a gourmet flavor. No recipe takes over 100
minutes to prepare from start to finish, and the
ingredients needed are usually staples. Spiral bound
book has 169 pages with over 400 recipes.

$8.95 Retail price
$ .47 Tax for Florida residents
$1.50 Postage and handling
Make check payable to The Junior League of Tampa, Inc.
ISBN 0-9609556-1-5

THROUGH OUR KITCHEN WINDOWS

WMSC Council, Bahia Vista Mennonite Church
2548 53rd Street
Sarasota, FL 33580 813/351-1050

Over 500 recipes, 200 plus pages of recipes for basic,
down-to-earth good Mennonite cooking with an
attractive, easy-to-keep-clean plastic binder. Makes
beautiful birthday, anniversary, Valentine, Mother's Day,
Christmas, or just-because-you're-you gifts.

$7.50 Retail price
$1.25 Postage and handling
Make check payable to *Through Our Kitchen Windows*
ISBN 0-918544-53-X

THYME WAVES

Junior Museum of Bay County
P. O. Box 977
Panama City, FL 32401 904/769-6128

A time and energy saving cookbook on the wave length
of our times. All recipes are both conventional and
microwave, each coded, i.e., Jiffy, Do Ahead, No Watch,
and all designed to help us utilize our time and energy
saving kitchen equipment. 282 pages. 425 recipes.

$8.95 Retail price
$ .45 Tax for Florida residents
$1.25 Postage and handling
Make check payable to *Thyme Waves*
ISBN 0-9612774-0-8

The yucca plant is commonly referred to as "Spanish bayonet"—early Spanish settlers actually used the spiky plants as part of their fortification.

"Best of the Best" Cookbook Series:

Best of the Best from **Mississippi** $12.95   0-937552-09-7
Best of the Best from **Tennessee** $12.95   0-937552-20-8
Best of the Best from **Florida** $12.95   0-937552-16-X
Best of the Best from **Louisiana** $12.95   0-937552-13-5
Best of the Best from **Kentucky** $12.95   0-937552-27-5
Best of the Best from **Georgia** $12.95   0-937552-30-5
Best of the Best from **Alabama** $12.95   0-937552-28-3
Best of the Best from **Texas** $14.95   0-937552-14-3

The Quail Ridge Press Cookbook Series:

The Little Gumbo Book $6.95   0-937552-17-8
Gourmet Camping $10.95   0-937552-23-2
Hors D'Oeuvres Everybody Loves $5.95   0-937552-11-9
The Seven Chocolate Sins $5.95   0-937552-01-1
A Salad A Day $5.95   0-937552-02-X
Quickies for Singles $5.95   0-937552-03-8
Twelve Days of Christmas Cookbook $5.95   0-937552-00-3
Country Mouse Cheese Cookbook $5.95   0-937552-10-0

Send check, money order, or VISA/MasterCard number with
expiration date to:

QUAIL RIDGE PRESS
P. O. Box 123
Brandon, MS 39043

Please add $1.50 postage and handling for first book; $.50
per additional book. Gift wrap with enclosed card add $1.00.
Mississippi residents add 6% sales tax.
Phone orders call: 601/825-2063.
Write or call for free catalog of all QRP books and cookbooks.